THE NORTON MIX

AMERICAN VOICES

EDITORS

KAREN DUNN-HALEY
GENERAL EDITOR
UNIVERSITY OF CALIFORNIA, DAVIS

STEVE DAVIS
LONE STAR COLLEGE, KINGWOOD

MATTHEW SCHOENBACHLER
UNIVERSITY OF NORTH ALABAMA

WENDY WALL
STATE UNIVERSITY OF NEW YORK AT BINGHAMTON

THE NORTON MIX

AMERICAN VOICES

TIDEWATER COMMUNITY COLLEGE

EDITED BY

FRAN JACOBSON, TIM KONHAUS,

AND SCOTT WADE

NORTON CUSTOM

W. W. NORTON & COMPANY, INC.

NEW YORK • LONDON

W. W. Norton & Company has been independent since its founding in 1923, when William Warder Norton and Mary D. Herter Norton first published lectures delivered at the People's Institute, the adult education division of New York City's Cooper Union. The Nortons soon expanded their program beyond the Institute, publishing books by celebrated academics from America and abroad. By mid-century, the two major pillars of Norton's publishing program—trade books and college texts—were firmly established. In the 1950s, the Norton family transferred control of the company to its employees, and today—with a staff of four hundred and a comparable number of trade, college, and professional titles published each year—W. W. Norton & Company stands as the largest and oldest publishing house owned wholly by its employees.

Editor: Jon Durbin
Custom editor: Katie Hannah
Associate editor: Justin Cahill
Managing editor, College: Marian Johnson
Project editor: Erica Wnek
Editorial assistant: Elizabeth Dana
Production associate: Diana Spiegle
Design director: Rubina Yeh
Book designers: Chris Welch, Hope Miller Goodell
Text permissions editor: Nancy Rodwan
Photo researcher: Stephanie Romeo
Copyeditor: Mike Fleming
Proofreaders: Barbara Necol, Ann Kirschner
Composition: Westchester Publishing Services
Manufacturing: Quad Graphics - Versailles

ISBN 978-0-393-13791-0

W. W. Norton & Company, Inc., 500 Fifth Avenue, New York, NY 10110
www.wwnorton.com
W. W. Norton & Company, Ltd., Castle House, 75/76 Wells Street, London W1T3QT

CONTENTS

★ REVOLUTIONARY ERA

★ EARLY NATIONAL PERIOD

✶ SECTIONALISM

✶ MANIFEST DESTINY

★ ANTEBELLUM PERIOD

★ CIVIL WAR AND RECONSTRUCTION

EARLY AMERICA

The Founding of the Iroquois League (ca. 1600)

North of the beautiful lake, in the land of the Crooked Tongues . . . in the village lived a good woman who had a virgin daughter. Now strangely this virgin conceived. . . . The daughter about this time went into a long sleep and dreamed that her child should be a son whom she should name Dekanawida. The messenger in her dream told her that he should become a great man and that he should go among the Flint people to live and that he should also go to the Many Hill Nation and there raise up the Great Tree of Peace.

The Ongwe-oweh had fought long and bravely. All the Ongwe-oweh fought other nations sometimes together and sometimes singly and ofttimes they fought among themselves. The nation of the Flint had little sympathy for the Nation of the Great Hill, and sometimes they raided one another's settlements. Thus did brothers and Ongwe-oweh fight. The nation of the Sunken Pole fought the Nation of the Flint and hated them. . . . Everywhere there was peril and everywhere mourning. Men were ragged with sacrifice and the women scarred with the flints, so everywhere there was misery. Feuds with one another, feuds with outer nations, feuds with brother nations, feuds of sister towns, and feuds of families and of clans made every warrior a stealthy man who liked to kill.

Then in those days there was no great law. Our founder had not yet come to create peace and give united strength to the Real Men, the Ongwe-oweh.

In those same days, the Onondagas had no peace. A man's life was valued as nothing. For any slight offense a man or woman was killed by his enemy and in this manner feuds started between families and clans. At night, none dared leave their doorways, lest they be struck down by an enemy's war club. Such was the condition when there was no Great Law.

South of the Onondaga town lived an evil-minded man. . . . His body was distorted by seven crooks and his long tangled locks were adorned by writhing living serpents. Moreover, this monster was a devourer of raw meat, even of human flesh. He was also a master of wizardry, and by his magic he destroyed men but he could not be destroyed. Adodarhoh was the name of the evil man.

Notwithstanding the evil character of Adodarhoh the people of Onondaga, the Nation of Many Hills, obeyed his commands and though it cost many lives they satisfied his insane whims, so much did they fear him for his sorcery. . . .

Dekanawida requested some of the Mohawk chiefs to call a council, so messengers were sent out among the people and the council was convened.

Dekanawida said, "I, with my co-worker, have a desire to now report on what we have done on five successive midsummer days, of five successive years. We have obtained the consent of five nations. These are the Mohawks, the Oneidas, the Onondagas, the Cayugas, and the Senecas. Our desire is to form a compact for a union of our nations. Our next step is to seek out Adodarhoh. It is he who has always set at naught all plans for the establishment of the Great Peace. We must seek his fire and look for his smoke. . . .

Then Dekanawida taught the people the Hymn of Peace and the other songs. He stood before the door of the longhouse and walked before it singing the new songs. Many came and learned them so that many were strong by the magic of them when it was time to carry the Great Peace to Onondaga. . . .

The frontier of the Onondaga country was reached and the expedition halted to kindle a fire, as was customary. Then the chiefs of the Onondagas, with their head men, welcomed them and a great throng marched to the fireside of Adodarhoh, the singer of the Peace Hymn leading the multitude. . . .

Then Dekanawida himself sang and walked before the door of Adodarhoh's house. When he finished his song he walked toward Adodarhoh and held out his hand to rub it on his body and to know its inherent strength and life. Then Adodarhoh was made straight and his mind became healthy. When Adodarhoh was made strong in rightful powers and his body had been healed, Dekanawida addressed the three nations. He said, "We have overcome a great obstacle. It has long stood in the way of peace. The mind of Adodarhoh is now made right and his crooked parts are made straight. Now indeed may we establish the great peace.

"Before we do firmly establish our union each nation must appoint a certain number of its wisest and purest men who shall be rulers, Rodiyaner. They shall be the advisers of the people and make the new rules that may be needful. These men shall be selected and confirmed by their female relations in whose line the titles shall be hereditary."

FROM *The Saga of Eirik the Red*
(13th century)

The Saga of Eirik the Red, *most likely written sometime in the thirteenth century, tells the story of Norsemen who, two centuries earlier, were the first known Europeans to set foot in North America. Eirik the Red (ca. 950–ca. 1002) was a Norseman expelled from both Norway and Iceland because of his penchant for manslaughter. Sailing westward, he established a settlement on the west coast of Greenland, where he died in 1002. His son, Leif Eriksson (ca. 970–ca. 1020), later sailed further westward and made landfall at a place he called Vinland, known today as Newfoundland. Until about fifty years ago, most historians believed the Norse sagas to be myth. However, in 1960, a Norwegian lawyer-turned-explorer named Helge Ingstad discovered a settlement at L'Anse aux Meadows on the northern tip of Newfoundland that dates to approximately 1000 CE. Most historians and archaeologists believe this is the place where Karlsefni and Eiriksdottir landed.*

The following excerpt tells of the Norse attempt to settle this region about a decade after the initial Norse landing in North America. The enterprise was led by Thorfinn Karlsefni, a brother-in-law of Leif Eriksson, and Freydis Eiriksdottir, the impulsive and impassioned illegitimate daughter of Eirik the Red. The account depicts the very dawn of recorded contact between Europeans and Native Americans, almost half a millennia before Columbus's voyage across the Atlantic.

The story now turns to Karlsefni, and tells how he sailed south along the land with Snorri and Bjarni and their crews.[1] They sailed a long way till they came to a river which flowed down from the land into a lake and so to the sea. . . . Karlsefni sailed with his men into the estuary and they called the place Hop. Ashore there they found self-sown fields of wheat where the ground was low-lying, and vines wherever there was high ground. Every brook was full of fish. . . . There were vast numbers of animals of every kind in the forest. They were there for a fortnight enjoying themselves and noticed nothing strange. They had their cattle with them.

1. Snorri Thorbrandsson, an associate of Karlsefni, and Bjarni Grimolfsson, captain of one of the expedition's ships.

Then one morning early, when they looked about them, they saw a multitude of skin-canoes. . . .

* * *

Their visitors rowed towards them, and were astonished at what they found, then came ashore. They were dark, ugly men who wore their hair in an unpleasant fashion. They had big eyes and were broad in the cheeks. They stayed there for a while, astonished at what they found, and afterwards rowed off south past the headland.

Karlsefni and his men had built themselves booths up above the lake. . . . They now spent the winter there. No snow fell, and the whole of their stock found its own food by grazing. But when spring came in they saw early one morning how a multitude of canoes came rowing from the south round the headland, so many that the bay looked as though sown with charcoal. . . . Karlsefni and his men raised their shields, and as soon as they met they began trading together. Most of all these people wanted to buy red cloth, in return for which they had furs to offer and grey skins. They also wanted to buy swords and spears, but this Karlsefni and Snorri would not allow. The Skrælings[2] were taking a span's length[3] of red cloth in exchange for an unblemished dark skin, and this they tied round their heads. Their trading continued thus for a while, when the cloth began to run short for Karlsefni and his men; they then cut it up into such small pieces that they were no wider than a finger-breadth, but the Skrælings even so gave just as much for it as before, or indeed more.

The next thing was that the bull belonging to Karlsefni and his mates ran out of the forest bellowing loudly. The Skrælings were terrified by this, raced out to their canoes, and then rowed south past the headland, and for three weeks running there was neither sight nor sound of them. But at the end of that period they saw a great multitude of Skræling boats coming up like a stream from the south. . . . The Skrælings were all yelling aloud, so Karlsefni and his men took red shields and held them out against them. The Skrælings ran from their boats and then they clashed together and fought. There was a heavy shower of missiles, for the Skrælings had warslings. Karlsefni and his men could see the Skrælings hoisting up on to a pole a very large ball, closely comparable to a sheep's paunch, and a deep blue-black in colour, which they let fly from the pole inland over Karlsefni's troop, and it made a hideous noise where it came down. A great fear now struck into Karlsefni and all his following, so that they had no other thought in their heads than to run away and make their escape up along the river, for they had the impression that the Skræling host was pouring in upon them from all sides. They made no stop till they reached some rocks, but there made a brave defence.

2. The Norse word for the Native Americans, which roughly translates to "ugly screaming people."
3. The distance between the thumb and pinky finger of a spread hand.

Freydis came out of doors and saw how they had run off. "Why are you running from wretches like these?" she cried. "Such gallant lads as you, I thought you would have knocked them on the head like cattle. Why, if I had a weapon, I think I could put up a better fight than any of you!"

They might as well not have heard her. Freydis was anxious to keep up with them, but was slow on her feet because of her pregnancy. Yet she kept moving after them to the forest, but the Skrælings now attacked her. She found a dead man in her path, Thorbrand Snorrason—he had a flat stone sticking out of his head. His naked sword lay beside him; she picked it up and prepared to defend herself. The Skrælings were making for her. She pulled out her breasts from under her clothes and slapped the naked sword on them, at which the Skrælings took fright, and ran off to their boats and rowed away. Karlsefni's men came up to her, praising her courage.

* * *

It now seemed plain to Karlsefni and his men that though the quality of the land was admirable, there would always be fear and strife dogging them there on account of those who already inhabited it. So they made ready to leave, setting their hearts on their own country, and sailed north along the land. . . .

Study Questions

1. When engaged in trading, what did the Norsemen want from the Native Americans? What did the Native Americans want from the Norsemen?

2. What did the Norsemen find attractive about the New World? Why did they leave?

3. What do Freydis's actions tell us about gender roles of her day, in both her own culture and that of the natives?

4. How does this narrative compare with those of other encounter narratives you've read, heard, or seen? What do such narratives teach us about both the encountered and the "discoverer"?

CHRISTOPHER COLUMBUS

FROM *The Log of Christopher Columbus* (1492)

Christopher Columbus's voyages to the Western Hemisphere changed the world, as most everyone knows. Also well known is that when he reached America, Columbus (ca. 1451–1506) thought he was exploring the islands off the coast of East Asia. Even after subsequent voyages led many to suspect that these lands were not Asian at all, Columbus—until the day he died—stubbornly denied that he had made contact with what the Europeans called the "New World." Less well understood, however, is that Columbus did not sail west to prove the world was round—in fact, most Europeans since the days of the ancient Greeks were well aware that the earth is a sphere—but to prove his mistaken notion that the planet was about two-thirds its actual size and Asia therefore lay about 3,000 miles to the west.

The log of Christopher Columbus is the only surviving document authored by Columbus himself that describes his voyages. The original diary has not survived—what we have, in fact, is a copy of a copy transcribed and summarized over a century later by a Dominican friar, Bartolomé de las Casas. Nonetheless, it is, by most scholars' reckoning, an accurate account corroborated by other surviving evidence.

Excerpts from "The Log of Christopher Columbus" from *The Log of Christopher Columbus* translated by Robert H. Fuson. Reprinted by permission of Amelia Fuson.

THE OUTWARD VOYAGE

3 August to 10 October 1492

Most Christian, exalted, excellent, and powerful princes, King and Queen of the Spains and of the islands of the sea, our Sovereigns[1]: It was in this year of 1492 that Your Highnesses . . . decided to send me, Christopher Columbus, to the regions of India, to see the Princes there and the peoples and the lands, and to learn of their disposition, and of everything, and the measures which could be taken for their conversion to our Holy Faith.

1. King Ferdinand II of Aragon (1452–1516) and Queen Isabella I of Castile (1451–1504).

* * *

Your Highnesses ordered me to go with a sufficient fleet to the said regions of India. For that purpose I was granted great favors and ennobled; from then henceforward I might entitle myself *Don* and be High Admiral of the Ocean Sea and Viceroy and perpetual Governor of all the islands and continental land that I might discover and acquire, as well as any other future discoveries in the Ocean Sea. Further, my eldest son shall succeed to the same position, and so on from generation to generation for ever after.

I left Granada on Saturday, the 12th day of the month of May in the same year of 1492 and went to the town of Palos, which is a seaport. There I fitted out three vessels, very suited to such an undertaking. I left the said port well supplied with a large quantity of provisions and with many seamen on the third day of the month of August in the said year, on a Friday, half an hour before sunrise.

* * *

THE DISCOVERY OF THE BAHAMAS

Thursday, 11 October 1492

* * *

After sunset I ordered the pilot to return to my original westerly course, and I urged the crew to be ever-vigilant. I took the added precaution of doubling the number of lookouts, and I reminded the men that the first to sight land would be given a silk doublet as a personal token from me. Further, he would be given an annuity of 10,000 maravedíes[2] from the Sovereigns.

About 10 o'clock at night, while standing on the sterncastle,[3] I thought I saw a light to the west. It looked like a little wax candle bobbing up and down. It had the same appearance as a light or torch belonging to fishermen or travellers who alternately raised and lowered it, or perhaps were going from house to house. I am the first to admit that I was so eager to find land that I did not trust my own senses, so I called for Pedro Gutiérrez, the representative of the King's household, and asked him to watch for the light. After a few moments, he too saw it. I then summoned Rodrigo Sánchez of Segovia, the comptroller of the fleet, and asked him to watch for the light. He saw nothing, nor did any other member of the crew. It was such an uncertain thing that I did not feel it was adequate proof of land.

2. Small silver coins worth about six cents.
3. A raised deck at the back of a ship.

* * *

I now believe that the light I saw earlier was a sign from God and that it was truly the first positive indication of land. When we caught up with the *Pinta*, which was always running ahead because she was a swift sailer, I learned that the first man to sight land was Rodrigo de Triana, a seaman from Lepe.

I hauled in all sails but the mainsail and lay-to till daylight. The land is about 6 miles to the west.

Friday, 12 October 1492

(Log entry for 12 October is combined with that of 11 October.)

At dawn we saw naked people, and I went ashore in the ship's boat, armed, followed by Martín Alonso Pinzón, captain of the *Pinta*, and his brother, Vincente Yáñez Pinzón, captain of the *Niña*. I unfurled the royal banner and the captains brought the flags which displayed a large green cross with the letters F and Y[4] at the left and right side of the cross. Over each letter was the appropriate crown of that Sovereign. These flags were carried as a standard on all of the ships. After a prayer of thanksgiving I ordered the captains of the *Pinta* and *Niña*, together with Rodrigo de Escobedo (secretary of the fleet), and Rodrigo Sánchez of Segovia (comptroller of the fleet) to bear faith and witness that I was taking possession of this island for the King and Queen. I made all the necessary declarations and had these testimonies carefully written down by the secretary. In addition to those named above, the entire company of the fleet bore witness to this act. To this island I gave the name *San Salvador*,[5] in honor of our Blessed Lord.

No sooner had we concluded the formalities of taking possession of the island than people began to come to the beach, all as naked as their mothers bore them, and the women also, although I did not see more than one very young girl. All those that I saw were young people, none of whom was over 30 years old. They are very well-built people, with handsome bodies and very fine faces, though their appearance is marred somewhat by very broad heads and foreheads, more so than I have ever seen in any other race. Their eyes are large and very pretty, and their skin is the color of Canary Islanders or of sunburned peasants, not at all black, as would be expected because we are on an east-west line with Hierro in the Canaries.[6] These are tall people and their legs, with no exceptions, are quite straight, and none of them has a paunch. They are, in fact, well proportioned. Their hair is not kinky, but straight, and coarse like horsehair. They wear it short over the eyebrows,

---

4. Ferdinand and Isabella (often spelled Ysabel).
5. Holy Savior (Spanish).
6. That is, the Canary Islands, off the northwestern coast of Africa.

but they have a long hank in the back that they never cut. Many of the natives paint their faces; others paint their whole bodies; some, only the eyes or nose. Some are painted black, some white, some red; others are of different colors.

The people here called this island *Guanahaní* in their language, and their speech is very fluent, although I do not understand any of it. They are friendly and well-dispositioned people who bare no arms except for small spears, and they have no iron. I showed one my sword, and through ignorance he grabbed it by the blade and cut himself. Their spears are made of wood, to which they attach a fish tooth at one end, or some other sharp thing.

I want the natives to develop a friendly attitude toward us because I know that they are a people who can be made free and converted to our Holy Faith more by love than by force. I therefore gave red caps to some and glass beads to others. They hung the beads around their necks, along with some other things of slight value that I gave them. And they took great pleasure in this and became so friendly that it was a marvel. They traded and gave everything they had with good will, but it seems to me that they have very little and are poor in everything. I warned my men to take nothing from the people without giving something in exchange.

This afternoon the people of San Salvador came swimming to our ships and in boats made from one log. They brought us parrots, balls of cotton thread, spears, and many other things, including a kind of dry leaf[7] that they hold in great esteem. For these items we swapped them little glass beads and hawks' bells.

Many of the men I have seen have scars on their bodies, and when I made signs to them to find out how this happened, they indicated that people from other nearby islands come to San Salvador to capture them; they defend themselves the best they can. I believe that people from the mainland come here to take them as slaves. They ought to make good and skilled servants, for they repeat very quickly whatever we say to them. I think they can easily be made Christians, for they seem to have no religion. If it pleases Our Lord, I will take six of them to Your Highnesses when I depart, in order that they may learn our language.

Saturday, 13 October 1492

* * *

I have been very attentive and have tried very hard to find out if there is any gold here. I have seen a few natives who wear a little piece of gold hanging from a hole made in the nose. By signs, if I interpret them correctly, I have learned that by

7. Tobacco.

going to the south, or rounding the island to the south, I can find a king who possesses a lot of gold and has great containers of it. I have tried to find some natives who will take me to this great king, but none seems inclined to make the journey.

* * *

I cannot get over the fact of how docile these people are. They have so little to give but will give it all for whatever we give them, if only broken pieces of glass and crockery. One seaman gave three Portuguese *ceitis* (not even worth a penny!) for about 25 pounds of spun cotton. I probably should have forbidden this exchange, but I wanted to take the cotton to Your Highnesses, and it seems to be in abundance. I think the cotton is grown on San Salvador, but I cannot say for sure because I have not been here that long. Also, the gold they wear hanging from their noses comes from here, but in order not to lose time I want to go to see if I can find the island of Japan.

When night came, all of the people went ashore in their boats.

* * *

Tuesday, 6 November 1492

Last night the two men I had sent inland to see the country returned and told me how they had gone 36 miles, to a village of 50 houses where there were a thousand inhabitants, as a great many live in one house. These houses are like very large pavilions.

The Spaniards said that the Indians received them with great solemnity, according to Indian custom, and all the men and women came to see them and lodged them in the best houses. The Indians touched them and kissed their hands and feet in wonderment, believing that we Spaniards came from Heaven, and so my men led them to understand. The Indians gave them to eat what they had.

The men said that on their arrival, the most distinguished persons in the village took them on their shoulders and carried them to the principal house and gave them two chairs in which to sit, and all the Indians seated themselves on the floor around them. These were most peculiar chairs. Each was made in one piece and in a strange shape, resembling a short-legged animal with a tail as broad as the seat. This tail lifted up to make a back to lean against. These seats are called *dujos* or *duchos* in their language.

The Indians who had gone with my men, that is, the one from Guanahaní and the one from here, told the people how the Christians lived and how we were good people. Afterwards the men left, and the women seated themselves in the same manner around them, kissing their hands and feet, trying to see if they were of flesh and bone like themselves. The women pleaded with them to stay there longer, at least for five days.

My men showed the Indians the cinnamon and pepper and other spices I had given them, and they were told by signs that there were many such spices nearby to the SE, but that they did not know if they had those things there in their own village. Having seen that there were no rich cities, my men returned to Puerto de Mares.

* * *

Wednesday, 12 December 1492

The wind remains contrary, and I am unable to depart. I placed a large cross at the entrance to the harbor, on a little rise the western side. This is a sign that Your Highnesses possess this land as your own and especially as an emblem of Jesus Christ, Our Lord, and in honor of Christianity. After erecting the cross, three sailors started up the mountain to see the trees and plants; and they heard a large crowd of people. These people were all naked like the others they had seen, and my men called to them and went after them, but the Indians fled. Finally they caught one woman who could go no farther: in doing so, they were carrying out my orders to take some of the Indians in order to show them honor and cause them to lose their fear of us. I also wanted to see if these Indians had anything worthwhile; it appeared that it could not be otherwise, judging from the beauty of the country.

So they brought the woman to the ship, a very young and beautiful girl, and she talked with those Indians with me, since they all have the same language. I clothed her and gave her glass beads, hawks' bells,[8] and brass rings, and sent her back to land, very honorably, the way I always do. I also sent some people from the ship with her, including three of the Indians with me, so that they could talk with those people. The sailors who took her to land said that she did not wish to leave the other Indian women on the ship, the ones we had taken at Puerto de Mares on the island of Juana.[9] All the Indians who had accompanied this Indian woman originally had come in a canoe, which is their caravel that they navigate everywhere; when they entered the harbor and saw the ships, they fled from my men, leaving the canoe, and ran back to their village overland. The Indian woman showed us the location of the village. She wore a small piece of gold in her nose, which is an indication that there is gold in this island.

8. Bells similar to what we might call a jingle bell used to track birds and often traded with Native Americans.
9. That is, Cuba.

Thursday, 13 December 1492

The Indians on my ship had told the Indian accompanying the sailors that I wanted a parrot, and he passed the word on to these other Indians. They brought many parrots and required no payment for them. The Indians begged my men not to leave that night and offered them many other things that they had in the mountains. When all these people were together, the sailors saw a great multitude of Indians coming with the husband of the woman whom I had honored and returned. They were carrying this woman on their shoulders, coming to thank me for the honor I had done her and the presents I had given her.

My men told me that these people were more handsome and of better disposition than any that we had seen up to now, but I do not know how this is possible. As to their appearance, the sailors said that there is no comparison with the ones we have seen before, either men or women. They are whiter than the others—indeed, they saw two young girls as white as any to be seen in Spain. As to the country, the best in Castile in beauty and fertility cannot compare with this. This land is as different from that surrounding Córdoba as day is from night.

All the land around the village is cultivated, and a river flows through the middle of the valley. It is very large and wide and could irrigate all the lands around. All the trees are green and full of fruit, and the plants are in flower and very tall. The roads are wide and good, and the breezes are like those in Castile in the month of April. The nightingales and other small birds sing as they do in Spain in the same month, and it is the greatest pleasure in the world. Small birds sing sweetly during the night, and one can hear many crickets and frogs. The fish are the same as in Spain. There are many mastic trees and aloes and cotton trees. No gold has been found, but this is not surprising since we have been here such a short time.

* * *

Our Lord willed that at midnight, when the crew saw me lie down to rest and also saw that there was a dead calm and the sea was as in a bowl, they all lay down to sleep and left the helm to [a] boy. The currents carried the ship upon one of these banks. Although it was night, the sea breaking on them made so much noise that they could be heard and seen at a 3-mile distance. The ship went upon the bank so quietly that it was hardly noticeable. When the boy felt the rudder ground and heard the noise of the sea, he cried out. I jumped up instantly; no one else had yet felt that we were aground. . . .

* * *

When I saw that some of my own crew were fleeing and that the sea was becoming more shallow, with my ship broadside to it, I did the only thing I could. I ordered the mast cut and the ship lightened as much as possible, to see if it could be refloated. But the water became even more shallow, and the ship settled more and more to one side. Although there was little or no sea, I could not save her. Then the seams opened, though she remained in one piece.

I took my crew to the *Niña* for their safety, and as there was a light land breeze and still half the night ahead of us, and since I did not know how far the banks extended, I beat about till daybreak and then went inside the bank to the ship. I also dispatched Diego de Arana, master-at-arms of the fleet, and Pedro Gutiérrez, representative of the Royal Household, to take the small boat and go directly to the King that had last Saturday invited me to his village. I instructed them to beg the King to come to this harbor with his boats.

The village of this King is about 5 miles beyond this bank. My men told me that the King wept when he heard of the disaster. He sent all his people from the village with many large canoes to help us unload the ship. The King displayed great haste and diligence, and everything was unloaded in a very brief space of time. He himself personally assisted the unloading, along with his brothers and relatives, and guarded what was taken ashore in order that everything might be completely secure.

From time to time the King sent one of his relatives to me, weeping, to console me, and they said that I was not to be troubled or annoyed, for the King would give me whatever he possessed. I certify to Your Highnesses that in no part of Castile could things be so secure; not even a shoe string was lost!

The King ordered everything placed near the houses, even emptying some in order that everything could be stored and guarded. He ordered armed men placed around the houses to guard everything all night. He, with all his people in the village, wept a great deal. They are an affectionate people, free from avarice and agreeable to everything. I certify to Your Highnesses that in all the world I do not believe there is a better people or a better country. They love their neighbors as themselves, and they have the softest and gentlest voices in the world and are always smiling. They may go naked, but Your Highnesses may be assured that they have very good customs among themselves, and the King maintains a most marvelous state, where everything takes place in an appropriate and well-ordered manner. It is a pleasure to see all of this. These people have good memories and want to see everything; they ask what things are and for what purpose they are used.

Wednesday, 26 December 1492

Today at sunrise the King of this country came to the *Niña*, where I was, and almost in tears told me not to be dismayed because he would give me whatever he had. He had already given two very large houses to my men, and he would give us more if we needed them. And yesterday he gave us as many canoes as we needed and the labor to unload the ship, and not even a breadcrumb was taken. They are so loyal and so respectful of the property of others, and this King is even more honest than the others.

While we were talking, another canoe came from some other place and brought some pieces of gold, which the Indians wished to trade for a hawk's bell, for they valued hawks' bells above everything else. The canoe had not even reached the *Niña*'s side when they called out and showed the pieces of gold, saying, "*Chuque, chuque,*" which means hawks' bells, which they are crazy about. When they saw the difficulty we were having, these Indians from the other place departed, begging me to keep a hawk's bell for them until tomorrow. They said that they would bring four pieces of gold as large as the hand. I was pleased to hear this. Then a sailor who had come from land told me that the wonderful pieces of gold my men were trading for in the village were costing practically nothing. For a leather thong the Indians gave pieces of gold worth more than two *castellanos*,[1] and by the end of the month things should get even better.

The King was delighted to see me happy, and he understood that I desired a great deal of gold. He indicated by signs that he knew where there was a lot of it nearby and that I should be of good cheer, for he would give me as much of it as I desired. He told me all about this gold, specifically, that it is found in Japan, which they call *Cibao*. The people there have so much of it that they place no value on it at all and will bring it here. Also, the King told me, there is much gold here in the Isla Española,[2] which they call Bohío, and in the province of Caribata.

The King dined with me on the *Niña* and afterwards went ashore with me, where he paid me great honor. Later we had a meal with two or three kinds of ajes,[3] served with shrimp, game, and other foods they have, including their bread; which they call *cazabe*. Then the King took me to see some groves of trees near the houses, and fully 1,000 people, all naked, went with us. The King was already wearing a shirt and a pair of gloves which I had given him, and he was more excited about the

---

1. Gold coins worth about 490 maravedís.
2. That is, Hispaniola, comprised of present-day Haiti and the Dominican Republic.
3. Type of vegetable similar to or the same as the sweet potato.

gloves than anything else that had been given him. By his manner of eating, his decent behavior, and his exceptional cleanliness, he showed himself to be of good birth.

After the meal we remained at the table for some time, and we were brought some herbs with which to rub our hands—I believe they use these to soften the skin. We were also given water for our hands. Later, after we had eaten, the Indians took me to the beach, and I sent for a Turkish bow and a handful of arrows. I had a man from my company who was a skilled archer shoot the arrows. Inasmuch as the King did not know what arms are, since his people neither possess nor use them, the demonstration impressed him very much. This all came about because we had had a conversation about the people of Caniba, whom they call *Caribes*, who come to seize them and who carry bows and arrows without iron tips. Nowhere in these lands is there knowledge of iron or steel, nor of any other metal except gold and copper, and I have seen very little of the latter. I told the King by signs that the Sovereigns of Castile would order the destruction of the Caribes, commanding the Caribes to be brought before them with their hands tied.

I ordered that a lombard[4] and a musket be fired, and the King was spellbound when he saw the effect of their force and what they penetrated. When the people heard the shots, they fell to their knees. They brought me a large mask, which had large pieces of gold in the ears and eyes and in other places, which the King himself presented to me. He placed this, along with other jewels of gold, on my head and around my neck. They also gave many things to the men with me. I derived a great deal of pleasure and consolation from these things, and when I realized that this mitigated the trouble and affliction I had experienced by losing the ship, I recognized that Our Lord had caused me to run aground at this place so that I might establish a settlement here. And so many things came to hand here that the disaster was a blessing in disguise. Certainly, if I had not run aground here, I would have kept out to sea without anchoring at this place because it is situated inside a large bay containing two or three banks of shoals. Neither would I have left any of my people here on this voyage; even if I had desired to leave them, I could not have outfitted them well enough, nor given them enough ammunition, provisions, and materials for a fort. It is quite true that many of the people with me have pleaded with me to permit them to remain here.

Now I have ordered that a tower and a fortress be constructed, very well built, with a large moat. This is not because I believe this to be necessary with these Indians, for I am sure that I could subjugate the entire island—which I believe is

---

4. A cannon.

larger than Portugal with twice the population—with the men that I have in my company. These Indians are naked, unarmed, and cowardly beyond help. But it is right that this tower be built, and what must be, must be. Since these Indians are so far from Your Highnesses, it is necessary that the people here know your people and what they can do, in order that the Indians may obey Your Highnesses with love and fear.

The men remaining have timbers with which to construct the fortress and provisions of bread and wine for more than a year, as well as seeds for sowing, and the ship's boat. I am leaving a caulker, a carpenter, a gunner, and a caskmaker among the many men who desire zealously to serve Your Highnesses and who will please me greatly if they find the mine where the gold comes from. Thus, everything that has happened was for this purpose, that this beginning may be made.

All this was the will of God: the ship's running aground so easily that it could not be felt, with neither wind nor wave; the cowardice of the ship's master and some of the crew (who were mostly from his part of Spain), who refused my order to cast the stern anchor to draw the ship off and save it; the discovery of this country.

Without God's intervention this country would not have been known as it has come to be known during our time here, and as it will be known by the people I intend to leave here. I had been sailing all the time with the intention of making discoveries and not remaining anywhere longer than a day unless there was no wind because the *Santa María* was very cumbersome and not suited to the work of discovery. The reason I took that ship in the first place was due to the people of Palos, who did not fulfill to me what they had promised the King and Queen. I should have been given ships suitable for this journey, and the people of Palos did not do that. Of the *Santa María*'s contents, not a leather strap was lost, nor a board, nor a nail, because the ship remained as sound as when she started except that we chopped and split her some in order to remove the large casks and all the cargo. All these things have been placed on land and are well secured.

I hope to God that when I come back here from Castile, which I intend on doing, that I will find a barrel of gold, for which these people I am leaving will have traded, and that they will have found the gold mine, and the spices, and in such quantities *that within three years the Sovereigns will prepare for and undertake the conquest of the Holy Land. I have already petitioned Your Highnesses to see that all the profits of this, my enterprise, should be spent on the conquest of Jerusalem, and Your Highnesses smiled and said that the idea pleased them, and that even without this expedition they had the inclination to do it.*

* * *

Wednesday, 2 January 1493

I went ashore this morning to take leave of King Guacanagari and to depart in the name of the Lord. I gave the King one of my shirts and showed him the force of the lombards and their effect. For this purpose I ordered one loaded and fired at the side of the *Santa María*, which was aground. This all came about as a result of a conversation about the Caribes, with whom they were at war. The King saw how far the lombard shot reached and how it passed through the side of the ship. I also had the people from the ship fight a mock battle with their arms, telling the Cacique not to fear the Caribes if they came. I did all this so that the King would consider those I am leaving as friends, and also that he might fear them. The King escorted me and the men with me to his house to eat with him.

I left on this Isla Española, which the Indians call Bohío, 39 men in the fortress, under the command of three officers, all of whom are very friendly with King Guacanagari. In command is Diego de Arana, a native of Córdoba, whom I have given all of the powers I have received from the Sovereigns, in full. Next in line, if something should happen to him, is his lieutenant, Pedro Gutiérrez, the representative of the Royal Household. Next in the line of succession is the lieutenant Rodrigo de Escobedo, secretary of the fleet and a native of Segovia, nephew of the friar Rodrigo Pérez.

I have left with them all the merchandise which the Sovereigns had ordered purchased for trading, of which there is a large quantity. With this they may trade and barter for gold, together with everything the grounded ship carried. I also left them sufficient biscuits for a year and wine and much artillery. I also left the ship's boat, since most of them are sailors, so they can go find the gold mine when they see that the time is favorable. In this manner, when I return, I might find a lot of gold waiting and a place to establish a settlement, for this harbor is not to my liking. Since the gold that is brought here comes from the east, the more they went to the east the closer to Spain they would be. I also left seeds for sowing, and I left my officers, including the secretary and the master-at-arms, and among the others a ship's carpenter, a caulker, a good gunner who knows a great deal about machines, a caskmaker, a physician, and a tailor. All these men are also seamen.

* * *

Friday, 15 March 1493

Yesterday after sunset I continued on my course until dawn, with a light wind; by sunrise I was off Saltes. At noon, with the tide rising, I entered the bar of Saltes until I was inside the harbor from which I had departed on August 3 of the past year. Thus, the writing is now completed, except that I intend to go by sea to Barcelona, where, I have been informed, Your Highnesses are staying. This is in order to give them a full account of my voyage, which Our Lord has permitted me to make, and for which He inspired me. His Divine Majesty does all good things, and everything is good except sin, and nothing can be imagined or planned without His consent. This voyage has miraculously proven this to be so, as can be learned from this writing, by the remarkable miracles which have occurred during the voyage and for me, who has been in the court of Your Highnesses for such a long time, with opposition and against the advice of so many of the principal persons of your household, who were all against me and treated this undertaking as a folly. I hope to Our Lord that it will be the greatest honor for Christianity, although it has been accomplished with such ease.

Study Questions

1. What is Columbus's reaction to the Natives? How did the Natives react to the Spaniards?

2. What features of the New World were of particular interest to Columbus?

3. What role does religion play in Columbus's understanding of his voyage?

4. The settlement established by Columbus's men on Hispaniola—known as La Navidad because the ship grounded on Christmas Day—was completely destroyed by the Indians and all thirty-nine Spaniards killed. Why, then, do you think Columbus described the natives as "docile" and "cowardly beyond help"? Why do you think Columbus painted such an optimistic picture of the New World and its inhabitants? What other evidence can you find that Columbus might have been carefully tailoring his narrative to appeal to his intended audience?

AMERIGO VESPUCCI

FROM On His First Voyage (1497)

I was chosen by his Highness to go in that fleet to aid in making discovery: and we set out from the port of Cadiz on the 10 day of May 1497, and took our route through the great gulph of the Ocean-sea: in which voyage we were 18 months [*engaged*]: and discovered much continental land and innumerable islands, and great part of them inhabited: whereas there is no mention made by the ancient writers of them: I believe, because they had no knowledge thereof: for, if I remember well, I have read in some one [*of those writers*] that he considered that this Ocean-sea was an unpeopled sea: and of this opinion was Dante our poet in the xxvi. chapter of the Inferno, where he feigns the death of Ulysses: in which voyage I beheld things of great wondrousness, as your Magnificence shall understand. As I said above, we left the port of Cadiz four consort ships: and began our voyage in a direct course to the Fortunate Isles, which are called to-day *la gran Canaria*, which are situated in the Ocean-sea at the extremity of the inhabited west, [*and*] set in the third climate: over which the North Pole has an elevation of 27 and a half degrees beyond their horizon: and they are 280 leagues distant from this city of Lisbon, by the wind between *mezzo di* and *libeccio*: where we remained eight days, taking in provision of water, and wood, and other necessary things: and from here, having said our prayers, we weighed anchor, and gave the sails to the wind, beginning our course to westward, taking one quarter by south-west: and so we sailed on till at the end of 37 days we reached a land which we deemed to be a continent: which is distant westwardly from the isles of Canary about a thousand leagues beyond the inhabited region.

BARTOLOMÉ DE LAS CASAS

FROM *A Short Account of the Destruction of the Indies* (1542)

Bartolomé de Las Casas (ca. 1484–1566) was Dominican friar who spent most of his adult life attempting to protect Native Americans from the shattering effects of the Spanish invasion. Born in Seville, Spain, Las Casas traveled to the Caribbean when he was eighteen and witnessed firsthand the brutal subjugation of the Indians. In his early twenties, he was ordained a priest, and thereafter became a relentless critic of his countrymen's atrocities. In 1521, he unsuccessfully attempted to create model communities based on cooperation between Spaniards and Native Americans in present-day Venezuela.

In 1542, fifty years after Columbus first made contact with the Americas, Las Casas wrote A Short Account of the Destruction of the Indies, *which was not published for another ten years. A catalog of Spanish atrocities against the indigenous peoples of the Western Hemisphere, the book became the basis for the "Black Legend," semi-mythic accounts of Spanish inhumanity that were enthusiastically embraced by European Protestants locked in an unrelenting war against Catholic countries led by Spain.*

The Americas were discovered in 1492, and the first Christian settlements established by the Spanish the following year. It is accordingly forty-nine years now since Spaniards began arriving in numbers in this part of the world. They first settled the large and fertile island of Hispaniola,[1] which boasts six hundred leagues of coastline and is surrounded by a great many other large islands, all of them, as I saw for myself, with as high a native population as anywhere on earth. . . . It would seem, if we are to judge by those areas so far explored, that, the Almighty selected this part of the world as home to the greater part of the human race.

---

1. The island the Spanish named Hispaniola is today split into two nation-states: Haiti and the Dominican Republic.

God made all the peoples of this area, many and varied as they are, as open and as innocent as can be imagined. The simplest people in the world—unassuming, long-suffering, unassertive, and submissive—they are without malice or guile, and are utterly faithful and obedient both to their own native lords and to the Spaniards in whose service they now find themselves. Never quarrelsome or belligerent or boisterous, they harbour no grudges and do not seek to settle old scores; indeed, the notions of revenge, rancour, and hatred are quite foreign to them. At the same time, they are among the least robust of human beings: their delicate constitutions make them unable to withstand hard work or suffering and render them liable to succumb to almost any illness, no matter how mild. Even the common people are no tougher than princes or than other Europeans born with a silver spoon in their mouths and who spend their lives shielded from the rigours of the outside world. They are also among the poorest people on the face of the earth; they own next to nothing and have no urge to acquire material possessions. As a result they are neither ambitious nor greedy, and are totally uninterested in worldly power. Their diet is every bit as poor and as monotonous, in quantity and in kind, as that enjoyed by the Desert Fathers.[2] Most of them go naked, save for a loincloth to cover their modesty; at best they may wrap themselves in a piece of cotton material a yard or two square. Most sleep on matting, although a few possess a kind of hanging net, known in the language of Hispaniola as a hammock. They are innocent and pure in mind and have a lively intelligence, all of which makes them particularly receptive to learning and understanding the truths of our Catholic faith and to being instructed in virtue; indeed, God has invested them with fewer impediments in this regard than any other people on earth. Once they begin to learn of the Christian faith they become so keen to know more, to receive the Sacraments, and to worship God, that the missionaries who instruct them do truly have to be men of exceptional patience and forbearance; and over the years I have time and again met Spanish laymen who have been so struck by the natural goodness that shines through these people that they frequently can be heard to exclaim: 'These would be the most blessed people on earth if only they were given the chance to convert to Christianity.'

It was upon these gentle lambs, imbued by the Creator with all the qualities we have mentioned, that from the very first day they clapped eyes on them the Spanish fell like ravening wolves upon the fold, or like tigers and savage lions who have not eaten meat for days. The pattern established at the outset has remained unchanged to this day, and the Spaniards still do nothing save tear the natives to shreds, murder them and inflict upon them untold misery, suffering and distress, tormenting, harrying and persecuting them mercilessly. We shall in due course describe some of the many ingenious methods of torture they have invented and refined for this purpose, but one can get some idea of the effectiveness of their

2. Various Christian hermits and monks, including St. Anthony, who lived as ascetics in the Egyptian desert in the third century and created the model for Christian monasticism.

methods from the figures alone. When the Spanish first journeyed there, the indigenous population of the island of Hispaniola stood at some three million; today only two hundred survive. The island of Cuba . . . is now to all intents and purposes uninhabited; and two other large, beautiful and fertile islands, Puerto Rico and Jamaica, have been similarly devastated. Not a living soul remains today on any of the islands of the Bahamas, which lie to the north of Hispaniola and Cuba, even though every single one of the sixty or so islands in the group, as well as those known as the Isles of Giants and others in the area, both large and small, is more fertile and more beautiful than the Royal Gardens in Seville and the climate is as healthy as anywhere on earth. The native population, which once numbered some five hundred thousand, was wiped out by forcible expatriation to the island of Hispaniola, a policy adopted by the Spaniards in an endeavour to make up losses among the indigenous population of that island. One God-fearing individual was moved to mount an expedition to seek out those who had escaped the Spanish trawl and were still living in the Bahamas and to save their souls by converting them to Christianity, but, by the end of a search lasting three whole years, they had found only the eleven survivors I saw with my own eyes. A further thirty or so islands in the region of Puerto Rico are also now uninhabited and left to go to rack and ruin as a direct result of the same practices. All these islands, which together must run to over two thousand leagues, are now abandoned and desolate.

On the mainland, we know for sure that our fellow-countrymen have, through their cruelty and wickedness, depopulated and laid waste an area which once boasted more than ten kingdoms, each of them larger in area than the whole of the Iberian Peninsula. The whole region, once teeming with human beings, is now deserted over a distance of more than two thousand leagues: a distance, that is, greater than the journey from Seville to Jerusalem and back again.

At a conservative estimate, the despotic and diabolical behaviour of the Christians has, over the last forty years, led to the unjust and totally unwarranted deaths of more than twelve million souls, women and children among them, and there are grounds for believing my own estimate of more than fifteen million to be nearer the mark.

There are two main ways in which those who have travelled to this part of the world pretending to be Christians have uprooted these pitiful peoples and wiped them from the face of the earth. First, they have waged war on them: unjust, cruel, bloody and tyrannical war. Second, they have murdered anyone and everyone who has shown the slightest sign of resistance, or even of wishing to escape the torment to which they have subjected him. This latter policy has been instrumental in suppressing the native leaders, and, indeed, given that the Spaniards normally spare only women and children, it has led to the annihilation of all adult males, whom they habitually subject to the harshest and most iniquitous and brutal slavery that man has ever devised for his fellow-men, treating them, in fact, worse than animals. All the many and infinitely varied ways that have been devised for

oppressing these peoples can be seen to flow from one or other of these two diabolical and tyrannical policies.

The reason the Christians have murdered on such a vast scale and killed anyone and everyone in their way is purely and simply greed. They have set out to
line their pockets with gold and to amass private fortunes as quickly as possible so
that they can then assume a status quite at odds with that into which they were
born. Their insatiable greed and overweening ambition know no bounds; the land
is fertile and rich, the inhabitants simple, forbearing and submissive. The Spaniards have shown not the slightest consideration for these people, treating them
(and I speak from first-hand experience, having been there from the outset) not
as brute animals—indeed, I would to God they had done and had shown them
the consideration they afford their animals—so much as piles of dung in the
middle of the road. They have had as little concern for their souls as for their
bodies, all the millions that have perished having gone to their deaths with no
knowledge of God and without the benefit of the Sacraments. One fact in all this
is widely known and beyond dispute, for even the tyrannical murderers themselves acknowledge the truth of it: the indigenous peoples never did the Europeans any harm whatever; on the contrary, they believed them to have descended
from the heavens, at least until they or their fellow-citizens had tasted, at the
hands of these oppressors, a diet of robbery, murder, violence, and all other manner of trials and tribulations.

Hispaniola

As we have said, the island of Hispaniola was the first to witness the arrival of
Europeans and the first to suffer the wholesale slaughter of its people and the
devastation and depopulation of the land. It all began with the Europeans taking
native women and children both as servants and to satisfy their own base appetites; then, not content with what the local people offered them of their own free
will (and all offered as much as they could spare), they started taking for themselves the food the natives contrived to produce by the sweat of their brows,
which was in all honesty little enough. Since what a European will consume in a
single day normally supports three native households of ten persons each for a
whole month, and since the newcomers began to subject the locals to other vexations, assaults, and iniquities, the people began to realize that these men could
not, in truth, have descended from the heavens. Some of them started to conceal
what food they had, others decided to send their women and children into hiding,
and yet others took to the hills to get away from the brutal and ruthless cruelty
that was being inflicted on them. The Christians punched them, boxed their ears
and flogged them in order to track down the local leaders, and the whole shameful
process came to a head when one of the European commanders raped the wife

of the paramount chief of the entire island.[3] It was then that the locals began to think up ways of driving the Europeans out of their lands and to take up arms against them. Their weapons, however, were flimsy and ineffective both in attack and in defence (and, indeed, war in the Americas is no more deadly than our jousting, or than many European children's games) and, with their horses and swords and lances, the Spaniards easily fended them off, killing them and committing all kind of atrocities against them.

They forced their way into native settlements, slaughtering everyone they found there, including small children, old men, pregnant women, and even women who had just given birth. They hacked them to pieces, slicing open their bellies with their swords as though they were so many sheep herded into a pen. They even laid wagers on whether they could manage to slice a man in two at a stroke, or cut an individual's head from his body, or disembowel him with a single blow of their axes. They grabbed suckling infants by the feet and, ripping them from their mothers' breasts, dashed them headlong against the rocks. Others, laughing and joking all the while, threw them over their shoulders into a river, shouting: 'Wriggle, you little perisher.' They slaughtered anyone and everyone in their path, on occasion running through a mother and her baby with a single thrust of their swords. They spared no one, erecting especially wide gibbets on which they could string their victims up with their feet just off the ground and then burn them alive thirteen at a time, in honour of our Saviour and the twelve Apostles, or tie dry straw to their bodies and set fire to it. Some they chose to keep alive and simply cut their wrists, leaving their hands dangling, saying to them: 'Take this letter'—meaning that their sorry condition would act as a warning to those hiding in the hills. The way they normally dealt with the native leaders and nobles was to tie them to a kind of griddle consisting of sticks resting on pitchforks driven into the ground and then grill them over a slow fire, with the result that they howled in agony and despair as they died a lingering death.

It once happened that I myself witnessed their grilling of four or five local leaders in this fashion (and I believe they had set up two or three other pairs of grills alongside so that they might process other victims at the same time) when the poor creatures' howls came between the Spanish commander and his sleep. He gave orders that the prisoners were to be throttled, but the man in charge of the execution detail, who was more bloodthirsty than the average common hangman (I know his identity and even met some relatives of his in Seville), was loath to cut short his private entertainment by throttling them and so he personally went round ramming wooden bungs into their mouths to stop them making such a racket and deliberately stoked the fire so that they would take just as long to die as he himself chose. I saw all these things for myself and many others besides. And, since all those who could do so took to the hills and mountains in order to escape

---

3. A reference to Guarionex ("Brave Noble Lord"), chief who led his Taino tribe's resistance against the Spanish.

The execution of an Indian chieftain of Cuba. *bpk, Berlin/Art Resource, NY.*

the clutches of these merciless and inhuman butchers, these mortal enemies of human kind trained hunting dogs to track them down—wild dogs who would savage a native to death as soon as look at him, tearing him to shreds and devouring his flesh as though he were a pig. These dogs wrought havoc among the natives and were responsible for much carnage. And when, as happened on the odd occasion, the locals did kill a European, as, given the enormity of the crimes committed against them, they were in all justice fully entitled to, the Spanish came to an unofficial agreement among themselves that for every European killed, one hundred natives would be executed.

* * *

For forty-two years[4] now, these matters have been constantly before my eyes and on my mind, and I can honestly say, as God is my witness, that I have solid grounds for believing that the depredations, the harm, the destruction, the

4. Las Casas arrived in the New World in 1502. As he finished his work in 1542, his account is off the mark by two years.

depopulation, the atrocities and massacres, the horrible cruelty and barbarism, the violence, the injustice, the plunder and the wholesale murder that all these territories have witnessed and their people suffered (and still suffer) are on such a scale that what I have here been able to relate is no more than a thousandth part of the reality of what has been taking place and continues to take place.

Recognition of the truth will make the reader more compassionate towards the sufferings and the predicament of these poor innocent peoples and oblige him to adopt an even more stern and censorious attitude towards the abominable greed, ambition and brutality of their Spanish oppressors; and no Christian who reads this should be in any doubt, even for a moment, that there has ever been a single instance, from the date of the discovery of the New World down to the present, when the indigenous people have committed even the slightest offence against the Europeans without due provocation, and that it has been the wicked plunder and the treachery of the Europeans that have given rise to all the evils we have described. Indeed, the natives believed the Europeans immortal and to be descended from the heavens and they welcomed them as such, at least until the actions of these celestial beings finally revealed what sort of creatures they were and what it was they were after.

There is one other factor which merits a mention and it is that, from the very outset, the Spanish have taken no more trouble to preach the Christian faith to these peoples than if they had been dealing with dogs or other animals. Indeed, they have done their level best to prevent missionaries from preaching, presumably because they felt that the spread of the Gospel would in some way stand between them and the gold and wealth they craved. Today, the peoples of the New World are as ignorant of God as they were a hundred years ago: they have no idea of whether He is made of wood, or of air, or of earth. The only place where the missionaries have enjoyed a modicum of success is New Spain, but we are talking here of a very small corner of the New World and, for the most part, the local people have died and still die in the blackest ignorance of the faith and without the benefit of the Sacraments.

Study Questions

1. How, according to Las Casas, did the natives greet the Spaniards?

2. Why, according to Las Casas, did the Spanish lay waste to the Caribbean islands and its inhabitants?

3. Does anything in Las Casas's narrative contradict his description of the natives as "simple" and "submissive"?

4. How does religion influence Las Casas's interpretation of the Spanish conquest of the Caribbean?

Instructions for the Virginia Colony (1606)

As we doubt not but you will have especial care to observe the ordinances set down by the King's Majesty and delivered unto you under the Privy Seal; so for your better directions upon your first landing we have thought good to recommend unto your care these instructions and articles following.

When it shall please God to send you on the coast of Virginia, you shall do your best endeavour to find out a safe port in the entrance of some navigable river, making choice of such a one as runneth farthest into the land, and if you happen to discover divers portable rivers, and amongst them any one that hath two main branches, if the difference be not great, make choice of that which bendeth most toward the North-West for that way you shall soonest find the other sea.

When you have made choice of the river on which you mean to settle, be not hasty in landing your victuals and munitions; but first let Captain Newport discover how far that river may be found navigable, that you make election of the strongest, most wholesome and fertile place; for if you make many removes, besides the loss of time, you shall greatly spoil your victuals and your caske, and with great pain transport it in small boats.

But if you choose your place so far up as a bark of fifty tuns will float, then you may lay all your provisions ashore with ease, and the better receive the trade of all the countries about you in the land; and such a place you may perchance find a hundred miles from the river's mouth, and the further up the better. For if you sit down near the entrance, except it be in some island that is strong by nature, an enemy that may approach you on even ground, may easily pull you out; and if he be driven to seek you a hundred miles [in] the land in boats, you shall from both sides of the river where it is narrowest, so beat them with your muskets as they shall never be able to prevail against you.

And to the end that you be not surprised as the French were in Florida by Melindus, and the Spaniard in the same place by the French, you shall do well to make this double provision. First, erect a little stoure at the mouth of the river that may lodge some ten men; with whom you shall leave a light boat, that when any fleet shall be in sight, they may come with speed to give you warning. Secondly, you must in no case suffer any of the native people of the country to inhabit between you and the sea coast; for you cannot carry yourselves so towards them, but they will grow discontented with your habitation, and be ready to guide and assist any nation that shall come to invade you; and if you neglect this, you neglect your safety.

When you have discovered as far up the river as you mean to plant yourselves, and landed your victuals and munitions; to the end that every man may know his charge, you shall do well to divide your six score men into three parts; whereof one party of them you may appoint to fortifie and build, of which your first work must be your storehouse for victuals; the other you may imploy in preparing your ground and sowing your corn and roots; the other ten of these forty you must leave as centinel at the haven's mouth. The other forty you may imploy for two months in discovery of the river above you, and on the country about you; which charge Captain Newport and Captain Gosnold may undertake of these forty discoverers. When they do espie any high lands or hills, Captain Gosnold may take twenty of the company to cross over the lands, and carrying a half dozen pickaxes to try if they can find any minerals. The other twenty may go on by river, and pitch up boughs upon the bank's side, by which the other boats shall follow them by the same turnings. You may also take with them a wherry, such as is used here in the Thames; by which you may send back to the President for supply of munition or any other want, that you may not be driven to return for every small defect.

You must observe if you can, whether the river on which you plant doth spring out of mountains or out of lakes. If it be out of any lake, the passage to the other sea will be more easy, and [it] is like enough, that out of the same lake you shall find some spring which run[s] the contrary way towards the East India Sea; for the great and famous rivers of Volga, Tan[a] is and Dwina have three heads near joynd; and yet the one falleth into the Caspian Sea, the other into the Euxine Sea, and the third into the Paelonian Sea.

In all your passages you must have great care not to offend the naturals [natives], if you can eschew it; and imploy some few of your company to trade with them for corn and all other . . . victuals if you have any; and this you must do before that they perceive you mean to plant among them; for not being sure how your own seed corn will prosper the first year, to avoid the danger of famine, use and endeavour to store yourselves of the country corn.

Your discoverers that pass over land with hired guides, must look well to them that they slip not from them: and for more assurance, let them take a compass with them, and write down how far they go upon every point of the compass; for that country having no way nor path, if that your guides run from you in the great woods or desert, you shall hardly ever find a passage back.

And how weary soever your soldiers be, let them never trust the country people with the carriage of their weapons; for if they run from you with your shott, which they only fear, they will easily kill them all with their arrows. And whensoever any of yours shoots before them, be sure they may be chosen out of your best marksmen; for if they see your learners miss what they aim at, they will think the weapon not so terrible, and thereby will be bould to assault you.

Above all things, do not advertize the killing of any of your men, that the country people may know it; if they perceive that they are but common men, and that with the loss of many of theirs they diminish any part of yours, they will make many adventures upon you. If the country be populous, you shall do well also, not to let them see or know of your sick men, if you have any; which may also encourage them to many enterprizes.

You must take especial care that you choose a seat for habitation that shall not be over burthened with woods near your town; for all the men you have, shall not be able to cleanse twenty acres a year; besides that it may serve for a covert for your enemies round about.

Neither must you plant in a low or moist place, because it will prove unhealthfull. You shall judge of the good air by the people; for some part of that coast where the lands are low, have their people blear eyed, and with swollen bellies and legs; but if the naturals be strong and clean made, it is a true sign of a wholesome soil.

You must take order to draw up the pinnace that is left with you, under the fort: and take her sails and anchors ashore, all but a small kedge to ride by; least some ill-dispositioned persons slip away with her.

You must take care that your marriners that go for wages, do not mar your trade; for those that mind not to inhabite, for a little gain will debase the estimation of exchange, and hinder the trade for ever after; and therefore you shall not admit or suffer any person whatsoever, other than such as shall be appointed by the President and Counsel there, to buy any merchandizes or other things whatsoever.

It were necessary that all your carpenters and other such like workmen about building do first build your storehouse and those other rooms of publick and necessary use before any house be set up for any private person: and though the workman may belong to any private persons yet let them all work together first for the company and then for private men.

And seeing order is at the same price with confusion, it shall be adviseably done to set your houses even and by a line, that your street may have a good breadth, and be carried square about your market place and every street's end opening into it; that from thence, with a few field pieces, you may command every street throughout; which market place you may also fortify if you think it needfull.

You shall do well to send a perfect relation by "Captain Newport of all that is done, what height you are seated, how far into the land, what commodities you find, what soil, woods and their several kinds, and so of all other things else to advertise particularly; and to suffer no man to return but by pasport from the

President and Counsel, nor to write any letter of anything that may discourage others.

Lastly and chiefly the way to prosper and achieve good success is to make yourselves all of one mind for the good of your country and your own, and to serve and fear God the Giver of all Goodness, for every plantation which our Heavenly Father hath not planted shall be rooted out.

On the Divine Rights of Kings (1609)

But as ye are clothed with two callings, so must ye be alike careful for the discharge of them both: that as yee are a good Christian, so yee may be a good King, discharging your Office . . . in the points of Iustice and Equitie: which in two sundrie waies ye must doe: the one, in establishing and excuting, (which is the life of the Law) good Lawes among your people: the other, by your behauiour in your owne person, and with your seruants, to teach your people by your example: for people are naturally inclined to counterfaite (like apes) their Princes maners. . . .

For the part of making, and executing of Lawes, consider first the trew difference betwixt a lawful good King, and an usurping Tyran, and yee shall the more easily vnderstand your duetie herein:. . . . The one acknowledgeth himselfe ordained for his people, hauing receiued from God a burthen of gouernment, whereof he must be countable: the other thinketh his people ordeined for him, a prey to his passons and inordinate appetites, as the fruites of his magnanimitie: And therefore, as their ends are directly contraries, so are their whole actions, as meanes, whereby the preasse to attaine to their endes. . . .

The State of Monarchie is the supremest thing vpon earth: For Kings are not onely Gods Lietuenants vpon earth, and fit vpon Gods throne, but euen by God himselfe thy are called Gods. . . . In the Scriptures Kings are called Gods, and so their power after a certaine relation compared to the Diuine power. . . .

Kings are iuftly called Gods, for that they exercise a manner or resemblance of Diuine power vpon earth: For if you wil consider the Attributes to God, you shall see how they agree in the person of a King. God hath power to create, or destroy, make, or vnmake at his pleasure, to giue life, or send death, to iudge all, and to bee judged nor accomptable to none: To raise low things, and to make high things law at his pleasure, and to God are both soule and body due. And the like power haue Kings: They make and vnmake their subiects: they haue power of raining, and casting downe: of life, and of death: Iudges ouer all their subiects, and in all causes, and yet accomptable to none but God onely. The haue power to exalt low things, and abase high things, and make of their subiects like men at the Chesse; A pawne to take bishop or a Knight, and to cry vp, or downe any of their subiects, as they do their money. And to the King is due both the affection of the soule, and the seruice of the body of his subiects. . . .

But now in these our times we are to distinguish betweene the state of Kings in their first originall, and betweene the state of setled Kings and Monarches, that doe at this time gouerene in ciuill Kingdomes: For euen as God, during the time of the olde Testament, spake by Oracles, and wrought by Miracles; yet how soone it pleased him to setle a *Church* which was bought, and redeemed by the blood of his onely Sonne *Crift*, then was there a cessation of both; Hee euer after gouerning his people and Church within the limits of his reueiledwill. So in the first originall of Kings, whereof some had their beginning by Conquest, and some by election of the people, their wills at that time serued for Law; Yet how soone Kingdomes began to be setled in ciuilitie and policie, then did Kings set downe their minds by Lawes, which are properly made by the King onely; but at the rogation of the people, the Kings grant being obteined thereunto. And so the King became to be *Lex loquens*, after a sort, binding himselfe by a double oath to the obseuation of the fundamentall Lawes of his kingdome: Tacitly, as by being a King, and so bound to protect aswell the people, as the Lawes of his Kingdome; and *Expresly*, by his oath at his Coronation. . . . Therefore all Kings that are not tyrants, or periured, wil be glad to bound themselues within the limits of their Lawes: and they that perswade them the contrary, are vipers, and pests, both against them and the Commonwealth. For it is a great difference between a Kings gouernment in a setled State, and what Kings in their originall power might doe. . . . As for my part, I thanke God, I

Pocahontas Engraving (1616)

Pocahontas (ca. 1596–1617), whose actual name was Matoaka, was a daughter of the powerful Indian leader Wahunsonacock, a man the English called Powhatan. In 1614 Pocahontas converted to Christianity, took the name Rebecca, and married John Rolfe, an Englishman best known today for developing a new and profitable strain of tobacco. Their son, Thomas, was born in early 1615. The next year, all three Rolfes traveled to England where Pocahontas became a something of a celebrity and earned the respect of well-bred Englishmen; the Reverend Samuel Purchas thought she "carried herself as the daughter of a King."

While in London, Pocahontas sat for a sketch portrait by a young Dutch artist named Simon Van de Passe, who afterward made the engraving on the following page based on the sitting. Van de Passe portrayed Pocahontas as an aristocrat: she is wearing fine clothing and pearl earrings, and is holding a fan made of ostrich feathers—a European symbol of royalty. Van de Passe, unlike many later artists, did not try to Anglicize Pocahontas completely—she is recognizably Native American. Although the inscription claims that she was twenty-one years old (the Latin "Ætatis suæ 21 A. 1616" translates to "at the age of 21 in the year 1616"), Pocahontas was in all likelihood only nineteen. Shortly after the portrait was made, Pocahontas died of unknown causes just as her ship was about to embark upon the voyage back to her home in Virginia.

Pocahontas, engraving by Simon Van De Passe. *Library of Congress.*

Study Questions

1. The Virginia Company struggled to get colonists to come to their colony. How might this portrait have encouraged such migration?

2. Pocahontas was considered a Native American "princess." What styles and symbols in the portrait suggest her social standing, and why might these have been incomprehensible to a Native American audience?

3. Given the technology of the day, why do you think Van De Passe might have chosen to make an engraving rather than, say, a painting or a sculpture of Pocahontas's likeness?

An Indentured Servant's Letter
to His Parents (1623)

The typical migrant to England's North American colonies in the seventeenth century was an indentured servant—a young man or woman desperate enough to agree to work for a master for a set amount of time (usually four to seven years) in return for transportation to North America, food, clothing, lodging, and, in some cases, money or land at the end of the contract.

Richard Frethorne was one of the thousands of such indentured servants who poured into Virginia in the seventeenth century. Like the vast majority of these migrants, we know very little about Frethorne himself. He came to Virginia shortly after the colony experienced a horrific Indian attack in 1622, and he worked at Martin's Hundred, a large tobacco plantation located on the James River about ten miles downriver from Jamestown. The following are excerpts from three letters Frethorne wrote to his parents in March and April of 1623. Shortly afterward, the young man died.

From Susan Myra Kingsbury, ed., *The Records of the Virgina Company of London* (Washington, D.C.: US Government Printing Office, 1935), 4:58–60.

March 20, April 2 and 3, 1623

Loveing and kind father and mother my most humble duty remembred to you hopeing in God of yor good health . . . this is to let you understand that I yor Child am in a most heavie Case by reason of the nature of the Country is such that it Causeth much sicknes, as the scurvie and the bloody flix,[1] and divers other diseases, wch[2] maketh the bodie very poore, and Weake, and when wee are sicke there is nothing to Comfort us; for since I came out of the ship, I never ate anie thing but pease, and loblollie (that is water gruell) as for deare or venison I never saw anie since I came into this land, ther is indeed some foule, but Wee are not allowed to goe, and get yt, but must Worke hard both earelie, and late for a messe of water gruell, and a mouthfull of bread, and beife,

---

1. Bloody flux—dysentery, a severe and often fatal intestinal disorder.
2. Which.

a mouthfull of bread for a pennie loafe must serve for 4 men wch is most pitifull if you did knowe as much as I, when people crie out day, and night, Oh that they were in England without their lymbes and would not care to loose anie lymbe to bee in England againe, yea though they beg from doore to doore, for wee live in feare of the Enimy[3] everie houer,[4] yet wee have had a Combate with them on the Sunday before Shrovetyde,[5] and wee tooke two alive, and make slaves of them, but it was by pollicie, for wee are in great danger, for or Plantacon is very weake, by reason of the dearth, and sicknes, of or Companie, for wee came but Twentie for the marchaunts, and they are halfe dead Just; and wee looke everie houer. When two more should goe, yet there came some for other men yet to lyve with us, of which ther is but one alive, and our Leiftenant is dead, and his father, and his brother, and there was some 5 or 6 of the last yeares 20 of wch there is but 3 left, so that wee are faine to get other men to plant with us, and yet wee are but 32 to fight against 3000 if they should Come, and the nighest helpe that Wee have is ten miles of us, and when the rogues overcame this place last,[6] they slew 80 Persons how then shall wee doe for wee lye even in their teeth, they may easilie take us but that God is mercifull, and can save with few as well as with many; . . . ther is nothing to be gotten here but sicknes, and death, except that one had money to lay out in some thinges for profit; But I have nothing at all, no not a shirt to my backe, but two Ragges nor no Clothes, but one poore suite, nor but one paire of shooes, but one paire of stockins, but one Capp, but two bands, my Cloke is stollen by one of my owne fellowes, and to his dying houer would not tell mee what he did with it but some of my fellows saw him have butter and beife out of a ship, wch my Cloke I doubt[7] paid for, so that I have not a penny, nor a a penny Worth to helpe me to either spice, or sugar, or strong Waters, without the wch one cannot lyve here, for as strong beare in England doth fatten and strengthen them so water here doth wash and weaken theis here, onelie keepe life and soule togeather. But I am not halfe a quarter so strong as I was in England, and all is for want of victualls, for I doe protest unto you, that I have eaten more in day at home then I have allowed me here for a Weeke. You have given more then my dayes allowance to a beggar at the doore; and if

---

3. The enemy—Native Americans.

4. Every hour.

5. Shrovetide—a carnival-like celebration during the three days before Ash Wednesday.

6. A devastating Indian attack on March 22, 1622, killed about one-third of all Virginian settlers.

7. Think, believe.

Mr Jackson[8] had not releived me, I should bee in a poore Case, but he like a father and shee like a loveing mother doth still helpe me.

* * *

Goodman Jackson pityed me & made me a Cabbin to lye in always when I come up, and he would give me some poore Jacks home with me wch Comforted mee more then pease, or water gruell. Oh they bee verie godlie folkes, and love me verie well, and will doe anie thing for me, and he much marvailed that you would send me a servaunt to the Companie,[9] he saith I had beene better knockd on the head, and Indeede so I fynd it now to my greate greife and miserie, and saith, that if you love me you will redeeme me suddenlie, for wch I doe Intreate and begg, and if you cannot get the marchaunts to redeeme me for some litle money then for Gods sake get a gathering or intreat some good folks to lay out some little Sum of moneye, in meale, and Cheese and butter, and beife, anie eating meate will yeald great profit, oile and vyniger is verie good, but father ther is greate losse in leakinge, but for Gods sake send beife and Cheese and butter.

* * *

If I die before it Come I have intreated Goodman Jackson to send you the worth of it, who hath promised he will; If you send you must direct yor letters to Goodman Jackson, at James Towne a Gunsmith. (you must set downe his frayt) because there bee more of his name there; good father doe not forget me, but have mercie and pittye my miserable Case. I know if you did but see me you would weepe to see me, for I have but one suite, but it is a strange one, it is very well guarded, wherefore for Gods sake pittie me, I pray you to remember my love my love to all my freinds, and kindred, I hope all my Brothers and Sisters are in good health, and as for my part I have set downe my resolucon that certaine-lie Wilbe, that is, that the Answeare of this letter wilbee life or death to me, therefore good father send as soone as you can, and if you send me anie thing let this bee the marke.

Richard Frethorne
Martyns Hundred

8. John Jackson, a gunsmith at Jamestown.
9. Virginia Company.

Study Questions

1. What specifically does Frethorne complain of?

2. What does Frethorne ask of his parents?

3. Although America is often described as the land of opportunity, Frethorne's story suggests that such a description is simplistic, to say the least. How would you formulate a description of early America that would take into account not only opportunity but also frustration, disappointment, and danger?

4. Describe the tone of Frethorne's letter. How might it differ from an account written by his employer? How might Frethorne have written differently to friends at home, or to his sweetheart?

JOHN SMITH

The Starving Time in Jamestown (1624)

Captain John Smith (1580–1631) was one of the original 104 English colonists who founded Jamestown, the first permanent English settlement in Virginia, in 1607. Jamestown's earliest period was extremely difficult; more than half of the settlers died of disease and poor nutrition. With the colony near collapse by 1608 as a result of mismanagement and lack of necessary skills such as farming, Smith gained control and instituted policies that brought discipline and order to the colony, including his famous proclamation that "He that will not work shall not eat." Badly injured in an accidental explosion of gunpowder, Smith returned to England for treatment in October 1609. He never returned to the colony.

Meanwhile shiploads of ill-prepared settlers continued to arrive at Jamestown, now without Smith's able leadership. The subsequent winter of 1609–10, a time of terrible hardship during which all but 60 of the 500 colonists died, became known as the "starving time." More than a decade later, when Smith wrote A General Historie of Virginia *to memorialize those who had been at Jamestown, he had few reliable records to draw upon. As you read the following selection, consider why the Jamestown colony struggled initially. What fundamental mistakes do the colonists appear to have made?*

I t might well be thought, a Countrie so faire (as Virginia is) and a people so tractable, would long ere this have beene quietly possessed, to the satisfaction of the adventurers, & the eternizing of the memory of those that effected it. But because all the world doe see a defailement;[1] this following Treatise shall give satisfaction to all indifferent Readers, how the businesse hath bin carried: where no doubt they will easily understand and answer to their question, how it came to passe there was no better speed and successe in those proceedings.

* * *

The day before Captaine Smith returned for England with the ships, Captaine Davis arrived in a small Pinace,[2] with some sixteene proper men more. . . . For the Salvages[3] no sooner understood Smith was gone, but they all revolted, and did

1. Failure.
2. Small boat.
3. Savages; that is, the Native Americans.

spoile and murther all they incountered. Now wee were all constrained to live onely on that Smith had onely for his owne Companie, for the rest had consumed their proportions. . . . Sickelmore upon the confidence of Powhatan,[4] with about thirtie others as carelesse as himselfe, were all slaine, onely Jeffrey Shortridge escaped, and Pokahontas the Kings daughter saved a boy called Henry Spilman, that lived many yeeres after, by her meanes, amongst the Patawomekes. . . . Now we all found the losse of Captaine Smith, yea his greatest maligners could now curse his losse: as for corne, provision and contribution from the Salvages, we had nothing but mortall wounds, with clubs and arrowes; as for our Hogs, Hens, Goats, Sheepe, Horse, or what lived, our commanders, officers & Salvages daily consumed them, some small proportions sometimes we tasted, till all was devoured; then swords, armes, pieces, or any thing, wee traded with the Salvages, whose cruell fingers were so oft imbrewed in our blouds, that what by their crueltie, our Governours indiscretion, and the losse of our ships, of five hundred within six moneths after Captaine Smiths departure, there remained not past sixtie men, women and children, most miserable and poore creatures; and those were preserved for the most part, by roots, herbes, acornes, walnuts, berries, now and then a little fish: they that had startch[5] in these extremities, made no small use of it; yea, even the very skinnes of our horses. Nay, so great was our famine, that a Salvage we slew, and buried, the poorer sort tooke him up againe and eat him, and so did divers one another boyled and stewed with roots and herbs: And one amongst the rest did kill his wife, powdered her, and had eaten part of her before it was knowne, for which hee was executed, as hee well deserved; now whether shee was better roasted, boyled or carbonado'd,[6] I know not, but of such a dish as powdered wife I never heard of. This was that time, which still to this day we called the starving time; it were too vile to say, and scarce to be beleeved, what we endured.

Study Questions

1. What reasons does Smith give for the hardships the colonists suffered? Does he offer any solutions?

2. What do you think they could have done to prevent starvation?

3. Why do you think Smith refers to himself in the third person in this excerpt?

4. The document was written in 1624, 15 years after Smith left Jamestown. How do you think Smith's account was affected by the passage of time, and especially by the facts that Smith was absent during the worst of the colony's hardships and that, by 1624, the colony was prospering?

4. Smith's name for the chief of the Powhattan Indians.
5. Plant starch, a tasteless powder normally used to stiffen fabric.
6. Scored with a knife and then grilled.

A Model of Christian Charity (1630)

John Winthrop (1588–1649) was easily the most important figure in the early years of the Massachusetts Bay Colony, serving as the colony's governor for most of its first twenty years. Born in England and trained as a lawyer, Winthrop in the 1620s became increasingly disheartened with his country. After years in which King Charles I clashed with the Puritans (a hostility that would erupt into civil war in the 1640s), Winthrop despaired that "this lande growes weary of her Inhabitantes" and helped organize the Massachusetts Bay Company, a corporation designed to establish a haven for Puritans in America. Yet as he prepared to leave for America, Winthrop struggled to explain that he and his followers were not Separatist Puritans like the Pilgrims who had settled Plymouth Colony ten years earlier. This raised an obvious question: if the Massachusetts Bay settlers were not giving up on England, then why were they leaving for North America?

For an answer, Winthrop turned to the Bible: "Ye are the light of the world. A city that is set on an hill cannot be hid" (Matthew 5:14). In this sermon, delivered either onboard the Arbella bound for America or just before Winthrop departed England with seven hundred others, Winthrop expressed his fondest hopes and darkest fears for the Christian commonwealth he envisioned. In so doing, he helped lay the groundwork for American exceptionalism, the controversial idea that America has a special destiny among the world's peoples.

From Edmund Clarence Stedman and Ellen MacKay Hutchinson, ed., *A Library of American Literature* (New York: Charles L. Webster & Co, 1892), 1:304–7.

God almighty in his most holy and wise providence, hath so disposed of the condition of mankind, as in all times some must be rich, some poor, some high and eminent in power and dignity; others mean and in submission.

* * *

All men being thus (by divine providence) ranked into two sorts, rich and poor; under the first are comprehended all such as are able to live comfortably by their own means duly improved; and all others are poor according to the former distribution. There are two rules whereby we are to walk one towards another: Justice and Mercy. . . . Sometimes there may be an occasion of showing mercy to a rich man in some sudden danger or distress, and also doing of mere justice to a poor man in regard of some particular contract, etc.

* * *

Herein are four things to be propounded: First, the persons; secondly, the work; thirdly, the end; fourthly, the means. First, for the persons. We are a company professing ourselves fellow-members of Christ, in which respect only, though we were absent from each other many miles, and had our employments as far distant, yet we ought to account ourselves knit together by this bond of love, and live in the exercise of it, if we would have comfort of our being in Christ. . . . Secondly, for the work we have in hand. It is by a mutual consent, through a special overvaluing providence and a more than an ordinary approbation of the Churches of Christ, to seek out a place of cohabitation and Consortship under a due form of Government both civil and ecclesiastical. In such cases as this, the care of the public must oversway all private respects, by which, not only conscience, but mere civil policy, doth bind us. For it is a true rule that particular estates cannot subsist in the ruin of the public.

Thirdly, the end is to improve our lives to do more service to the Lord; the comfort and increase of the body of Christ, whereof we are members; that ourselves and posterity may be the better preserved from the common corruptions of this evil world, to serve the Lord and work out our salvation under the power and purity of his holy ordinances. Fourthly, for the means whereby this must be effected. They are twofold, a conformity with the work and end we aim at. These we see are extraordinary, therefore we must not content ourselves with usual ordinary means. Whatsoever we did, or ought to have done, when we lived in England, the same must we do, and more also, where we go. That which the most in their churches maintain as truth in profession only, we must bring into familiar and constant practice; as in this duty of love, we must love brotherly without dissimulation, we must love one another with a pure heart fervently. We must bear one another's burdens. We must not look only on our own things, but also on the things of our brethren. Neither must we think that the Lord will bear with such failings at our hands as he doth from those among whom we have lived; and that for these three Reasons: First, in regard of the more near bond of marriage between him and us, wherein he hath taken us to be his, after a most strict and peculiar manner, which will make them the more jealous of our love and obedience. So he tells the people of Israel, "You only have I known of all the families of the Earth, therefore will I punish you for your Transgressions."[1] Secondly, because the Lord will be sanctified in them that come near him. We know that there were many that corrupted the service of the Lord; some setting up altars before his own; others offering both strange fire and strange sacrifices also; yet there came no fire from

1. Amos 3:2.

heaven, or other sudden judgment upon them, as did upon Nadab and Abihu,[2] who yet we may think did not sin presumptuously. Thirdly, when God gives a special commission he looks to have it strictly observed in every article. When he gave Saul a commission to destroy Amalek,[3] He indented with him upon certain articles, and because he failed in one of the least, and that upon a fair pretence, it lost him the kingdom, which should have been his reward, if he had observed his commission.

Thus stands the cause between God and us. We are entered into Covenant with him for this work. We have taken out a commission. The Lord hath given us leave to draw our own articles. We have professed to enterprise these and those accounts, upon these and those ends. We have hereupon besought him of favor and blessing. Now if the Lord shall please to hear us, and bring us in peace to the place we desire, then hath He ratified this covenant and sealed our Commission, and will expect a strict performance of the articles contained in it; but if we shall neglect the observation of these articles which are the ends we have propounded, and, dissembling with our God,[4] shall fall to embrace this present world and prosecute our carnal intentions, seeking great things for ourselves and our posterity, the Lord will surely break out in wrath against us; be revenged of such a [sinful] people and make us know the price of the breach of such a covenant.

Now the only way to avoid this shipwreck, and to provide for our posterity, is to follow the counsel of Micah, to do justly, to love mercy, to walk humbly with our God. For this end, we must be knit together, in this work, as one man. We must entertain each other in brotherly affection. We must be willing to abridge ourselves of our superfluities, for the supply of others' necessities. We must uphold a familiar commerce together in all meekness, gentleness, patience and liberality. We must delight in each other; make others' conditions our own; rejoice together, mourn together, labor and suffer together, always having before our eyes our commission and community in the work, as members of the same body. So shall we keep the unity of the spirit in the bond of peace. The Lord will be our God, and delight to dwell among us, as his own people, and will command a blessing upon us in all our ways. So that we shall see much more of his wisdom, power, goodness and truth, than formerly we have been acquainted with. We shall find that the God of Israel is among us, when ten of us shall be able to resist a thousand of our enemies; when he shall make us a praise and glory that men shall say of succeeding plantations, "The Lord make it likely that of New England." For we must consider that we shall be as a city upon a hill. The eves of all people are upon us.

2. Sons of Aaron, who, according to Leviticus 10:1–2, offered "a strange fire before the Lord, which he had not commanded them. Therefore a fire went out from the Lord, and devoured them, so they died before the Lord" (Geneva Bible).

3. The story of Saul and Amalek is told in Exodus 17:8–16, Deuteronomy 25:17–19, and 1 Samuel 15:2–9.

4. Micah 6:8.

So that if we shall deal falsely with our God in this work we have undertaken, and so cause him to withdraw his present help from us, we shall be made a story and a byword through the world. We shall open the mouths of enemies to speak evil of the ways of God, and all professors for God's sake. We shall shame the faces of many of God's worthy servants, and cause their prayers to be turned into curses upon us till we be consumed out of the good land whither we are agoing.

I shall shut up this discourse with that exhortation of Moses, that faithful servant of the Lord, in his last farewell to Israel (Deut. xxx.): Beloved, there is now set before us life and good, Death and evil, in that we are commanded this day to love the Lord our God, and to love one another, to walk in his ways and to keep his Commandments and his Ordinance and his laws, and the articles of our Covenant with him, that we may live and be multiplied, and that the Lord our God may bless us in the land whither we go to possess it. But if our hearts shall turn away, so that we will not obey, but shall be seduced, and worship and serve other gods, our pleasure and profits, and serve them; it is propounded unto us this day, we shall surely perish out of the good land whither we pass over this vast sea to possess it;

> Therefore let us choose life
> that we, and our seed
> may live, by obeying His
> voice and cleaving to Him,
> for He is our life and
> our prosperity.

Study Questions

1. According to Winthrop, what was the purpose of the Massachusetts Bay Colony? What sort of relationship between church and state does Winthrop envision?

2. Why do you think Winthrop begins his sermon with an extended discussion of the divine origin of social and economic inequalities? Who or what is responsible for inequalities among men? What is his attitude toward democracy?

3. What did Winthrop mean when he declared that "we shall be as a city upon a hill"? What does Winthrop suggest will happen if the settlers fail to live up to God's standards?

4. Winthrop wrote that the settlers of Massachusetts Bay "must delight in each other; make others' conditions our own; rejoice together, mourn together, labor and suffer together, always having before our eyes our commission and community in the work, as members of the same body." What does this sentiment suggest about the colonial attitudes toward individualism?

5. Many Americans today embrace the notion that America is unique in world history, that the country has a special mission—that the United States is a chosen nation. This idea, known as American exceptionalism, has come under strong attack in the past half century. What do you think?

The Examination of Mrs. Anne Hutchinson at the Court at Newton (1637)

Anne Hutchinson (ca. 1591–1643) moved from England to the Massachusetts Bay Colony in 1634 with her husband, William, and their twelve children. Settling in Boston, across the street from Governor John Winthrop, Hutchinson began hosting gatherings at her home during which she discussed religious matters. At these meetings, which drew as many as sixty people and included high-ranking authorities of the colony, Hutchinson claimed to possess a direct connection with the divine—what she would call in her trial "immediate revelation"—and questioned whether certain ministers were in fact among those God had selected for eternal salvation. For the authorities of Massachusetts Bay, such claims were profoundly alarming; if one could commune directly with God, what use was there for the church, the state, or any man-made authority? Hutchinson's claim to channel the will of God—a claim that rendered the laws of man irrelevant at best—is the core of the so-called antinomian heresy. Such teachings not only flew in the face of orthodox Calvinist theology—which held that humans, inescapably mired in sin, could not know the mind of God and thus could not know their fate—they also threatened the very foundations of the Massachusetts Bay Colony.

In November 1637, Hutchinson was summoned to appear before a council of leading ministers and magistrates of the Massachusetts Bay Colony to defend her unorthodox beliefs and teachings. Although Hutchinson's intelligence and quick wit were more than her persecutors bargained for, she and her family were expelled from the colony in early 1638. After living briefly in Rhode Island—a colony established by another nonconforming expatriate from Massachusetts, Roger Williams—the Hutchinsons removed to Long Island in present-day New York State. In 1643, Anne Hutchinson and five of her children were killed by Indians.

From David D. Hall, ed., *The Antinomian Controversy, 1636–1638: A Documentary History, Second Edition* (Durham and London: Duke University Press, 1990), 312–318, 333–334, 336–341, 347–348.

M R. WINTHROP, GOVERNOR: Mrs. Hutchinson, you are called here as one of those that have troubled the peace of the commonwealth and the churches here; you are known to be a woman that hath had a great share in the promoting and divulging of those opinions that are causes of this trouble, and to be nearly joined not only in affinity and affection with some of those the court had taken notice of and passed censure upon, but you have spoken divers things as we have been informed very prejudicial to the honour of the churches and ministers thereof, and you have maintained a meeting and an assembly in your house that hath been condemned by the general assembly as a thing not tolerable nor comely in the sight of God nor fitting for your sex, and notwithstanding that was cried down you have continued the same, therefore we have thought good to send for you to understand how things are, that if you be in an erroneous way we may reduce you that so you may become a profitable member here among us, otherwise if you be obstinate in your course that then the court may take such course that you may trouble us no further, therefore I would intreat you to express whether you do not hold and assent in practice to those opinions and factions that have been handled in court already, that is to say, whether you do not justify Mr. Wheelwright's[1] sermon and the petition.

* * *

MRS. HUTCHINSON: What law have I broken?

Gov.: Why the fifth commandment.[2]

MRS. H.: I deny that for he saith in the Lord.

Gov.: You have joined with them in the faction.

MRS. H.: In what faction have I joined with them?

Gov.: In presenting the petition.

MRS. H.: Suppose I had set my hand to the petition what then?

Gov.: You saw that case tried before.

MRS. H.: But I had not my hand to the petition.

Gov.: You have councelled them.

MRS. H.: Wherein?

Gov.: Why in entertaining them.

MRS. H.: What breach of law is that Sir?

Gov.: Why dishonouring of parents.

MRS. H.: But put the case Sir that I do fear the Lord and my parents, may not I entertain them that fear the Lord because my parents will not give me leave?

---

1. John Wheelwright (c. 1592–1679) Puritan minister in the Massachusetts Bay Colony; along with Anne Hutchinson, his sister-in-law, Wheelwright was expelled from the colony during the antinomian controversy.

2. Honor thy father and thy mother (Exodus 20:12).

Gov.: If they be the fathers of the commonwealth, and they of another religion, if you entertain them then you dishonour your parents and are justly punishable.

Mrs. H.: If I entertain them, as they have dishonoured their parents I do.

Gov.: No but you by countenancing them above others put honor upon them.

Mrs. H.: I may put honor upon them as the children of God and as they do honor the Lord.

Gov.: We do not mean to discourse with those of your sex but only this; you do adhere unto them and do endeavour to set forward this faction and so you do dishonour us.

Mrs. H.: I do acknowledge no such thing neither do I think that I ever put any dishonour upon you.

Gov.: Why do you keep such a meeting at your house as you do every week upon a set day?

Mrs. H.: It is lawful for me so to do, as it is all your practices and can you find a warrant for yourself and condemn me for the same thing? The ground of my taking it up was, when I first came to this land because I did not go to such meetings as those were, it was presently reported that I did not allow of such meetings but held them unlawful and therefore in that regard they said I was proud and did despise all ordinances, upon that a friend came unto me and told me of it and I to prevent such aspersions took it up, but it was in practice before I came therefore I was not the first.

* * *

Gov.: Suppose that a man should come and say Mrs. Hutchinson I hear that you are a woman that God hath given his grace unto and you have knowledge in the word of God I pray instruct me a little, ought you not to instruct this man?

Mrs. H.: I think I may.—Do you think it not lawful for me to teach women and why do you call me to teach the court?

Gov.: We do not call you to teach the court but to lay open yourself.

Mrs. H.: I desire you that you would then set me down a rule by which I may put them away that come unto me and so have peace in so doing.

* * *

Gov.: Your course is not to be suffered for, besides that we find such a course as this to be greatly prejudicial to the state, besides the occasion that it is to seduce many honest persons that are called to those meetings and your opinions being known to be different from the word of God may seduce many simple souls that resort unto you, besides that the occasion which hath come of late hath come from none but such as have frequented your meetings, so that now they are flown off from magistrates and ministers and this since they have come to you, and besides that it will not well stand with the commonwealth that families should be neglected for so many neighbours and dames and so much time spent, we see no rule of God for this, we see not that any should have authority to set up any other exercises besides what authority hath already set up and so what hurt comes of this you will be guilty of and we for suffering you.

MRS. H.: Sir I do not believe that to be so.

GOV.: Well, we see how it is we must therefore put it away from you, or restrain you from maintaining this course.

MRS. H.: If you have a rule for it from God's word you may.

GOV.: We are your judges, and not you ours and we must compel you to it.

* * *

MR. DUDLEY, DEPUTY GOVERNOR: Here hath been much spoken concerning Mrs. Hutchinson's meetings and among other answers she saith that men come not there, I would ask you this one question then, whether never any man was at your meeting?

GOV.: There are two meetings kept at their house.

DEP. GOV.: How is there two meetings?

MRS. H.: Ey Sir, I shall not equivocate, there is a meeting of men and women and there is a meeting only for women.

DEP. GOV.: Are they both constant?

MRS. H.: No, but upon occasions they are deferred.

MR. ENDICOT: Who teaches in the men's meetings?

MRS. H.: None but men.

MR. ENDICOT: Do not women sometimes?

MRS. H.: Never as I heard, not one.

DEP. GOV.: I would go a little higher with Mrs. Hutchinson. About three years ago we were all in peace. Mrs. Hutchinson from that time she came hath made a disturbance, and some that came over with her in the ship did inform me what she was as soon as she was landed. I being then in place dealt with the pastor and teacher of Boston and desired them to enquire of her, and then I was satisfied that she held nothing different from us, but within half a year after, she had vented divers of her strange opinions and had made parties in the country, and at length it comes that Mr. Cotton and Mr. Vane[3] were of her judgment, but Mr. Cotton hath cleared himself that he was not of that mind, but now it appears by this woman's meeting that Mrs. Hutchinson hath so forestalled the minds of many by their resort to her meeting that now she hath a potent party in the country.

* * *

3. John Cotton (1585–1652), Puritan minister; an early supporter of Anne Hutchinson, he turned against her later in her trial. Henry Vane (1613–62), a proponent of religious tolerance, was governor of the Massachusetts Bay Colony during Hutchinson's trial.

Gov.: Mr. Cotton, the court desires that you declare what you do remember of the conference which was at that time and is now in question.

Mr. Cotton: I did not think I should be called to bear witness in this cause and therefore did not labour to call to remembrance what was done; but the greatest passage that took impression upon me was to this purpose. The elders spake that they had heard that she had spoken some condemning words of their ministry, and among other things they did first pray her to answer wherein she thought their ministry did differ from mine, how the comparison sprang I am ignorant, but sorry I was that any comparison should be between me and my brethren and uncomfortable it was, she told them to this purpose that they did not hold forth a covenant of grace as I did, but wherein did we differ? why she said that they did not hold forth the seal of the spirit as he doth. Where is the difference there? say they, why saith she speaking to one or other of them, I know not to whom. You preach of the seal of the spirit upon a work and he upon free grace without a work or without respect to a work, he preaches the seal of the spirit upon free grace and you upon a work. I told her I was very sorry that she put comparisons between my ministry and theirs, for she had said more than I could myself, and rather I had that she had put us in fellowship with them and not have made that discrepancy. She said, she found the difference. Upon that there grew some speeches upon the thing and I do remember I instanced to them the story of Thomas Bilney[4] in the book of martyrs how freely the spirit witnessed unto him without any respect unto a work as himself professes. Now upon this other speeches did grow. If you put me in mind of any thing I shall speak it, but this was the sum of the difference, nor did it seem to be so ill taken as it is and our brethren did say also that they would not so easily believe reports as they had done and withal mentioned that they would speak no more of it, some of them did; and afterwards some of them did say they were less satisfied than before. And I must say that I did not find her saying they were under a covenant of works, nor that she said they did preach a covenant of works.

* * *

Mrs. H.: If you please to give me leave I shall give you the ground of what I know to be true. Being much troubled to see the falseness of the constitution of the church of England, I had like to have turned separatist; whereupon I kept a day of solemn humiliation and pondering of the thing; this scripture was brought unto me—he that denies Jesus Christ to be come in the flesh is

---

4. Bilney (c. 1495–1531), an English religious dissenter burned at the stake in 1531. *Book of martyrs: Acts and Monuments* (1563) by John Foxe, popularly known as *Foxe's Book of Martyrs*, told the stories of Protestant martyrs persecuted by Roman Catholics.

antichrist[5] —This I considered of and in considering found that the papists did not deny him to be come in the flesh, nor we did not deny him—who then was antichrist? Was the Turk antichrist only? The Lord knows that I could not open scripture; he must by his prophetical office open it unto me. So after that being unsatisfied in the thing, the Lord was pleased to bring this scripture out of the Hebrews. He that denies the testament denies the testator,[6] and in this did open unto me and give me to see that those which did not teach the new covenant had the spirit of antichrist, and upon this he did discover the ministry unto me and ever since. I bless the Lord, he hath let me see which was the clear ministry and which the wrong. Since that time I confess I have been more choice and he hath let me to distinguish between the voice of my beloved and the voice of Moses, the voice of John Baptist and the voice of antichrist, for all those voices are spoken of in scripture. Now if you do condemn me for speaking what in my conscience I know to be truth I must commit myself unto the Lord.

MR. NOWELL: How do you know that that was the spirit?

MRS. H.: How did Abraham know that it was God that bid him offer his son, being a breach of the sixth commandment?

DEP. GOV.: By an immediate voice.

MRS. H.: So to me by an immediate revelation.

DEP. GOV.: How! an immediate revelation.

MRS. H.: By the voice of his own spirit to my soul.

* * *

MR. STOUGHTON: Behold I turn away from you.

MRS. H.: But now having seen him which is invisible I fear not what man can do unto me.

GOV.: Daniel was delivered by miracle do you think to be deliver'd so too?

MRS. H.: I do here speak it before the court. I look that the Lord should deliver me by his providence.

MR. HARLAKENDEN: I may read scripture and the most glorious hypocrite may read them and yet go down to hell.

MRS. H.: It may be so.

* * *

DEP. GOV.: I desire Mr. Cotton to tell us whether you do approve of Mrs. Hutchinson's revelations as she hath laid them down.

MR. COTTON: I know not whether I do understand her, but this I say, if she doth expect a deliverance in a way of providence—then I cannot deny it.

DEP. GOV.: No Sir we did not speak of that.

5. 1 John 2:18.
6. Hebrews 9:16.

MR. COTTON: If it be by way of miracle then I would suspect it.

DEP. GOV.: Do you believe that her revelations are true?

MR. COTTON: That she may have some special providence of God to help her is a thing that I cannot bear witness against.

DEP. GOV.: Good Sir I do ask whether this revelation be of God or no?

MR. COTTON: I should desire to know whether the sentence of the court will bring her to any calamity, and then I would know of her whether she expects to be delivered from that calamity by a miracle or a providence of God.

MRS. H.: By a providence of God I say I expect to be delivered from some calamity that shall come to me.

* * *

GOV.: The court hath already declared themselves satisfied concerning the things you hear, and concerning the troublesomeness of her spirit and the danger of her course amongst us, which is not to be suffered. Therefore if it be the mind of the court that Mrs. Hutchinson for these things that appear before us is unfit for our society, and if it be the mind of the court that she shall be banished out of our liberties and imprisoned till she be sent away, let them hold up their hands. All but three.

Those that are contrary minded hold up yours,

Mr. Goddington and Mr. Colborn, only.

MR. JENNISON: I cannot hold up my hand one way or the other, and I shall give my reason if the court require it.

GOV.: Mrs. Hutchinson, the sentence of the court you hear is that you are banished from out of our jurisdiction as being a woman not fit for our society, and are to be imprisoned till the court shall send you away.

MRS. H.: I desire to know wherefore I am banished?

GOV.: Say no more, the court knows wherefore and is satisfied.

Study Questions

1. What specifically did Hutchinson say and do that so threatened the authorities of the Massachusetts Bay Colony? How well did Hutchinson defend herself?

2. How did the fact that it was a woman who was challenging authority shape the response of Winthrop and the other authorities?

3. What did Hutchinson mean when she claimed to have experienced "immediate revelation"? Why did the claim so agitate her accusers?

4. What does the banishment of Hutchinson—a private citizen—say about the Massachusetts Bay Colony? Was the settlement established to foster religious freedom?

Virginia Ruling on Lifetime Servitude (1640)

The first labor supply in Virginia in the seventeenth century consisted of indentured servants both white and black. The indenture was a contract—commonly an agreement that a "servant" would provide several years of labor in exchange for the cost of passage to America and, eventually, a grant of land. These servants had little freedom but were not slaves, and had the promise of freedom at the end of their contract. More than half of all the European immigrants to the British colonies began their lives in America as indentured servants.

In 1640, three servants fled a Virginia plantation. Caught and returned to their owner, the two European servants had their servitude extended by four years each. However, the third runaway, a black man named John Punch, was sentenced to "serve his said master or his assigns for the time of his natural life." The John Punch case is considered by many historians to be a legal landmark in that it made a racial distinction among indentured servants. It's also possible that Punch was the first documented person forced to be a "servant"—a slave—for the duration of his life. As you read the following selection, consider why the rulings for the three men differed, and what impact this case would have on the future of American slavery.

The Robinson Manuscript, "Decisions of the General Court," *Virginia Magazine of History and Biography*, V (January, 1898), 236.

9th of July, 1640. Whereas Hugh Gwyn hath, by order from this board, Brought back from Maryland three servants formerly run away from the said Gwyn, the court doth therefore order that the said three servants shall receive the punishment of whipping and to have thirty stripes[1] apiece; one called Victor, a dutchman, the other a Scotchman called James Gregory, shall first serve out their times with their master according to their Indentures, and one whole year apiece after the time of their service is Expired By their said Indentures in recompence of his Loss sustained by their absence, and after that service to their said Master is Expired to serve the colony for three whole years apiece, and that the third being a negro named John Punch shall serve his said master of his assigns for the time of his natural life here or elsewhere.

---

1. Lashes.

Study Questions

1. What punishments were given to the three runaways? How do they differ?

2. Why do think John Punch was sentenced to serve "for the time of his natural life"?

3. What is the significance of the court case in regards to the codification of race based slavery?

4. Why would the General Court concern itself with what might be considered a contractual dispute between a master and his servants, treating it not as a civil case but as a criminal matter? What does the Virginia ruling imply about state (that is, government) involvement in the "servitude" of individuals?

Quaker Resolution Against Slavery (1652)

At a General Court held at Warwick, the 18th of May, 1652.

Whereas there is a common course practised among Englishmen, to buy negroes to that end they may have them for service or slaves for ever; for the preventing of such practices among us, let it be ordered, that no black mankind or white being shall be forced, by covenant, bond, or otherwise, to serve any man or his assignees longer than ten years, or until they come to be twenty-four years of age, if they be taken in under fourteen, from the time of their coming within the liberties of this Colony—at the end or term of ten years, to set them free, as the manner is with the English servants. And that man that will not let them go free, or shall sell them away elsewhere, to that end they may be enslaved to others for a longer time, he or they shall forfeit to the colony forty pounds.

Slave Laws in Virginia

(1661, 1691, and 1705)

Slavery evolved over time in the American colonies. In the first half of the seventeenth century, indentured servants (laborers working to repay the cost of their passage to America) in the Chesapeake colonies could reasonably hope for their freedom, but as economic conditions changed and more labor was needed for the farming of tobacco, indentured servitude gave way to race-based slavery. Over the first century of settlement, the authorities began to codify increasingly severe new slave laws that limited the rights of African slaves and cut off legal paths to freedom. The laws and customs governing slavery in Virginia became the model for the other colonies.

The following documents demonstrate this progression of legal codes, from legislation regarding runaway indentured servants, through laws to deal with anxiety over miscegenation and the possible presence of free blacks, to an excerpt from the 1705 slave code that pieced together laws passed over the previous century, ruling definitively that slaves were property for life. Take note of the terms used to describe slaves and servants and their races, and how these terms changed over the course of the forty-year span of time represented by these documents.

MARCH 1661

Whereas there are diverse loytering runaways in this country who very often absent themselves from their masters service and sometimes in a long time cannot be found, that losse of the time and the charge in the seeking them often exceeding the value of their labor: Bee it therefore enacted that all runaways that shall absent themselves from their said masters service shall be lyable to make satisfaction by service after the times by custome or indenture is expired (vizt.)[1] double their times of service soe neglected, and if the time of their running away was in the crop[2] or the charge of recovering them extraordinary the court shall lymitt a longer time of service proportionable to the damage the master shall make appeare he hath susteyned, . . . it is enacted that the master of any runaway that intends to take the benefitt of this act, shall as soone as he hath recovered him carry him to the next commissioner and there

---

1. Abbreviation of *videlicet* (Latin), "namely."
2. That is, during harvest time.

declare and prove the time of his absence, . . . and the court on that certificate passe judgment for the time he shall serve for his absence; and in case any English servant shall run away in company of any negroes who are incapable of making satisfaction by addition of a time, it is enacted that the English soe running away in the company with them shall at the time of service to their owne masters expired, serve the masters of the said negroes for their absence soe long as they should have done by this act if they had not beene slaves, every christian in company serving his proportion; and if the negroes be lost or dye in such time of their being run away, the christian servants in company with them shall by proportion among them, either pay fower thousand five hundred pounds of tobacco and caske or fower yeares service for every negroe soe lost or dead.

APRIL 1691

. . . And for prevention of that abominable mixture and spurious issue which hereafter may encrease in this dominion, as well by negroes, mulattoes, and Indians intermarrying with English, or other white women, as by their unlawfull accompanying with one another, Be it enacted . . . that for the time to come, . . . whatsoever English or other white man or woman being free shall intermarry with a negroe, mulatto, or Indian man or woman bond or free shall within three months after such marriage be banished and removed from this dominion forever, . . .

. . . and be it further enacted . . . That if any English woman being free shall have a bastard child by any negro or mulatto, she pay the sume of fifteen pounds sterling,[3] within one moneth after such bastard child be born, to the Church wardens of the parish . . . , and in default of such payment she shall be taken into the possession of the said Church wardens and disposed of for five yeares, and the said fine of fifteen pounds, or whatever the woman shall be disposed of for, shall be paid, one third part to their majesties for and towards the support of the government . . . , and one other third part to the use of the parish where the offence is committed, and the other third part to the informer, and that such bastard child be bound out as a servant by the said Church wardens untill he or she shall attaine the age of thirty yeares, and in case such English woman that shall have such bastard child be a servant, she shall be sold by the said church wardens, (after her time is expired that she ought by law to serve her master) for five yeares, and the money she shall be sold for divided as is before appointed, and the child to serve as aforesaid.

. . . Be it enacted . . . That no negro or mulatto be . . . set free by any person or persons whatsoever, unless such person or persons, their heires, executors or administrators pay for the transportation of such negro or negroes out of the countrey within six moneths after such setting them free, upon penalty of paying of

3. Nearly $4,000 in today's U.S. currency.

tenn pounds sterling[4] to the Church wardens of the parish where such person shall dwell with, which money, or so much thereof as shall be necessary, the said Church wardens are to cause the said negro or mulatto to be transported out of the countrey, and the remainder of the said money to imploy to the use of the poor of the parish.

OCTOBER 1705

. . . be it enacted . . . That all servants imported and brought into this country, by sea or land, who were not Christians in their native country, (except Turks and Moors in amity with her majesty, and others that can make due proof of their being free in England, or any other Christian country, before they were shipped, in order to transportation hither) shall be accounted and be slaves, and as such be here bought and sold notwithstanding a conversion to Christianity afterwards.

Study Questions

1. What would happen to the child of an English woman and an African American father? Why do you think the law was created that based a slave's condition upon that of the mother, not the father?

2. What issues of sex and religion are addressed by the laws? What incentives do you see in the documents to report others who commit these infractions?

3. Why do you think it was important to colonial Virginians to emphasize that conversion to Christianity would not exempt a slave from bondage?

4. Considering them together, why do you think these laws were enacted? Evaluate the changes you see in attitudes toward servants and slaves, and connect them to what you know about the evolving economy of the Chesapeake colonies.

---

4. Nearly $2,600 in today's U.S. currency.

WILLIAM BYRD

The Secret Diary of William Byrd of Westover (1675)

William Byrd II (1674–1744) was one of the leading politician planters in seventeenth-century Virginia. He is probably best known for helping to survey the boundary between Virginia and North Carolina, and he is credited with establishing the town of Richmond, Virginia. Educated in England as a young man, Byrd had a lifelong passion for learning, mastering Greek and collecting more than 3,000 books to create one of the largest libraries in colonial America. He was a prolific writer who wrote several books and kept a diary, written in a shorthand code, that was only deciphered and published in the twentieth century.

The entries in this diary contain an intermingling of mundane details of day-to-day life (his customary breakfast, friendly visits to the governor in Williamsburg), hints of his work as master of a large plantation, and punishments for slaves that today would be considered brutal and inhumane. The diary is a window into Byrd's world, where he wielded absolute power over his "family," including his slaves. As you read this selection, think about what these private diary entries tell us about Byrd's true opinions on life in colonial Virginia.

Louis B. Wright and Marion Tinlin, eds., *The Secret Diary of William Byrd of Westover, 1709–1712* (Richmond, VA.: Dietz Press, 1941).

FEBRUARY, 1709

8. I rose at 5 o'clock this morning and read a chapter in Hebrew and 200 verses in Homer's *Odyssey*. I ate milk for breakfast. I said my prayers. Jenny and Eugene were whipped. I danced my dance. I read law in the morning and Italian in the afternoon. I ate tough chicken for dinner. The boat came with the pork from Appomattox and was cut. In the evening I walked about the plantation. I said my prayers. I had good thoughts, good health, and good humor this day, thanks be to God Almighty.

22. I rose at 7 o'clock and read a chapter in Hebrew and 200 verses in Homer's *Odyssey*. I said my prayers, and ate milk for breakfast. I threatened Anaka with a whipping if she did not confess the intrigue between Daniel and Nurse, but she

prevented by a confession. I chided Nurse severely about it, but she denied, with an impudent face, protesting that Daniel only lay on the bed for the sake of the child. I ate nothing but beef for dinner. The Doctor went to Mr. Dick Cocke who was very dangerously sick. I said my prayers. I had good health, good thoughts, and good humor, thanks be to God Almighty.

MARCH, 1709

30. It rained very much this morning. I rose about 7 o'clock and said my prayers shortly. I ate milk for breakfast and about 10 I returned from Falling Creek to Mr. Anderson's, where I ate some fish for dinner, and about 4 o'clock came home in the rain where I found all things in good order but only Jenny had run into the river last night but came out again of herself and was severely whipped for it. In the evening I ate some milk. I neglected to say my prayers, for which God forgive me. I had good health, good thoughts, and good humor, thanks be to God almighty.

31. I rose at 6 o'clock and read a chapter in Hebrew and 200 verses in Homer's *Odyssey*. I said my prayers and ate milk for breakfast. I danced my dance. Mr. Haynes came to see me and I appointed him to receive the President's tobacco. We made an end of sowing the oats. I ate nothing but boiled beef for dinner. My wife was out of humor for nothing. However I endeavored to please her again, having consideration for a woman's weakness. I played at billiards with the ladies. I read Italian. In the evening we walked about the plantation. My wife was out of order so we went to bed soon. I had good health, good thoughts, and good humor, thanks be to God Almighty. I said my prayers. This month was remarkable for abundance of rain and wind without frost.

JUNE, 1709

10. . . . In the evening I took a walk about the plantation. Eugene was whipped for running away and had the [bit] put on him. . . .

SEPTEMBER, 1709

3. I rose at 5 o'clock and was hindered from reading Hebrew by the company; however, I read some Greek in Josephus. I said my prayers and ate chocolate with Mr. Taylor for breakfast. Then he went away. I read some geometry. We had no court this day. My wife was indisposed again but not to much purpose. I ate roast chicken for dinner. In the afternoon I beat Jenny for throwing water on the couch. I took a walk to Mr. Harrison's who told me he heard the peace was concluded in the last month. After I had been courteously entertained with wine and cake I

returned home, where I found all well, thank God. I neglected to say my prayers but had good health, good thoughts, and good humor, thanks be to God Almighty.

6. About one o'clock this morning my wife was happily delivered of a son, thanks be to God Almighty. I was awake in a blink and rose and my cousin Harrison met me on the stairs and told me it was a boy. We drank some French wine and went to bed again and rose at 7 o'clock. I read a chapter in Hebrew and then drank chocolate with the women for breakfast. I returned God humble thanks for so great a blessing and recommended my young son to His divine protection. . . .

MAY, 1710

27. I rose at 5 o'clock and read two chapters in Hebrew and some Greek in Anacreon.[1] I said my prayers and ate milk for breakfast. I danced my dance. Evie took a purge which worked but a little and my son had a little fever. . . . I went about 11 o'clock to Colonel Randolph's to visit him because he was sick, and I found him better than he had been. We had bacon and green peas for dinner. I let the Colonel know anything I had was at his service and took my leave about 5 o'clock and got home about 7 where I found the boy in his fever but Evie was better, thank God Almighty. . . .

31. I rose at 5 o'clock and read a chapter in Hebrew and some Greek in Anacreon. I said my prayers and ate milk for breakfast. The child had a fever still. I danced my dance. I read some Italian and wrote a letter. I ate hashed mutton for dinner. In the afternoon I played at billiards with my wife and was exceedingly griped in my belly. I ate as many cherries as I could get for it, but they did no good. I read more Italian, and in the evening took a walk to my cousin Harrison's whom I found very melancholy. She told me she was much alone and little company came near her. When I returned I found the child a little better. I said my prayers and had good health, good thoughts, and good humor, thanks be to God Almighty. The weather of this month was generally cold, notwithstanding for about a week of it, it was very hot. The wind was often east and northeast and northwest, which did much injury to the fruit trees and made the weather unseasonable and the people sickly.

JUNE, 1710

3. I rose at 6 o'clock and as soon as I came out news was brought that the child was very ill. We went out and found him just ready to die and he died about 8 o'clock in the morning. God gives and God takes away; blessed be the name of God. Mrs. Harrison and Mr. Anderson and his wife and some other company

---

1. Greek lyric poet (c. 570–c. 485 BCE).

came to see us in our affliction. My wife was much afflicted but I submitted to His judgment better, notwithstanding I was very sensible[2] of my loss, but God's will be done. . . . My poor wife and I walked in the garden. In the evening I neglected to say my prayers, had indifferent health, good thoughts, and good humor, thanks be to God almighty.

NOVEMBER, 1710

13. I rose at 7 o'clock and said a short prayer. Then I took a little walk about the plantation. I ate toast and cider for breakfast. Colonel Digges sent for a white negro for us to see who except the color was featured like other negroes. She told us that in her country, which is called Aboh near Calabar,[3] there were many whites as well as blacks. We played at dice till about 12 o'clock and then we [went] to Williamsburg, but I was so dusted with dirt that I was forced to change my clothes. Yesterday Mr. Ingles had a child burnt to death by fire taking hold of its clothes. We went to the capitol and stayed there about two hours and then I went and dined with the Governor where I ate roast mutton. I had a letter from home which told me all was well except a negro woman who ran away and was found dead. I said my prayers and had good thoughts, good health, and good humor, thank God Almighty.

FEBRUARY, 1711

27. I rose at 6 o'clock and read two chapters in Hebrew and some Greek in Lucian.[4] I said my prayers and ate boiled milk for breakfast. I danced my dance and then went to the brick house to see my people pile the planks and found them all idle for which I threatened them soundly but did not whip them. The weather was cold and the wind at northeast. I wrote a letter to England. Then I read some English till 12 o'clock when Mr. Dunn and his wife came. I ate boiled beef for dinner. In the afternoon Mr. Dunn and I played at billiards. Then we took a long walk about the plantation and looked over all my business. In the evening my wife and little Jenny had a great quarrel in which my wife got the worst but at last by the help of the family Jenny was overcome and soundly whipped. At night I ate some bread and cheese. I said my prayers and had good health, good thoughts, and good humor, thank God Almighty.

2. That is, keenly aware.
3. Port in present-day Nigeria.
4. Greek prose satirist (c. 120–c. 180 CE).

Study Questions

1. What does Byrd's diary tell us about the relationship the head of a household and his family, as well as that between masters and slaves?

2. How do you account for an educated person such as Byrd meting out punishments such as the entries describe? How would he justify such punishments?

3. Why might Byrd have used a shorthand code for his diary? From whom was he concealing these entries? What might be meant by "I danced my dance"?

4. What can his diary tell us about the values and the daily life among the planter elite in colonial Virginia?

NATHANIEL BACON

Declaration of the People (1676)

In 1676 Nathaniel Bacon (1647–1676), a twenty-nine-year-old English gentleman and habitual troublemaker, led a revolt against the Virginian government. He had arrived in the colony two years earlier and was quickly appointed to the Governor's Council, largely because his cousin was married to the governor, Sir William Berkeley. But when the ambitious Bacon moved to the western edge of the Virginia settlement and demanded the authority to attack nearby Indian tribes, Governor Berkeley refused. Bacon nonetheless raised an army of land-hungry frontier farmers and waged a private war against the natives. After the governor declared Bacon a rebel, he led five hundred armed followers into Jamestown, forcing colonial authorities to give him permission to wage war. Bacon thereafter senselessly massacred a number of Native Americans who had never attacked any Virginia settlements. In September, Bacon again marched on Jamestown and ordered his men to burn it to the ground. Five weeks later, however, Bacon died of dysentery and the rebellion collapsed. Berkeley, upon regaining control, ordered the execution of almost two dozen rebels.

At the height of the rebellion in the summer of 1676, Bacon issued the following "Declaration of the People," an attempt to rally popular support for his rebellion against Governor Berkeley and his supporters among the well-to-do tobacco planters.

From *Virginia Magazine of History and Biography* (Virginia Historical Society, 1893), 59–61.

For having upon specious pretences of Publick works raised unjust Taxes upon the Commonalty for the advancement of private Favourits and other sinnister ends but noe visible effects in any measure adequate.

For not having dureing the long time of his Government in any measure advanced this hopefull Colony either by Fortification, Townes or Trade.

For having abused and rendered Contemptible the Majesty of Justice, of advancing to places of judicature scandalous and Ignorant favourits.

For having wronged his Majesties Prerogative and Interest by assuming the monopoley of the Beaver Trade.[1]

---

1. A highly profitable commerce in which European-Americans traded manufactured goods for beaver skins supplied by the Native Americans. In Europe, the pelts were used mainly in the manufacture of headwear.

By having in that unjust gaine Bartered and sould his Majesties Country and the lives of his Loyal Subjects to the Barbarous Heathen.[2]

For haveing protected favoured and Imboldened the Indians against his Majesties most Loyall subjects never contriveing requireing or appointing any due or proper meanes of satisfaction for their many Invasions Murthers and Robberies Committed upon us.

For having when the Army of the English was Just upon the Track of the Indians, which now in all places Burne Spoyle and Murder, and when wee might with ease have destroyed them who then were in open Hostility for having expresly Countermanded and sent back our Army by passing his word for the peaceable demeanour of the said Indians, who imediately prosecuted their evill Intentions Committing horrid Murders and Robberies in all places being protected by the said Engagement and word pass'd of him the said S'r William Berkley having ruined and made desolate a great part of his Majesties Country, have now drawne themselves into such obscure and remote places and are by their successes soe imboldened and confirmed and by their Confederacy soe strengthened that the cryes of Bloud are in all places and the Terrour and consternation of the People soe great, that they are now become not only a difficult, but a very formidable Enemy who might with Ease have been destroyed &c.[3] When upon the Loud Outcries of Blood the Assembly had with all care raised and framed an Army for the prevention of future Mischiefs and safeguard of his Majesties Colony.

For having with only the privacy of some few favourits without acquainting the People, only by the Alteration of a Figure forged a Commission by wee know not what hand, not only without but against the Consent of the People, for raising and effecting of Civill Warrs and distractions, which being happily and without Bloodshedd prevented.

For haveing the second tyme attempted the same thereby, calling downe our Forces from the defence of the Frontiers, and most weake Exposed Places, for the prevention of civill Mischief and Ruine amongst ourselves, whilst the barbarous Enemy in all places did Invade murder and spoyle us his Majesties most faithfull subjects.

Of these the aforesaid Articles wee accuse S'r William Berkely, as guilty of each and every one of the same, and as one, who hath Traiterously attempted, violated and Injured his Majesties Interest here, by the losse of a great Part of his Colony, and many of his Faithfull and Loyall subjects by him betrayed, and in a barbarous and shamefull manner exposed to the Incursions and murthers of the Heathen.

---

2. Native Americans.

3. Et cetera (Latin for "and other things").

And we further declare these the Ensueing Persons in this List, to have been his wicked, and pernicious Councellors, Aiders and Assisters against the Commonalty in these our Cruell Commotions

Sr Henry Chicherly, Knt.,	Jos. Bridger,
Col. Charles Wormley,	Wm Clabourne,
Phil. Dalowell,	Thos. Hawkins, Juni'r,
Robert Beverly,	William Sherwood,
Robert Lee,	Jos. Page, Clerk,
Thos. Ballard,	Jo. Cliffe, Clerk
William Cole,	Hubberd Farrell,
Richard Whitacre,	John West,
Nicholas Spencer,	Thos. Reade,

Mathew Kemp.

And wee doe further demand, That the said S'r William Berkley, with all the Persons in this List, be forthwith delivered upp, or surrender themselves, within foure dayes, after the notice hereof, or otherwise wee declare, as followeth. That in whatsoever house, place, or shipp, any of the said Persons shall reside, be hide, or protected, Wee doe declare, that the Owners, masters, or Inhabitants of the said places, to be Confederates, and Traitors to the People, and the Estates of them, as alsoe of all the aforesaid Persons to be Confiscated, This wee the Commons of Virginia doe declare desiring a prime Union among ourselves, that wee may Joyntly, and with one Accord defend ourselves against the Common Enemye. And Let not the Faults of the guilty, be the Reproach of the Innocent, or the Faults or Crimes of ye Oppressors divide and separate us, who have suffered by theire oppressions.

These are therefore in his Majesties name, to Command you forthwith to seize, the Persons above mentioned, as Traytors to ye King and Countrey, and them to bring to Middle Plantation,[4] and there to secure them, till further Order, and in Case of opposition, if you want any other Assistance, you are forthwith to demand it in the Name of the People of all the Counties of Virginia

NATH BACON, Gen'l.

By the Consent of ye People.

---

4. Present-day Williamsburg, Virginia.

Study Questions

1. How does Bacon attempt to justify his rebellion? What reasons did he give for leading the uprising? What changes did he call for?

2. What were Bacon's complaints about the Indians? What complaints might an Indian have had against the English settlers?

3. What gave Bacon the right to speak for "the people" and the "commons of Virginia"? On what grounds did Bacon claim to have the authority to depose Governor Berkeley?

4. Do you think Bacon's own privileged background gave him the sense that he could challenge the rule of the Virginia authorities and impose his own will on the colony? What does Bacon's writing reveal about his assumptions concerning himself and his intended readers?

FRANCIS DANIEL PASTORIUS, GARRET HENDERICH, DERICK OP DEN GRAEFF, AND ABRAHAM OP DEN GRAEFF

Resolutions of the Germantown Quakers (1688)

In 1683, a group of twenty-five German and Dutch Quaker families migrated to the English colony of Pennsylvania and founded Germantown a few miles north of Philadelphia. Pennsylvania had been established three years before as a haven for Quakers—officially the Society of Friends. The Quakers had been persecuted in England for their unorthodox beliefs, particularly their concept of the "Inner Light"—in essence, the presence of God existing within all humans—that led them to the radical ideas that all people—male or female, black, white, or Native American—were equal in the eyes of God.

In 1688 leaders of Germantown, including the settlement's founder Francis Daniel Pastorius (1651–ca. 1719), authored the following anti-slavery document. It was the first systematic, organized protest against slavery written in the New World, one that argued that slavery—which existed in all of Britain's North American colonies—was immoral on the basis of a common humanity. The authors presented the petition to the monthly Quaker meeting held in Dublin, Pennsylvania, at the house of Richard Worrell. The Dublin Quakers, unsure of how to handle a petition of such potentially radical significance, forwarded the resolution to the Philadelphia Yearly Meeting, which refused to act. Filed away, the petition wasn't rediscovered until 1844.

From P.G. Mode, ed., "The Resolutions of the Germantown Mennonites, February 8, 1688," *Source Book and Bibliographical Guide for American Church History* (Menasha, Wisconsin: George Banta Publishing Company, ca. 1921).

This is to the monthly meeting held at Richard Worrell's:

These are the reasons why we are against the traffic of men-body, as followeth: Is there any that would be done or handled at this manner? viz.,[1] to be sold or made a slave for all the time of his life? How fearful and faint-hearted are many at sea, when they see a strange vessel, being afraid it should be a Turk, and

1. Abbreviation for *videlicet*, namely (Latin).

they should be taken, and sold for slaves into Turkey. Now, what is this better done, than Turks[2] do? Yea, rather it is worse for them, which say they are Christians; for we hear that the most part of such negers[3] are brought hither against their will and consent, and that many of them are stolen. Now, though they are black, we cannot conceive there is more liberty to have them slaves, as it is to have other white ones. There is a saying, that we should do to all men like as we will be done ourselves,[4] making no difference of what generation, descent, or colour they are. And those who steal or rob men, and those who buy or purchase them, are they not all alike? Here is liberty of conscience, which is right and reasonable; here ought to be likewise liberty of the body, except of evil-doers, which is another case. But to bring men hither, or to rob and sell them against their will, we stand against. In Europe there are many oppressed for conscience sake; and here there are those oppressed which are of a black colour. And we who know that men must not commit adultery some do commit adultery in others, separating wives from their husbands, and giving them to others: and some sell the children of these poor creatures to other men. Ah! do consider well this thing, you who do it, if you would be done at this manner and if it is done according to Christianity! You surpass Holland and Germany in this thing. This makes an ill report in all those countries of Europe, where they hear of [it], that the Quakers do here handel men as they handel there the cattle. And for that reason some have no mind or inclination to come hither. And who shall maintain this your cause, or plead for it? Truly, we cannot do so, except you shall inform us better hereof, viz.: that Christians have liberty to practice these things. Pray, what thing in the world can be done worse towards us, than if men should rob or steal us away, and sell us for slaves to strange countries; separating husbands from their wives and children. Being now this is not done in the manner we would be done at; therefore, we contradict, and are against this traffic of men-body. And we who profess that it is not lawful to steal, must, likewise, avoid to purchase such things as are stolen, but rather help to stop this robbing and stealing, if possible. And such men ought to be delivered out of the hands of the robbers, and set free as in Europe. Then is Pennsylvania to have a good report, instead, it hath now a bad one, for this sake, in other countries; Especially whereas the Europeans are desirous to know in what manner the Quakers do rule in their province; and most of them do look upon us with an envious eye. But if this is done well, what shall we say is done evil?

If once these slaves (which they say are so wicked and stubborn men,) should join themselves fight for their freedom, and handel their masters and mistresses, as they did handel them before; will these masters and mistresses take the sword

2. The Barbary pirates of North Africa, who had seized ships and enslaved Europeans since the sixteenth century. ("Turk" was often a general term meaning "Muslim" in the seventeenth century.)
3. The German word for Negro.
4. Matthew 7:12.

at hand and war against these poor slaves, like, as we are able to believe, some will not refuse to do? Or, have these poor negers not as much right to fight for their freedom, as you have to keep them slaves?

Now consider well this thing, if it is good or bad. And in case you find it to be good to handel these blacks in that manner, we desire and require you hereby lovingly, that you may inform us herein, which at this time never was done, viz., that Christians have such a liberty to do so. To the end we shall be satisfied on this point, and satisfy likewise our good friends and acquaintances in our native country, to whom it is a terror, or fearful thing, that men should be handelled so in Pennsylvania.

This is from our meeting at Germantown, held ye 18th of the 2d month, 1688, to be delivered to the monthly meeting at Richard Worrell's.

Garret Henderich,
Derick op de Graeff,
Francis Daniel Pastorius,
Abram op de Graeff.

Study Questions

1. What Biblical arguments do the Quakers present against slavery?

2. How do the resolutions demonstrate the authors' belief in the equality of all mankind?

3. What more practical arguments do the Germantowners give for their opposition to slavery?

4. Do you think the Dutch Quakers' own experience with persecution led them to be more sympathetic to the plight of the slaves?

5. Do the arguments in the resolution appear to reflect extensive personal observation of the practice of slavery, or is the authors' objection to slavery mainly theoretical?

The Bill of Rights and the Supremacy
of the English Parliament (1689)

The Bill of Rights of 1689, Old South Leaflets (Boston, n.d.), No. 19, 3–4.

n Act for Declaring the Rights and Liberties of the Subject, and Settling the succession of the Crown. 1689.

1. That the pretended power of suspending of laws, or the execution of laws, by regal authority, without consent of Parliament, is illegal.
2. That the pretended power of dispensing with laws, or the execution of laws by regal authority, as it hath been assumed and exercised of late, is illegal.
3. That the commission for erecting the late Court of Commissioners for Ecclesiastical Causes, and all other commissions and courts of like nature, are illegal and pernicious.
4. That levying money for or to the use of the Crown by pretence of prerogative, without grant of Parliament, for longer time or in other manner than the same is or shall be granted, is illegal.
5. That it is the right of the subjects to petition the King, and all commitments and prosecutions for such petitioning are illegal.
6. That the raising or keeping a standing army within the kingdom in time of peace, unless it be with consent of Parliament, is against law.
7. That the subjects which are Protestants may have arms for their defence suitable to their conditions, and as allowed by law.
8. That election of members of Parliament ought to be free.
9. That the freedom of speech, and debates or proceedings in Parliament, ought not to be impeached or questioned in any court or place out of Parliament.
10. That excessive bail ought not to be required, nor excessive fines imposed; nor cruel and unusual punishments inflicted.
11. That jurors ought to be duly impanelled and returned, and jurers which pass upon men in trials for high treason ought to be freeholders.
12. That all grants and promises of fines and forfeitures of particular persons before conviction are illegal and void.
13. And that for redress of all grievances, and for the amending, strengthening, and preserving of the laws, Parliaments ought to be held frequently.

And they do claim, demand, and insist upon all and singular the premises, as their undoubted rights and liberties; and that no declarations, judgements, doings or proceedings, to the prejudice of the people in any of the said premises, ought in any wise to be drawn hereafter into consequence or example.

JONATHAN EDWARDS

Sinners in the Hands of an Angry God (1741)

The First Great Awakening—a series of fervent religious revivals that emphasized the sinfulness of mankind and the power of faith to initiate a spiritual rebirth— swept the American colonies for two decades beginning in the 1730s. Many Americans, who came to be known as "New Lights," were thrilled with the new religious style and its emphasis on sudden and powerful conversion. However, many other Americans—"Old Lights"—were appalled by what they saw as ecstatic, frenzied forms of worship. Often the two groups were members of the same congregation, and conflict between them convulsed churches throughout the thirteen colonies.

Jonathan Edwards (1703–1758), the Congregationalist minister at Northampton, Massachusetts, tirelessly promoted the revivals, and is today considered colonial America's most brilliant theologian. In the summer of 1741, Peter Reynolds, the minister at Enfield, Connecticut, offered his pulpit to Edwards, hoping that he would be able to rouse his apathetic congregation and convince them that their spiritual indifference had placed their souls in mortal jeopardy. And so on July 8, the thirty-seven-year-old Edwards delivered the following sermon in a measured, quiet tone. It had an electrifying effect on the congregation. According to one eyewitness, "before the sermon was done there was a great moaning and crying went out through the whole House. . . . 'What shall I do to be saved,' 'Oh, I am going to Hell,' 'Oh, what shall I do for Christ,' and so forth. So yet the minister was obliged to desist, the shrieks and cry were piercing and amazing." Although it was not typical of Edwards's preaching—he was more likely to stress God's love rather than His wrath—"Sinners in the Hands of an Angry God" has become the most famous sermon in American history.

From *The Works of President Edwards* (New York: Leavitt & Allen, 1852), 4:313–18, 321.

There is nothing that keeps wicked men at any one moment out of hell, but the mere pleasure of God. . . .

The truth of this observation may appear by the following considerations.

1. There is no want[1] of power in God to cast wicked men into hell at any moment. Men's hands cannot be strong when God rises up: the strongest have no power to resist him, nor can any deliver out of his hands.

He is not only able to cast wicked men into hell, but he can most easily do it. Sometimes an earthly prince meets with a great deal of difficulty to subdue a rebel, that has found means to fortify himself, and has made himself strong by the number of his followers. But it is not so with God. There is no fortress that is any defence against the power of God. Though hand join in hand, and vast multitudes of God's enemies combine and associate themselves, they are easily broken in pieces: they are as great heaps of light chaff before the whirlwind; or large quantities of dry stubble before devouring flames. We find it easy to tread on and crush a worm that we see crawling on the earth; so it is easy for us to cut or singe a slender thread that any thing hangs by; thus easy is it for God, when he pleases, to cast his enemies down to hell. What are we, that we should think to stand before him, at whose rebuke the earth trembles, and before whom the rocks are thrown down!

2. They deserve to be cast into hell; so that divine justice never stands in the way, it makes no objection against God's using his power at any moment to destroy them. Yea, on the contrary, justice calls aloud for an infinite punishment of their sins. Divine justice says of the tree that brings forth such grapes of Sodom, "Cut it down, why cumbereth it the ground?" Luke xiii. 7. The sword of divine justice is every moment brandished over their heads, and it is nothing but the hand of arbitrary mercy, and God's mere will, that holds it back.

3. They are already under a sentence of condemnation to hell. They do not only justly deserve to be cast down thither, but the sentence of the law of God, that eternal and immutable rule of righteousness that God has fixed between him and mankind, is gone out against them; and stands against them; so that they are bound over already to hell: John iii. 18. "He that believeth not is condemned already. . . ."

4. They are now the objects of that very same anger and wrath of God, that is expressed in the torments of hell: and the reason why they do not go down to hell at each moment, is not because God, in whose power they are, is not then very angry with them; as angry, as he is with many of those miserable creatures that he is now tormenting in hell, and do there feel and bear the fierceness of his wrath. Yea, God is a great deal more angry with great numbers that are now on earth; yea, doubtless, with many that are now in this congregation, that, it may be, are at ease and quiet, than he is with many of those that are now in the flames of hell.

---

1. Lack.

So that it is not because God is unmindful of their wickedness, and does not resent it, that he does not let loose his hand and cut them off. God is not altogether such a one as themselves, though they may imagine him to be so. The wrath of God burns against them; their damnation does not slumber; the pit is prepared; the fire is made ready; the furnace is now hot; ready to receive them; the flames do now rage and glow. The glittering sword is whet, and held over them, and the pit hath opened her mouth under them.

5. The devil stands ready to fall upon them, and seize them as his own, at what moment God shall permit him. They belong to him; he has their souls in his possession, and under his dominion.

* * *

6. There are in the souls of wicked men those hellish principles reigning, that would presently kindle and flame out into hell-fire, if it were not for God's restraints.

* * *

7. It is no security to wicked men for one moment, that there are no visible means of death at hand. It is no security to a natural man, that he is now in health, and that he does not see which way he should now immediately go out of the world by any accident, and that there is no visible danger in any respect in his circumstances. The manifold and continual experience of the world in all ages, shows that this is no evidence that a man is not on the very brink of eternity, and that the next step will not be into another world. The unseen, unthought of ways and means of persons' going suddenly out of the world are innumerable and inconceivable. Unconverted, men walk over the pit of hell on a rotten covering, and there are innumerable places in this covering so weak that they will not bear their weight, and these places are not seen. The arrows of death fly unseen at noonday; the sharpest sight cannot discern them. God has so many different, unsearchable ways of taking wicked men out of the world and sending them to hell, that there is nothing to make it appear, that God had need to be at the expense of a miracle, or go out of the ordinary course of his providence, to destroy any wicked man, at any moment. . . .

8. Natural men's prudence and care to preserve their own lives, or the care of others to preserve them, do not secure them a moment. This, divine providence and universal experience do also bear testimony to. There is this clear evidence that men's own wisdom is no security to them from death; that if it were otherwise we should see some difference between the wise and politic men of the world, and others, with regard to their liableness to early and unexpected death; but how is it in fact? Eccles. ii. 16, "How dieth the wise man? As the fool."

9. All wicked men's pains and contrivance they use to escape hell, while they continue to reject Christ, and so remain wicked men, do not secure them from hell one moment. Almost every natural man that hears of hell, flatters himself that he shall escape it. . . .

* * *

But the foolish children of men do miserably delude themselves in their own schemes, and in their confidence in their own strength and wisdom, they trust to nothing but a shadow. The bigger part of those that heretofore have lived under the same means of grace, and are now dead, are undoubtedly gone to hell; and it was not because they were not as wise as those that are now alive; it was not because they did not lay out matters as well for themselves to secure their own escape.

* * *

10. God has laid himself under no obligation, by any promise, to keep any natural man out of hell one moment: God certainly has made no promises either of eternal life, or of any deliverance or preservation from eternal death, but what are contained in the covenant of grace,[2] the promises that are given in Christ, in whom all the promises are yea and amen.[3] But surely they have no interest in the promises of the covenant of grace that are not the children of the covenant, and that do not believe in any of the promises of the covenant, and have no interest in the Mediator of the covenant.

So that, whatever some have imagined and pretended about promises made to natural men's earnest seeking and knocking, it is plain and manifest, that whatever pains a natural man takes in religion, whatever prayers he makes, till he believes in Christ, God is under no manner of obligation to keep him a moment from eternal destruction.

So that thus it is, that natural men are held in the hand of God over the pit of hell; they have deserved the fiery pit, and are already sentenced to it; and God is dreadfully provoked, his anger is as great towards them as to those that are actually suffering the executions of the fierceness of his wrath in hell, and they have done nothing in the least, to appease or abate that anger, neither is God in the least bound by any promise to hold them up one moment; the devil is waiting for them, hell is gaping for them, the flames gather and flash about them, and would fain lay hold on them and swallow them up; the fire pent up in their own hearts is struggling to break out; and they have no interest in any Mediator, there are no means within reach that can be any security to them. In short, they have no refuge, nothing to take hold of; all that preserves them every momont is the mere arbitrary will, and uncovenanted, unobliged forbearance of an incensed God.

---

2. The idea that God saves humans because of their faith alone, not for their good works.
3. Corinthians 1:20: "For all the promises of God in him are yea, and in him Amen, unto the glory of God by us." That is, all God's promises will be fulfilled.

APPLICATION.

The use may be of awakening to unconverted persons in this congregation. This that you have heard is the case of every one of you that are out of Christ. That world of misery, that lake of burning brimstone, is extended abroad under you. There is the dreadful pit of the glowing flames of the wrath of God; there is hell's wide gaping mouth open; and you have nothing to stand upon, nor any thing to take hold of. There is nothing between you and hell but the air; it is only the power and mere pleasure of God that holds you up.

You probably are not sensible[4] of this; you find you are kept out of hell, but do not see the hand of God in it; but look at other things, as the good state of your bodily constitution, your care of your own life, and the means you use for your own preservation. But indeed these things are nothing; if God should withdraw his hand, they would avail no more to keep you from falling, than the thin air to hold up a person that is suspended in it.

Your wickedness makes you as it were heavy as lead, and to tend downwards with great weight and pressure towards hell; and if God should let you go, you would immediately sink and swiftly descend and plunge into the bottomless gulf, and your healthy constitution, and your own care and prudence, and best contrivance, and all your righteousness, would have no more influence to uphold you and keep you out of hell, than a spider's web would have to stop a falling rock. Were it not that so is the sovereign pleasure of God, the earth would not bear you one moment; for you are a burden to it; the creation groans with you.

* * *

There are the black clouds of God's wrath now hanging directly over your heads, full of the dreadful storm, and big with thunder; and were it not for the restraining hand of God, it would immediately burst forth upon you. The sovereign pleasure of God, for the present, stays his rough wind; otherwise it would come with fury, and your destruction would come like a whirlwind, and you would be like the chaff of the summer threshing floor.

* * *

The God that holds you over the pit of hell, much as one holds a spider, or some loathsome insect, over the fire, abhors you, and is dreadfully provoked; his wrath towards you burns like fire; he looks upon you as worthy of nothing else, but to be cast into the fire; he is of purer eyes than to bear to have you in his sight; you are ten thousand times so abominable in his eyes, as the most hateful and venomous serpent is in ours. You have offended him infinitely more than ever a stubborn

4. Conscious, aware.

rebel did his prince: and yet it is nothing but his hand that holds you from falling into the fire every moment: it is ascribed to nothing else, that you did not go to hell the last night; that you was suffered to awake again in this world, after you closed your eyes to sleep; and there is no other reason to be given, why you have not dropped into hell since you arose in the morning, but that God's hand has held you up: there is no other reason to be given why you have not gone to hell, since you have sat here in the house of God, provoking his pure eyes by your sinful wicked manner of attending his solemn worship: yea, there is nothing else that is to be given as a reason why you do not this very moment drop down into hell.

O sinner! consider the fearful danger you are in: it is a great furnace of wrath, a wide and bottomless pit, full of the fire of wrath, that you are held over in the hand of that God, whose wrath is provoked and incensed as much against you, as against many of the damned in hell: you hang by a slender thread, with the flames of divine wrath flashing about it, and ready every moment to singe it, and burn it asunder; and you have no interest in any Mediator, and nothing to lay hold of to save yourself, nothing to keep off the flames of wrath, nothing of your own, nothing that you ever have done, nothing that you can do, to induce God to spare you one moment.

* * *

How dreadful is the state of those that are daily and hourly in danger of this great wrath and infinite misery! But this is the dismal case of every soul in this congregation that has not been born again, however moral and strict, sober and religious, they may otherwise be. Oh that you would consider it, whether you be young or old! There is reason to think, that there are many in this congregation now hearing this discourse, that will actually be the subjects of this very misery to all eternity. We know not who they are, or in what seats they sit, or what thoughts they now have. It may be they are now at ease, and hear all these things without much disturbance, and are now flattering themselves that they are not the persons; promising themselves that they shall escape. If we knew that there was one person, and but one, in the whole congregation, that was to be the subject of this misery, what an awful thing it would be to think of! If we knew who it was, what an awful sight would it be to see such a person! How might all the rest of the congregation lift up a lamentable and bitter cry over him! But alas! Instead of one, how many is it likely will remember should not be in hell in a very short time, before this year is out. And it would be no wonder if some persons, that now sit here in some seats of this meeting-house in health, and quiet and secure, should be there before to-morrow morning.

Study Questions

1. In the opinion of Edwards, how does God look upon mankind? What is the character, according to Edwards, of "natural man"?

2. Why do you think the sermon so upset Edwards's listeners? Do you think it retains its power today? Why or why not?

3. How does Edwards's tone in "Sinners in the Hands of an Angry God" characterize—or contradict—the tone of the broader Awakening movement?

4. What do you think of Edwards's beliefs about humans' relationship with God and the nature of salvation?

ALEXANDER FALCONBRIDGE

FROM An Account of the Slave Trade on the Coast of Africa (1788)

As soon as the wretched Africans, purchased at the fairs, fall into the hands of the black traders, they experience an earnest of those dreadful sufferings which they are doomed in future to undergo. And there is not the least room to doubt, but that even before they can reach the fairs, great numbers perish from cruel usage, want of food, travelling through inhospitable deserts, &c. They are brought from the places where they are purchased to Bonny, &c. in canoes; at the bottom of which they lie, having their hands tied with a kind of willow twigs, and a strict watch is kept over them. Their usage in other respects, during the time of the passage, which generally lasts several days, is equally cruel. Their allowance of food is so scanty, that it is barely sufficient to support nature. They are, besides, much exposed to the violent rains which frequently fall here, being covered only with mats that afford but a slight defence; and as there is usually water at the bottom of the canoes, from their leaking, they are scarcely ever dry.

Nor do these unhappy beings, after they become the property of the Europeans (from whom, as a more civilized people, more humanity might naturally be expected) find their situation in the least amended. Their treatment is no lefs rigorous. The men negroes, on being brought aboard the ship, are immediately fastened together, two and two, by hand-cuffs on their wrists, and by irons rivetted on their legs. They are then sent down between the decks, and placed in an apartment partitioned off for that purpose. The women likewife are placed in a separate apartment between decks, but without being ironed. And an adjoining room, on the same deck, is besides appointed for the boys. Thus are they all placed in different apartments.

But at the same time, they are frequently stowed so close, as to admit of no other posture than lying on their sides. Neither will the height between decks, unless directly under the grating, permit them the indulgence of an exect posture; especially where there are platforms, which is generally the case. These platforms are a kind of shelf, about eight or nine feet in breadth, extending from the side of the ship towards the centre. They are placed nearly midway between the decks, at the distance of two or three feet from each deck. Upon these the negroes are stowed in the same manner as they are on the deck underneath.

* * *

About eight o'clock in the morning the negroes are generally brought upon deck. Their irons being examined, a long chain, which is locked to a ring-bolt, fixed in the deck, is run through the rings of the shackles of the men, and then locked to another ring-bolt, fixed also in the deck. By this means fifty or sixty, and sometimes more, are fastened to one chain, in order to prevent them from rising, or endeavouring to escape. If the weather proves favourable, they are permitted to remain in that situation till four or five in the afternoon, when they are disengaged from the chain; and sent down.

* * *

Upon the negroes refusing to take sustenance, I have seen coals of fire, glowing hot, put on a shovel, and placed so near their lips, as to scorch and burn them. And this has been accompanied with threats, of forcing them to swallow the coals, if they any longer persisted in refusing to eat. These means have generally had the desired effect. I have also been credibly informed, that a certain captain in the slave trade, poured melted lead on such of the negroes as obstinately refused their food.

Exercise being deemed necessary for the preservation of their health, they are sometimes obliged to dance, when the weather will permit their coming on deck. If they go about it reluctantly, or do not move with agility, they are flogged; a person standing by them all the time with a cat-o'-nine-tails in his hand for that purpose. Their musick, upon these occasions, consists of a drum, sometimes with only one head ; and when that is worn out, they do not scruple to make use of the bottom of one of the tubs before described. The poor wretches are frequently compelled to sing also; but when they do so, for their songs are generally, as may naturally be expected, melaneholy lamentations of their exile from their native country. . . .

On board some ships, the common sailors are allowed to have intercourse with such of the black women whose consent they can procure. And some of them have been known to take the inconstancy of their paramours so much to heart, as to leap overboard and drown themselves. The officers are permitted to indulge their passions among them at pleasure, and sometimes are guilty of such brutal excesses, as disgrace human nature.

The hardships and inconveniencies suffered by the negroes during the passage, are scarcely to be enumerated or conceived. They are far more violently affected by the sea-sickness, than the Europeans. It frequently terminates in death, especially among the women. But the exclusion of the fresh air is among the most intolerable. For the purpose of admitting this needful refreshment, most of the ships in the slave-trade are provided, between the decks, with five or six air-ports on each side of the ship, of about six inches in length, and four in breadth; in addition to which, some few ships, but not one in twenty, have what they denominate *wind-fails*. But whenever the sea is rough, and the rain heavy, it becomes necessary to shut these, and every other conveyance by which the air is admitted. The fresh air being thus excluded, the negroes rooms very soon grow intolerably hot. The confined air, rendered noxious by the effluvia exhaled from their bodies, and by being repeatedly breathed, soon produces fevers and fluxes, which generally carries off great numbers of them.

* * *

One morning, upon examining the place allotted for the sick negroes, I perceived that one of them, who was so emaciated as scarcely to be able to walk, was missing, and was convinced that he must have gone overboard in the night, probably to put a more expeditious period to his sufferings. And, to conclude on this subject, I could not help being sensibly affected, on a former voyage, at observing with what apparent eagerness a black woman seized some dirt from off an African yam, and put it into her mouth; seeming to rejoice at the opportunity of possessing some of her native earth.

From these instances I think it may be clearly deduced, that the unhappy Africans are not bereft of the finer feelings, but have a strong attachment to their native country, together with a just sense of the value of liberty. And the situation of the miserable beings above described, more forcibly urge the necessity of abolishing a trade which is the source of such evils, than the most eloquent harangue, or persuasive arguments could do.

CHARLES CHAUNCY

A Caveat Against Enthusiasm (1742)

By the 1730s, the American colonies were witness to a great wave of spiritual upheaval now known as the First Great Awakening. The revivalists, called "new lights," rejected the rationalist, hierarchical approach of the established Protestant churches and began preaching in a more extemporaneous style that was more personal and emotional—a style that many historians believe typified a growing individualistic and democratic temperament among colonists. The new manner of religious expression was just one reflection of a range of cultural, political, and economic changes in eighteenth-century colonial America that, collectively, posed a range of challenges to British authority.

Charles Chauncy (1705–1787) was born to an elite Puritan merchant family in Boston and received both an undergraduate degree and a master's in theology from Harvard University. He was one of many members of the established Congregational ministry who distrusted the new style of the revivalists, referring to them as "Enthusiasts." As you read this selection, consider why an "old light" like Chauncy might be concerned about the new style of preaching and the spiritual ferment of the age.

Charles Chauncy, *A Caveat Against Enthusiasm* (Boston, 1742), pp. 3–7.

The Enthusiast is one who has a conceit of himself as a person favored with the extraordinary presence of the Deity. He mistakes the workings of his own passions for divine communications, and fancies himself immediately inspired by the Spirit of God, when all the while, he is under no other influence than that of an overheated imagination.

The cause of this enthusiasm is a bad temperament of the blood and spirits;[1] 'tis properly a disease, a sort of madness: And there are few, perhaps none at all, but are subject to it; though none are so much in danger of it as those in whom melancholy is the prevailing ingredient in their constitution. In these it often reigns; and sometimes to so great a degree that they are really beside themselves, acting as truly by the blind impetus of a wild fancy, as though they had neither reason nor understanding.

---

1. Before the modern era in medical understanding, the generally accepted belief was that any physical or mental illness was the result of an imbalance of the four bodily fluids or "humors" and their associated emotional "temperaments": black bile (melancholy), yellow bile (anger), phlegm (peaceful), and blood (energetic).

And various are the ways in which their enthusiam discovers itself.

Sometimes, it may be seen in their countenance. A certain wildness is discernable in their general look and air, especially when their imaginations are moved and fired.

Sometimes, it strangely loosens their tongues, and gives them such an energy. . . .

Sometimes, it affects their bodies, throws them into convulsions and distortions, into quakings and tremblings, . . . violent agitations and foamings, . . .

Sometimes, it will unaccountably mix itself with their conduct and give it such a tincture of that which is freakish or furious as none can have an idea of, but those who have seen the behavior of a person in a frenzy.

Sometimes, it appears in their imaginary peculiar intimacy with heaven. They are, in their own opinion, the special favorites of God, have more familiar converse with Him than other good men, and receive immediate, extraordinary communications from him. The thoughts which suddenly rise up in their minds, they take for suggestions of the Spirit; their very fancies are divine illuminations; nor are they strongly inclined to anything, but 'tis an impulse from God, a plain revelation of his will.

. . . Many have fancied themselves acting by immediate warrant from heaven, while they have been committing the most undoubted wickedness. There is indeed scarce anything so wild, either in speculation or practice, but they have given in to it. They have, in many instances, been blasphemers of God and open disturbers of the peace of the world.

But in nothing does the enthusiasm of these persons discover itself more than in the disregard they express to the dictates of reason. They are above the force of argument, beyond conviction from a calm and sober address to their understandings. As for them, they are distinguished persons; God himself speaks inwardly and immediately to their souls. . . . And in vain will you endeavor to convince such persons of any mistakes they are fallen into. They are certainly in the right, and know themselves to be so. They have the Spirit opening their understandings and revealing the truth to them. They believe only as he has taught them: and to suspect they are in the wrong is to do dishonor to the Spirit; 'tis to oppose his dictates, to set up their own wisdom in opposition to his, and shut their eyes against that light with which he has shined into their souls. They are not, therefore, capable of being argued with; you had as good reason with the wind.

And as the natural consequence of their being thus sure of everything, they are not only infinitely stiff and tenacious, but impatient of contradiction, censorious, and uncharitable: they encourage a good opinion of none but such as are in their way of thinking and speaking. Those, to be sure, who venture to debate with them about their errors and mistakes, their weaknesses and indiscretions, run the hazard of being stigmatized by them as poor unconverted wretches, without the Spirit, under the government of carnal reason, enemies to God and religion, and in the broad way to hell.

They are likewise positive and dogmatical, vainly fond of their own imaginations, and invincibly set upon propagating them: . . . they sometimes exert themselves with a sort of ecstatic violence: and 'tis this that gives them the advantage, among the less knowing and judicious of these who are modest, suspicious of themselves, and not too assuming in matters of conscience and salvation. The extraordinary fervor of their minds, accompanied with uncommon bodily motions, and an excessive confidence and assurance, gains them great reputation among the populace, who speak of them as men of God in distinction from all others, and too commonly hearken to and revere their dictate, as though they really were, as they pretend, immediately communicated to them from the Divine Spirit.

This is the nature of Enthusiasm . . .

And much to be pitied are the persons who are seized with it. Our compassion commonly works towards those who, while under distraction fondly imagine themselves to be kings or emperors, fancy themselves to be prophets, inspired of God and immediately called and commissioned by him to deliver his messages to the world. . . . We should think as favorably of them as may be, and be disposed to judge with mercy, as we would hope to obtain mercy.

Study Questions

1. According to Charles Chauncy, what is an "Enthusiast?" What were the causes and symptoms of this "Enthusiasm?"

2. What does Chauncy claim to be the "natural consequences" of "Enthusiasm"?

3. What attitude does Chauncy want his readers to take toward those who are seized by "Enthusiasm"?

4. What was subversive about the First Great Awakening, and how might this period of spiritual upheaval have contributed to the political upheaval of the American Revolution?

BENJAMIN FRANKLIN

On Deism (1791)

In his famous Autobiography, *Benjamin Franklin (1706–1790) described a youthful encounter with a form of religion gaining popularity among the educated in Europe and America in the early eighteenth century: deism (literally "God-ism"). Deism essentially rejected the notion of supernatural intervention in the affairs of mankind, arguing instead that a rational and empirical study of God's creation is the best and, indeed, the only way to understand the Supreme Being. Deists typically conceived of God as comparable to a divine watchmaker—that is, an omnipotent force that had created the universe and everything in it, and then endowed it with the capability to run without His active intervention. Notably, deists also rejected the belief that Jesus was the literal son of God who performed miracles and rose from the dead.*

Although the Autobiography *suggests that Franklin disavowed deism, he continued to be skeptical of core Christian beliefs. For example, just before his death, in 1790, Franklin explained to the Reverend Ezra Stiles that "I have . . . some Doubts as to [Jesus's] divinity." As you read the following excerpt, consider whether "some error" had indeed "insinuated itself" into his "metaphysical reasonings."*

From John Bigelow, ed., *Autobiography of Benjamin Franklin* (Philadelphia: J. B. Lippincott & Co., 1896), 164–66.

My parents had early given me religious impressions, and brought me through my childhood piously in the Dissenting way.[1] But I was scarce fifteen, when, after doubting by turns of several points, as I found them disputed in the different books I read, I began to doubt of Revelation[2] itself. Some books against Deism fell into my hands; they were said to be the substance of sermons preached at Boyle's Lectures.[3] It happened that they wrought

1. Franklin, like most New Englanders of the day, was raised in a Calvinist Congregationalist church, the members of which were sometimes referred to as "dissenters" because they were not of the Church of England, the official religion of the empire.
2. God's disclosure of Himself and His will to His creatures.
3. Robert Boyle (1627–91) was a seventeenth-century English scientist remembered as the "father of chemistry." Deeply interested in religious matters, Boyle endowed a series of lectures designed to defend orthodox Christianity from rival belief systems such as Judaism, Islam, atheism, and deism.

an effect on me quite contrary to what was intended by them; for the arguments of the Deists, which were quoted to be refuted, appeared to me much stronger than the refutations; in short, I soon became a thorough Deist. My arguments perverted some others, particularly Collins and Ralph,[4] but, each of them having afterwards wrong'd me greatly without the least compunction, and recollecting Keith's conduct[5] towards me (who was another freethinker), and my own towards Vernon and Miss Read,[6] which at times gave me great trouble, I began to suspect that this doctrine, tho' it might be true, was not very useful. My London pamphlet,[7] which had for its motto these lines of Dryden:

> "Whatever is, is right. Though purblind man
> Sees but a part o' the chain, the nearest link:
> His eyes not carrying to the equal beam,
> That poises all above;"[8]

and from the attributes of God, his infinite wisdom, goodness and power, concluded that nothing could possibly be wrong in the world, and that vice and virtue were empty distinctions, no such things existing, appear'd now not so clever a performance as I once thought it; and I doubted whether some error had not insinuated itself unperceiv'd into my argument, so as to infect all that follow'd, as is common in metaphysical reasonings.

I grew convinc'd that *truth, sincerity* and *integrity* in dealings between man and man were of the utmost importance to the felicity of life; and I form'd written resolutions, which still remain in my journal book, to practice them ever while I lived. Revelation had indeed no weight with me, as such; but I entertain'd an opinion that, though certain actions might not be bad *because* they were forbidden by it, or good *because* it commanded them, yet probably those actions might be forbidden *because* they were bad for us, or commanded *because* they were beneficial to us, in their own natures, all the circumstances of things considered. And this persuasion, with the kind hand of Providence, or some guardian angel, or accidental favorable circumstances and situations, or all together, preserved me, thro' this

---

4. John Collins and James Ralph, two irresponsible friends of Franklin's.
5. Sir William Keith (1669–1749) was the governor of Pennsylvania in the 1720s who befriended young Franklin and promised to help him, but never followed through.
6. Vernon was an acquaintance of Franklin's from Newport, Rhode Island, who employed him to collect a debt in Pennsylvania. Deborah Read Franklin (1708–74) was Franklin's common-law wife.
7. In 1725 Franklin privately published a pamphlet, "A Dissertation upon Liberty and Necessity, Pleasure and Pain," in which he mused about the nature of God and man.
8. Franklin erroneously conflates quotations from two poems by two English poets. "Whatever is, is right" is from Alexander Pope's long poem *An Essay on Man* (1732–34). The rest of this passage, which Franklin gets slightly wrong, is from John Dryden's verse tragedy *Oedipus* (1679): Whatever is, is in its causes just,/Since all things are by fate. But purlind man/Sees but a part o' the chain, the nearest links,/His eyes not carrying to that equal beam/That poises above all.

dangerous time of youth, and the hazardous situations I was sometimes in among strangers, remote from the eye and advice of my father, without any willful gross immorality or injustice, that might have been expected from my want of religion.

Study Questions

1. How did Franklin come to learn about deism?

2. Why, according to Franklin, did he have second thoughts about deism?

3. What is the significance of Franklin's rejection of deism as "not very useful"? What does this suggest about his general attitude toward religion?

4. Why do you think Franklin, writing his *Autobiography* later in life, depicted himself as rejecting deism when he still held to its major tenets? Do you think he was considering the beliefs of the typical American who would be reading his story?

REVOLUTIONARY ERA

Resolutions of the Stamp Act Congress (1765)

Under the ministry of George Grenville (1712–1770), Parliament in 1765 for the first time directly taxed its North American colonies in order to pay the expense of defending them. This tax, enacted by the Stamp Act of 1765, mandated that duties be laid on a variety of legal documents: writs, warrants, bonds, petitions, attorneys' licenses, liquor licenses, and land grants—as well as college diplomas, playing cards, dice, almanacs, calendars, pamphlets, newspapers, and even newspaper advertisements. (It was called the "Stamp Tax" because all documents that had been taxed would be stamped, somewhat like tobacco products today.) According to the legislation, anyone who evaded the tax or interfered with its collection would be tried in juryless courts by an official who, should he render a guilty verdict, would get a portion of any confiscated commodities.

Remarkably, authorities in England had no clue that they were setting off a firestorm, in part because English citizens had been paying stamp taxes since 1694. But when they first learned of the tax, infuriated Americans refused to purchase English goods and took to the streets in protest. In October 1765, at the suggestion of the Massachusetts colonial legislature, representatives from nine of the thirteen British colonies met in New York to address the crisis. At this gathering, known as the Stamp Act Congress, the representatives laid forth their grievances in fourteen resolutions authored by Pennsylvania delegate John Dickinson (1732–1808). As an extralegal gathering of colonial representatives organized to express discontent against England, the Stamp Act Congress represented one of the first successful attempts of intercolonial cooperation and portended the increasing sophistication of future protests against the mother country.

From William MacDonald, ed., *Documentary Source Book of American History 1606–1913* (New York: The MacMillan Co., 1916), 136–139.

T he members of this Congress, sincerely devoted, with the warmest sentiments of affection and duty to his Majesty's person and government, inviolably attached to the present happy establishment of the Protestant succession, and with minds deeply impressed by a sense of the present and impending misfortunes of the British colonies on this continent; having considered as maturely as time will permit, the circumstances of the said colonies, esteem it our indispensible duty to make the following declarations of our humble opinion, respecting the most essential rights and liberties of the colonists, and of the grievances under which they labour, by reason of several late acts of parliament.

I. That his Majesty's subjects in these colonies, owe the same allegiance to the crown of Great Britain, that is owing from his subjects born within the realm, and all due subordination to that august body the parliament of Great-Britain.

II. That his Majesty's liege subjects[1] in these colonies, are intitled to all the inherent rights and liberties of his natural born subjects, within the kingdom of Great-Britain.

III. That it is inseparably essential to the freedom of a people, and the undoubted right of Englishmen, that no Taxes be imposed on them but with their own consent, given personally, or by their representatives.

IV. That the people of these colonies are not, and, from their local circumstances, cannot be, represented in the House of Commons in Great-Britain.

V. That the only representatives of the people of these colonies are persons chosen therein by themselves, and that no taxes ever have been, or can be constitutionally imposed on them, but by their respective legislatures.

VI. That all supplies to the crown being free gifts of the people, it is unreasonable and inconsistent with the principles and spirit of the British constitution, for the people of Great-Britain to grant to his Majesty the property of the colonists.

VII. That trial by jury, is the inherent and invaluable right of every British subject in these colonies.

VIII. That . . . [the Stamp Act] . . . , by imposing taxes on the inhabitants of these colonies, and the said act, and several other acts, by extending the jurisdiction of the courts of admiralty[2] beyond its ancient limits, have a manifest tendency to subvert the rights and liberties of the colonists.

IX. That the duties imposed by several late acts of parliament, from the peculiar circumstances of these colonies, will be extremely burthensome and grievous; and from the scarcity of specie,[3] the payment of them absolutely impracticable.

X. That as the profits of the trade of these colonies ultimately center in Great-Britain, to pay for the manufactures which they are obliged to take from thence, they eventually contribute very largely to all supplies granted there to the crown.

XI. That the restrictions imposed by several late acts of parliament on the trade of these colonies, will render them unable to purchase the manufactures of Great-Britain.

1. Feudal term for individuals who owe allegiance and service to a lord.
2. Juryless courts in which colonists accused of avoiding payment of the Stamp Tax were to be tried.
3. The Stamp Tax was payable only in gold or silver, which was scarce in the colonies. Most colonies issued their own paper currency, which the British authorities refused to accept.

XII. That the increase, prosperity and happiness of these colonies, depend on the full and free enjoyments of their rights and liberties, and an intercourse with Great-Britain mutually affectionate and advantageous.

XIII. That it is the right of the British subjects in these colonies to petition the king, or either house of parliament.

Lastly, That it is the indispensible duty of these colonies, to the best of sovereigns, to the mother country, and to themselves, to endeavour by a loyal and dutiful address to his Majesty, and humble applications to both houses of parliament, to procure the repeal of the act for granting and applying certain stamp duties, of all clauses of any other acts of parliament, whereby the jurisdiction of the admiralty is extended as aforesaid, and of the other late acts for the restriction of American commerce.

Study Questions

1. What specific arguments did the Stamp Act Congress set forth in opposing the Stamp Act and other acts of Parliament?

2. What measures besides the tax itself upset the colonists?

3. Why did the Stamp Act Congress go out of its way to profess its loyalty to England and the king?

4. Do the ideas expressed in the Resolutions strike you as radical? Why or why not? How do you think Parliament reacted to the document?

HANNAH GRIFFITTS

Women's Role in Boycotting English Goods (1768)

FROM *The Female Patriots*

After the 1763 Peace of Paris ended the Seven Years' War, Great Britain was faced with both an unprecedented national debt and the responsibility of governing a vastly enlarged empire. As a partial solution to these challenges, the British government passed a series of taxes on the American colonies—the Sugar Act (1764), the Stamp Act (1765), and the Townshend Duties (1767). Rather than accomplishing their purposes, however, the taxes triggered an escalating conflict between the British authorities and the colonists that eventually resulted in war and American independence.

American resistance to taxation took a number of forms, none more important than the boycotting of British goods either through non-importation—in which colonists pressured merchants not to import British goods—or non-consumption agreements, in which consumers themselves pledged not to buy goods from any merchant who sold British manufactures. The boycotts democratized protest in a number of ways. They not only invested day-to-day economic decisions with political meaning, but, crucially, they drew American women into the political arena. As the South Carolina patriot Christopher Gadsden remarked, "without the cooperation of 'our wives' in the boycotts, 'tis impossible to succeed." Moreover, if British goods were to be renounced, it necessarily meant that domestic manufactures—especially the household weaving of cloth, or homespun—must take the place of British imports. Thus women, who were traditionally assumed to be completely apart from politics, were accorded a crucial role in the protests against British policy.

When she wrote the following poem, Hannah Griffitts (1727–1817) was a forty-one-year-old single Quaker from Philadelphia. Although she forthrightly opposed the attempt to tax the colonies, Griffitts, as a Quaker, was necessarily a pacifist and could not support armed resistance against Britain. When the war began, she renounced the American cause and became a Loyalist. As you read, consider her identity as both a female and a Quaker.

From Hannah Griffitts, "The Female Patriots," *Pennsylvania Chronicle* 3.48 (1768).

To the PRINTERS of the P E N N S Y L V A N I A
C H R O N I C L E.

GENTLEMEN,

I send you the inclosed female Performance for a Place in
your Paper, if you think it may contribute any Thing to
the Entertainment or Reformation of your Male-
Readers, and am, Your's, &c.

The F E M A L E   P A T R I O T S.
Addressed to the Daughters of Liberty in America, 1768.

SINCE the Men, from a Party or Fear of a Frown.
Are kept by a *Sugar-plumb*[1] quietly down,
Supinely asleep and depriv'd of their Sight,
Are stripped of their Freedom, and robb'd of their Right;
[5]   If the Sons, so degenerate! the Blessings despise,
Let the *Daughters* of Liberty nobly arise;
And tho' we've no Voice but a Negative here,
The Use of the *Taxables*†, let us forbear:—
(Then Merchants import till your Stores are all full,
[10]   May the Buyers be few, and your Traffick be dull!)
Stand firmly resolv'd, and bid *Grenville*[2] to see,
That rather than Freedom we part with our *Tea*,[3]
And well as we love the dear Draught when a-dry
As American Patriots our Taste we deny—
[15]   Pennsylvania's gay Meadows can richly afford,
To pamper our Fancy or furnish our Board;
And Paper sufficient at *Home* still we have,
To assure the *Wiseacre*, we will not sign *Slave*;
When this *Homespun* shall fail, to remonstrate our Grief,
[20]   We can speak viva Voce,[4] or scratch on a Leaf;
Refuse all their Colours, tho' richest of Dye,
When the Juice of a Berry our Paint can supply,
To humour our Fancy—and as for our Houses,

---

1. An indirect reference to the Sugar Act of 1764, a three-pence tax on every imported gallon of molasses.
2. George Grenville (1712–70) was the prime minister of Great Britain from 1763 to 1765. Under his administration, Parliament enacted the Stamp Tax, which taxed a variety of paper goods in colonial America. [Ed.]
3. A reference to the Townshend Duties of 1767, which taxed paint, paper, glass, lead, and tea. Their purpose
was to raise revenue in order to pay British officials, thus freeing them from the control of the colonial legislatures. The references to paper and paint also allude to these taxes. [Ed.]
4. By word of mouth (Latin). [Ed.]
†. *Tea, Paper, Glass and Paints.*

> They'll do without Painting as well as our Spouses;
[25] While to keep out the Cold of a keen Winter Morn,
> We can screen[5] the North-west with a well polished Horn;
> And trust me a *Woman*, by honest Invention,
> Might give this *State-Doctor* a Dose of Prevention.
>   Join mutual in this—and but small as it seems,
[30] We may jostle a *Grenville*, and puzzle his Schemes;
> But a Motive more worthy our *Patriot-Pen*,
> Thus acting—we point out their Duty to *Men*;
> And should the *Bound-Pensioners*[6] tell us to hush,
> We can throw back the Satire, by bidding them blush.

A F E M A L E .

Study Questions

1. According to the poem, what specifically were men doing—or not doing—that upset Griffitts?

2. How does Griffitts propose that women, who had "no Voice but a Negative," influence the decisions of men? What does Griffitts believe to be the source of female power?

3. What does the poem suggest about women's political awareness and participation in the American Revolution?

---

5. A screen designed to ward off the heat of a fire or a draft of air. [Ed.]
6. Those who depended on the British government in some fashion. [Ed.]

JOHN MURRAY, FOURTH EARL OF DUNMORE

Dunmore's Proclamation (1775)

BY HIS EXCELLENCY THE RIGHT HONORABLE JOHN EARL
OF DUNMORE, HIS MAJESTY'S LIEUTENANT AND GOVERNOR
GENERAL OF THE COLONY AND DOMINION OF VIRGINIA,
AND VICE ADMIRAL OF THE SAME.

A PROCLAMATION.

As I have ever entertained Hopes, that an Accommodation might have taken Place between GREAT-BRITAIN and this Colony, without being compelled by my Duty to this most disagreeable but now absolutely necessary Step, rendered so by a Body of armed Men unlawfully assembled, firing on His MAJESTY'S Tenders, and the formation of an Army, and that Army now on their March to attack His MAJESTY'S Troops and destroy the well disposed Subjects of this Colony. To defeat such treasonable Purposes, and that all such Traitors, and their Abettors, may be brought to Justice, and that the Peace, and good Order of this Colony may be again restored, which the ordinary Course of the Civil Law is unable to effect; I have thought fit to issue this my Proclamation, hereby declaring, that until the aforesaid good Purposes can be obtained, I do in Virtue of the Power and Authority to ME given, by his MAJESTY, determine to execute Martial Law, and cause the same to be executed throughout this Colony: and to the end that Peace and good Order may the sooner be restored, I do require every Person capable of bearing Arms, to resort to His MAJESTY'S STANDARD, or be looked upon as Traitors to His MAJESTY'S Crown and Government, and thereby become liable to the Penalty the Law inflicts upon such Offences; such as forfeiture of Life, confiscation of Lands, etc., etc. And I do hereby further declare all indented Servants, Negroes, or others, (appertaining to Rebels,) free that are able and willing to bear Arms, they joining His MAJESTY'S Troops as soon as may be, for the more speedily reducing this Colony to a proper Sense of their Duty, to His MAJESTY'S Crown and Dignity. I do further order, and require, all His MAJESTY'S Leige Subjects, to retain their Quitrents, or any other Taxes due or that may become due, in their own Custody, till such Time as Peace may be again restored to this at present most unhappy Country, or demanded of them for their former salutary Purposes, by Officers properly authorised to receive the same. GIVEN under my Hand on board the Ship WILLIAM, off NORFOLK, the 7th Day of NOVEMBER, in the SIXTEENTH Year of His MAJESTY'S Reign.

DUNMORE.

(GOD save the KING.)

THOMAS PAINE

FROM *Common Sense* (1776)

By January 1776 the Thirteen Colonies had been at war with England for seven months. Many colonists—perhaps most—still thought of the conflict as a means of restoring Americans' rights within the British Empire. Thus the publication of Common Sense—*a pamphlet insisting not only that America should be independent but also should reject monarchy itself—quickly became a sensation. The pamphlet's author, Thomas Paine (1737–1809), was an Englishmen who had arrived in the colonies only fourteen months earlier and whose entire adult life was an unbroken story of personal and professional disappointments: two failed marriages, bankruptcy, and a series of jobs he couldn't keep. But once in America, Paine secured work with a Philadelphia printer and found his calling as a writer. Gaining attention for his pamphlets denouncing slavery, Paine began working on* Common Sense *in September 1775.*

Unlike earlier critics of English policy, Common Sense *paid no respect to the British system of government: in angry, impassioned prose, Paine condemned monarchy as inherently unjust. Indeed, it was not just his message that was remarkable; it was the style of the writing. Avoiding the flowery language and untranslated Greek and Latin phrases that were conventional among other pamphleteers, Paine aspired to speak directly to ordinary Americans, writing straightforward prose liberally sprinkled with references to scripture. Only forty-six pages long,* Common Sense *sold somewhere between 50,000 and 150,000 copies and went through twenty-five printings in seven colonies. In a country of about 2.5 million people, such numbers were unprecedented. Tens of thousands of Americans read it, and at least as many more came to understand Paine's argument by word of mouth. Despite its overwhelming success, Paine made little money on the pamphlet; what he did make he donated to the Continental Army. Most important was its effect:* Common Sense *brought clarity to a confused issue and a conflicted people, galvanizing resistance at a defining moment of American history.*

From Thomas Paine, *Common Sense* (New York: Solomon King, 1830), 1:33–40, 46–47, 56–57.

In the following pages I offer nothing more than simple facts, plain arguments, and common sense and have no other preliminaries to settle with the reader, than that he will divest himself of prejudice and prepossession, and suffer his reason and his feelings to determine for themselves; that he will put *on*, or rather that he will not put *off* the true character of a man, and generously enlarge his views beyond the present day.

Volumes have been written on the subject of the struggle between England and America. Men of all ranks have embarked in the controversy, from different motives, and with various designs: but all have been ineffectual, and the period of debate is closed. Arms, as the last resource, must decide the contest; the appeal was the choice of the king, and the continent hath accepted the challenge.

* * *

The sun never shone on a cause of greater worth. 'Tis not the affair of a city, a county, a province, or a kingdom, but of a continent—of at least one eighth part of the habitable globe. 'Tis not the concern of a day, a year, or an age; posterity are virtually involved in the contest, and will be more or less affected even to the end of time, by the proceedings now. Now is the seed-time of continental union, faith and honor. The least fracture now will be like a name engraved with the point of a pin on the tender rind of a young oak; the wound will enlarge with the tree, and posterity read it in full grown characters.

By referring the matter from argument to arms, a new area for politics is struck; a new method of thinking hath arisen. All plans, proposals, &c. prior to the nineteenth of April,[1] i.e. to the commencement of hostilities, are like the almanacks of last year; which, though proper then, are superceded and useless now.

* * *

As much hath been said of the advantages of reconciliation, which, like an agreeable dream, hath passed away and left us as we were, it is but right that we should examine the contrary side of the argument, and inquire into some of the many material injuries which these colonies sustain, and always will sustain, by being connected with and dependant on Great Britain. To examine that connection and dependance, on the principles of nature and common sense, to see what we have to trust to, if separated, and what we are to expect, if dependant.

I have heard it asserted by some, that as America has flourished under her former connexion with Great Britain, the same connexion is necessary towards her future happiness, and will always have the same effect. Nothing can be more fallacious than this kind of argument. We may as well assert that because a child has thrived upon milk, that it is never to have meat, or that the first twenty years of our lives is to become a precedent for the next twenty. But even this is admitting

---

1. The day in 1776 of the Battles of Lexington and Concord; the beginning of the Revolutionary War.

more than is true, for I answer roundly, that America would have flourished as much, and probably much more, had no European power had any thing to do with her. The articles of commerce, by which she has enriched herself, are the necessaries of life, and will always have a market while eating is the custom of Europe.

But she has protected us, say some. That she hath engrossed us is true, and defended the continent at our expense as well as her own, is admitted, and she would have defended Turkey from the same motives, *viz.*[2] for the sake of trade and dominion.

Alas! we have been long led away by ancient prejudices, and made large sacrifices to superstition. We have boasted the protection of Great Britain, without considering, that her motive was *interest* not *attachment*; and that she did not protect us from *our enemies* on *our account*, but from *her enemies* on *her own account*, from those who had no quarrel with us on any *other account* and who will always be our enemies on the *same account*. Let Britain waive her pretensions to the continent, or the continent throw off the dependance, and we should be at peace with France and Spain were they at war with Britain. The miseries of Hanover[3] last war ought to warn us against connexions.

* * *

But Britain is the parent country, say some. Then the more shame upon her conduct. Even brutes do not devour their young, nor savages make war upon their families; wherefore, the assertion, if true, turns to her reproach; but it happens not to be true, or only partly so. . . . Europe, and not England, is the parent country of America. This new world hath been the asylum for the persecuted lovers of civil and religious liberty from *every part* of Europe. Hither have they fled, not from the tender embraces of the mother, but from the cruelty of the monster; and it is so far true of England, that the same tyranny which drove the first emigrants from home, pursues their descendants still.

In this extensive quarter of the globe, we forget the narrow limits of three hundred and sixty miles (the extent of England) and carry our friendship on a larger scale; we claim brotherhood with every European Christian, and triumph in the generosity of the sentiment.

* * *

I challenge the warmest advocate for reconciliation, to show a single advantage that this continent can reap, by being connected with Great Britain. I repeat the

---

2. That is to say (abbreviation of *videlicet*, Latin for "namely").

3. During Europe's Seven Years' War (which played out in North America as the "French and Indian War"), the French invaded the German Principality of Hanover, which was allied with the British because the ruling family of England hailed from there.

challenge; not a single advantage is derived. Our corn will fetch its price in any market in Europe, and our imported goods must be paid for, buy them where we will.

But the injuries and disadvantages which we sustain by that connexion, are without number; and our duty to mankind at large, as well as to ourselves, instructs us to renounce the alliance; because, any submission to or dependance on Great Britain, tends directly to involve this continent in European wars and quarrels; and sets us at variance with nations, who would otherwise seek our friendship, and against whom, we have neither anger nor complaint. As Europe is our market for trade, we ought to form no partial connexion with any part of it. It is the true interest of America to steer clear of European contentions, which she never can do, while, by her dependance on Britain, she is made the make-weight in the scale of British politics.

Europe is too thickly planted with kingdoms to be long at peace, and whenever a war breaks out between England and any foreign power, the trade of America goes to ruin, *because of her connexion with Britain*. The next war may not turn out like the last, and should it not, the advocates for reconciliation now will be wishing for separation then, because, neutrality in that case, would be a safer convoy than a man of war.[4] Every thing that is right or natural pleads for separation. The blood of the slain, the weeping voice of nature cries, *'tis time to part*. Even the distance at which the Almighty hath placed England and America, is a strong and natural proof, that the authority of the one over the other, was never the design of heaven. The time likewise at which the continent was discovered, adds weight to the argument, and the manner in which it was peopled, increases the force of it. The reformation was preceded by the discovery of America, as if the Almighty graciously meant to open a sanctuary to the persecuted in future years, when home should afford neither friendship nor safety.

* * *

It is not in the power of Britain or of Europe to conquer America, if she does not conquer herself by *delay* and *timidity*. The present winter is worth an age if rightly employed, but if lost or neglected, the whole continent will partake of the misfortune; and there is no punishment which that man will not deserve, be he who, or what, or where he will, that may be the moans of sacrificing a season so precious and useful.

It is repugnant to reason, and the universal order of things, to all examples from former ages, to suppose that this continent can longer remain subject to any external power. The moat sanguine in Britain, do not think so. The utmost stretch of human wisdom cannot, at this time, compass a plan short of separation, which can promise the continent even a year's security. Reconciliation is *now* a fallacious dream. Nature hath deserted the connexion, and art cannot supply her place. For,

---

4. That is, a warship.

as Milton[5] wisely expresses, "never can true reconcilement grow, where wounds of deadly hate have pierced so deep."

Every quiet method for peace hath been ineffectual. Our prayers have been rejected with disdain; and only tended to convince us, that nothing flatters vanity, or confirms obstinacy in kings more than repeated petitioning—nothing hath contributed more than this very measure to make the kings of Europe absolute: Wherefore, since nothing but blows will do, for God's sake let us come to a final separation, and not leave the next generation to be cutting throats, under the violated unmeaning names of parent and child.

To say they will never attempt it again, is idle and visionary; we thought so at the repeal of the stamp act, yet a year or two undeceived us: as well may we suppose that nations, which have been once defeated, will never renew the quarrel.

As to government matters, it is not in the power of Britain to do this continent justice: the business of it will soon be too weighty and intricate to be managed with any tolerable degree of convenience, by a power so distant from us, and so very ignorant of us; for if they cannot conquer us, they cannot govern us. To be always running three or four thousand miles with a tale or a petition, waiting four or five months for an answer, which, when obtained, requires five or six more to explain it in, will in a few years be looked upon as folly and childishness—there was a time when it was proper, and there is a proper time for it to cease.

Small islands, not capable of protecting themselves, are the proper objects for kingdoms to take under their care; but there is something absurd, in supposing a continent to be perpetually governed by an island. In no instance hath nature made the satellite larger than its primary planet; and as England and America, with respect to each other, reverses the common order of nature, it is evident that they belong to different systems. England to Europe—America to itself.

* * *

But where, say some, is the king of America? I'll tell you, friend, he reigns above, and doth not make havoc of mankind like the royal brute of Britain. Yet that we may not appear to be defective even in earthly honors, let a day be solemnly set apart for proclaiming the charter; let it be brought forth placed on the divine law, the word of God; let a crown be placed thereon, by which the world may know, that so far as we approve of monarchy, that in America *the law is king.* For as in absolute governments the king is law, so in free countries the law ought to be king; and there ought to be no other. But lest any ill use should afterwards arise, let the crown at the conclusion of the ceremony be demolished, and scattered among the people whose right it is.

---

5. John Milton (1608–74), English poet. The quote is from Book IV of Milton's most famous work, the epic poem *Paradise Lost* (1667).

A government of our own is our natural right: and when a man seriously reflects on the precariousness of human affairs, he will become convinced, that it is infinitely wiser and safer, to form a constitution of our own in a cool deliberate manner, while we have it in our power, than to trust such an interesting event to time and chance.

* * *

Ye that tell us of harmony and reconciliation, can ye restore to us the time that is past? Can ye give to prostitution its former innocence? Neither can ye reconcile Britain and America. The last cord now is broken, the people of England are presenting addresses against us. There are injuries which nature cannot forgive; she would cease to be nature if she did. As well can the lover forgive the ravisher of his mistress, as the continent forgive the murders of Britain. The Almighty hath implanted in us these unextinguishable feelings, for good and wise purposes. They are the guardians of his image in our hearts, and distinguish us from the herd of common animals. The social compact would dissolve, and justice be extirpated from the earth, or have only a casual existence were we callous to the touches of affection. The robber, and the murderer, would often escape unpunished, did not the injuries which our tempers sustain, provoke us into justice.

* * *

To conclude. However strange it may appear to some, or however unwilling they may be to think so, matters not, but many strong and striking reasons may be given, to show, that nothing can settle our affairs so expeditiously as an open and determined declaration for independence. Some of which are,

1st, It is the custom of nations, when any two are at war, for some other powers, not engaged in the quarrel, to step in as mediators, and bring about the preliminaries of a peace; but while America calls herself the subject of Britain, no power, however well disposed she may be, can offer her mediation. Wherefore, in our present state, we may quarrel on for ever.

2d, It is unreasonable to suppose, that France or Spain will give us any kind of assistance, if we mean only to make use of that assistance for the purpose of repairing the breach, and strengthening the connexion between Britain and America; because, those powers would be sufferers by the consequences.

3d, While we profess ourselves the subjects of Britain, we must, in the eyes of foreign nations, be considered as rebels. The precedent is somewhat dangerous to *their peace*, for men to be in arms under the name of subjects; we, on the spot, can solve the paradox: but to unite resistance and subjection, requires an idea much too refined for common understanding.

4th, Should a manifesto be published, and despatched to foreign courts, setting forth the miseries we have endured, and the peaceful methods which we have ineffectually used for redress; declaring at the same time, that not being able, any longer, to live happily of safely under the cruel disposition of the British court, we had been driven to the necessity of breaking off all connexion with her; at the same time, assuring all such courts of our peaceable disposition towards them, and of our desire of entering into trade with them. Such a memorial would produce more good effects to this continent, than if a ship were freighted with petitions to Britain.

Under our present denomination of British subjects, we can neither be received nor heard abroad: the custom of all courts is against us, and will be so, until, by an independence, we take rank with other nations.

These proceedings may at first appear strange and difficult; but like all other steps, which we have already passed over, will in a little time become familiar and agreeable; and, until an independence is declared, the continent will feel itself like a man who continues putting off some unpleasant business from day to day, yet knows it must be done, hates to set about it, wishes it over, and is continually haunted with the thoughts of its necessity.

Study Questions

1. What, according to Paine, was Britain's real interest in having colonies?

2. What "injuries and disadvantages" did America endure because of its relationship with Britain? Why, according to Paine, should America refuse to reconcile with Britain?

3. What arguments against independence did Paine anticipate? How did he refute them?

4. Why do you think Paine cited the Bible—rather than the work of political theorists or ancient authorities on republicanism—to support the case for an independent American republic?

The Virginia Declaration
of Rights (1776)

Adopted unanimously June 12, 1776 Virginia Convention of Delegates drafted by Mr. George Mason.

JUNE 12, 1776

I. That all men are by nature equally free and independent, and have certain inherent rights, of which, when they enter into a state of society, they cannot, by any compact, deprive or divest their posterity; namely, the enjoyment of life and liberty, with the means of acquiring and possessing property, and pursuing and obtaining happiness and safety.

II. That all power is vested in, and consequently derived from, the people; that magistrates are their trustees and servants, and at all times amenable to them.

III. That government is, or ought to be, instituted for the common benefit, protection, and security of the people, nation or community; of all the various modes and forms of government that is best, which is capable of producing the greatest degree of happiness and safety and is most effectually secured against the danger of maladministration; and that, whenever any government shall be found inadequate or contrary to these purposes, a majority of the community hath an indubitable, unalienable, and indefeasible right to reform, alter or abolish it, in such manner as shall be judged most conductive to the public weal.

IV. That no man, or set of men, are entitled to exclusive or separate emoluments or privileges from the community, but in consideration of public services; which, not being descendible, neither ought the offices of magistrate, legislator, or judge be hereditary.

V. That the legislative and executive powers of the state should be separate and distinct from the judicative; and, that the members of the two first may be restrained from oppression by feeling and participating the burthens of the people, they should, at fixed periods, be reduced to a private station, return into that body from which they were originally taken, and the vacancies be supplied by frequent, certain, and regular elections in which all, or any part of the former members, to be again eligible, or ineligible, as the laws shall direct.

VI. That elections of members to serve as representatives of the people in assembly ought to be free; and that all men, having sufficient evidence of permanent common interest with, and attachment to, the community have the right of suffrage and cannot be taxed or deprived of their property for public uses without their own consent or that of their representatives so elected, nor bound by any law to which they have not, in like manner, assented, for the public good.

VII. That all power of suspending laws, or the execution of laws, by any authority without consent of the representatives of the people is injurious to their rights and ought not to be exercised.

VIII. That in all capital or criminal prosecutions a man hath a right to demand the cause and nature of his accusation to be confronted with the accusers and witnesses, to call for evidence in his favor, and to a speedy trial by an impartial jury of his vicinage, without whose unanimous consent he cannot be found guilty, nor can he be compelled to give evidence against himself; that no man be deprived of his liberty except by the law of the land or the judgement of his peers.

IX. That excessive bail ought not to be required, nor excessive fines imposed; nor cruel and unusual punishments inflicted.

X. That general warrants, whereby any officer or messenger may be commanded to search suspected places without evidence of a fact committed, or to seize any person or persons not named, or whose offense is not particularly described and supported by evidence, are grievous and oppressive and ought not to be granted.

XI. That in controversies respecting property and in suits between man and man, the ancient trial by jury is preferable to any other and ought to be held sacred.

XII. That the freedom of the press is one of the greatest bulwarks of liberty and can never be restrained but by despotic governments.

XIII. That a well regulated militia, composed of the body of the people, trained to arms, is the proper, natural, and safe defense of a free state; that standing armies, in time of peace, should be avoided as dangerous to liberty; and that, in all cases, the military should be under strict subordination to, and be governed by, the civil power.

XIV. That the people have a right to uniform government; and therefore, that no government separate from, or independent of, the government of Virginia, ought to be erected or established within the limits thereof.

XV. That no free government, or the blessings of liberty, can be preserved to any people but by a firm adherence to justice, moderation, temperance, frugality, and virtue and by frequent recurrence to fundamental principles.

XVI. That religion, or the duty which we owe to our Creator and the manner of discharging it, can be directed by reason and conviction, not by force or violence; and therefore, all men are equally entitled to the free exercise of religion, according to the dictates of conscience; and that it is the mutual duty of all to practice Christian forbearance, love, and charity towards each other.

Slaves Petition for Freedom During the American Revolution (1773, 1774)

Boston, April 20th, 1773.

Sir,

The efforts made by the legislative of this province in their last sessions to free themselves from slavery, gave us, who are in that deplorable state, a high degree of satisfaction. We expect great things from men who have made such a noble stand against the designs of their *fellow-men* to enslave them. We cannot but wish and hope Sir, that you will have the same grand object, we mean civil and religious liberty, in view in your next session. The divine spirit of *freedom*, seems to fire every humane breast on this continent, except such as are bribed to assist in executing the execrable plan.

We are very sensible that it would be highly detrimental to our present masters, if we were allowed to demand all that of *right* belongs to us for past services; this we disclaim. Even the *Spaniards*, who have not those sublime ideas of freedom that English men have, are conscious that they have no right to all services of their fellowmen, we mean the *Africans*, whom they have purchased with their money; therefore they allow them one day in a week to work for themselve, to enable them to earn money to purchase the residue of their time, which they have a right to demand in such portions as they are able to pay for (a due appraizment of their services being first made, which always stands at the purchase money.) We do not pretend to dictate to you Sir, or to the honorable Assembly, of which you are a member : We acknowledge our obligations to you for what you have already done, but as the people of this province seem to be actuated by the principles of equity and justice, we cannot but expect your house will again take our deplorable case into serious consideration, and give us that ample relief which, *as men*, we have a natural right to.

But since the wise and righteous governor of the universe, has permitted our fellow men to make us slaves, we bow in submission to him, and determine to behave in such a manner, as that we may have reason to expect the divine approbation of, and assistance in, our peaceable and lawful attempts to gain our freedom.

We are willing to submit to such regulations and laws, as may be made relative to us, until we leave the province, which we determine to do as soon as we can from our joynt labours procure money to transport ourselves to some part of the coast of *Africa*, where we propose a settlement. We are very desirous that you should have instructions relative to us, from your town, therefore we pray you to communicate this letter to them, and ask this favor for us.

In behalf of our fellow slaves in this province,
And by order of their Committee.

Peter Bestes,
Sambo Freeman,
Felix Holbrook,
Chester Joie.

———————

For the Representative of the town of Taunton.

To his Excellency Thomas Gage Esq
Captain General and Governor in Chief in and
over This Province

To the Honourable his Majestys Council
and the Honourable House of Representatives
in General Court assembled may 25 1774

The Petition of a Grate [Great] Number of Blackes of this
Province who by divine permission are held in a state
of Slavery within the bowels of a free and Christian
Country Humbly Shewing
That your Petitioners apprehend we have in common
With all other men a naturel [natural] right to our freedoms without
Being depriv'd of them by our fellow men as we are a
freeborn Pepel [People] and have never forfeited this Blessing
by aney [any] compact or agreement whatever. But we were unjustly
dragged by the cruel hand of power from our dearest
frinds [friends] and others sum [some] of us stolen from the bosoms of
    our tender
Parents and from a Populous Pleasant and plentiful country and
Brought hither to be made slaves for Life in a Christian land
Thus are we deprived of every thing that hath a tendency to make
life even tolerable, the endearing ties of husband and wife we are
strangers to for we are no longer man and wife then our masters
or Mestreses [Mistresses] thinkes [think] proper marred [married] or
    onmarred

[unmarried]. Our Children
are also taken from us by force and sent maney [many] miles
from us wear [where] we seldom or ever see them again there
to be made slaves of fore [for] Life which sumtimes [sometimes] is verey
    [very]
short by Reson [reason] of Being dragged from their mothers
Breest [Breast] Thus our Lives are imbittered to us on these accounts by
    our deplorable situation we are rendered incapable
of shewing our obedience to Almighty God how can a
Slave perform the duties of a husband to a wife or parent
to his child How can a husband leave master and work and
Cleave to his wife How can the wife submit [theres ?] [there?] themselves
to there [their] Husbands in all things. How can the child obey
thear [their] parents in all things. There is a grat [great] number of us
Member Sencear [Sincere] thou [though] once [ov the?] members of
    Christs Church the
Church of Christ how can
the master and the Slave be said to fullfil [fulfill] that command
Live in love let Brotherly Love contuner [continue] and abound
Beare [Bear] yea onenothers [one another] Bordenes [Burdens] How can
    the master be said
to Beare my Borden [Burden] when he Beares [Bears] me down, whith the
Have chanes [chains] of slavery and operson [oppression] aganst my will
and How can we fullfill [fulfill] our parte [parte] of duty to him whilst
    in this
Condition and as we cannot searve [serve] our god as we ought whilst
in this situation Nither [Neither] can we reap an equal benefet [benefit]
from the laws of the Land which doth not justifi [justify] but condemes
    [condemns]
Slavery or if there had bin [been] aney [any] Law to hold us in Bondege
    [Bondage]
we are Humbely [Humbly] of the opinion ther never was aney [any] to
inslave our children for life when Born in a free Countrey [Country].
We therfor [therefore] Bage [Beg] your Excellency and Honours will give
this it its deu [due] weight and consideration and that you will
accordingly cause an act of the legislative to be pessed [passed]
that we may obtain our Natural right our freedoms
and our Children be set at lebety [liberty] at the yeare of Twenty
one for whoues [whose] sekes [sakes] more Petequeley [Particularly]
    your Petitioners is
is in Duty ever to Proy [Pray].

The Treaty of Paris (1783)

U.S. Department of State, *Treaties and Conventions Between the United States of America and Other Powers Since July 4, 1776* (Washington, D.C., 1889), pp. 375–379.

Concluded September 3, 1783; Ratified by the Continental Congress January 14, 1784; Proclaimed January 14, 1784. . . .

[ARTICLE I] His Britannic Majesty acknowledge the said United States, viz. New Hampshire, Massachusetts Bay, Rhode Island, and Province Plantations, Connecticut, New York, New Jersey, Pennsylvania, Delaware, Maryland, Virginia, North Carolina, South Carolina, and Georgia, to be free, sovereign and independent States; that he treats with them as such, and for himself, his heirs and successors, relinquishes all claims to the Government, propriety and territorial rights of the same, and every part thereof. . . .

[ARTICLE III] It is agreed that the people of the United States shall continue to enjoy unmolested the right to take fish of every kind on the Grand Bank, and on all the other banks of Newfoundland; also in the Gulph of Saint Lawrence, and at all other places in the sea where inhabitants of both countries used at any time theretofore to fish. And also that the inhabitants of the United States shall have liberty to take fish of every kind on such part of the coast of Newfoundland as British fishermen shall use (but not to dry or cure the same on that island) and also on the coasts, bays and creeks of all other of His Britannic Majesty's dominions in America; and that the American fishermen shall have liberty to dry and cure fish in any of the unsettled bays, harbours and creeks of Nova Scotia, Magdalen Islands, and Labrador, so long as the same shall remain unsettled; but so soon as the same or either of them shall be settled, it shall not be lawful for the said fishermen to dry or cure fish at such settlements, without a previous agreement for that purpose with the inhabitants, proprietors or possessors of the ground.

[ARTICLE IV] It is agreed that creditors on either side shall meet with no lawful impediment to the recovery of the full value in sterling money, of all bonafide debts heretofore contracted.

[ARTICLE V] It is agreed that the Congress shall earnestly recommend it to the legislatures of the respective States, to provide for the restitution of all estates, rights and properties which have been confiscated, belonging to real British subjects. . . .

[ARTICLE VI] That there shall be no future confiscations made, nor any prosecutions commenc'd against any person or persons for, or by reason of the part which he or they may have taken in the present war, and that no person shall, on that account, suffer any future loss or damage, either in his person, liberty or property; and that those who may be in confinement on such charges, at the time of the ratification of the treaty in America, shall be immediately set at liberty, and the prosecutions so commenced be discontinued.

[ARTICLE VII] There shall be a firm and perpetual peace between His Britannic Majesty and the said States, and between the subjects of the one and the citizens of the other, wherefore all hostilities, both by sea and land, shall henceforth cease: All prisoners on both sides shall be set at liberty, and His Britannic Majesty shall, with all convenient speed, and without causing any destruction, or carrying away any negroes or other property of the American inhabitants, withdraw all his armies, garrisons and fleets from the said United States, and from every post, place and harbour within the same; leaving in all fortifications the American artillery that may be therein: And shall also order and cause all archives, records, deeds and papers, belonging to any of the said states, or their citizens, which, in the course of the war, may have fallen into the hands of his officers, to be forthwith restored and deliver'd to the proper States and persons to whom they belong.

[ARTICLE VIII] The navigation of the river Mississippi, from its source to the ocean, shall for ever remain free and open to the subjects of Great Britain, and the citizens of the United States.

[ARTICLE IX] In case it should so happen that any place or territory belonging to Great Britain or to the United States, should have been conquer'd by the arms of either from the other, before the arrival of the said provisional articles in America, it is agreed, that the same shall be restored without difficulty, and without requiring any compensation. . . .

Done at Paris, this third day of September, in the year of our Lord one thousand seven hundred and eighty-three.

[Seal.]   D. Hartley

[Seal.]   John Adams

[Seal.]   B. Franklin

[Seal.]   John Jay

EARLY NATIONAL PERIOD

United States Foreign Policy:
The Beginning

FRANCES JACOBSON

The United States launched its foreign policy in 1789, the year the French Revolution began. By this time the nation had fought four wars as colonials and the American Revolution as rebels. Americans were disgusted with European affairs, and this helped to shape its foreign entanglements. It was anxious to mind its own business; but the idea of an innocent, isolationist America is a myth, although the United States did want to be free of Old World concerns. This was not to be, however, as it was swept up in the maelstrom of the French Revolution, going to war first with France, then Britain. The home front would have to wait.

By 1789 the basic tenets of United States foreign policy were that Americans were God's chosen people; European regimes were degenerate and corrupt; America would be neutral in Europe's quarrels, but would involve itself in trade. It also had a humanitarian spirit and would stand up for justice and fair play. To its chagrin, trade led it straight into the jaws of warfare. Unprepared, it struggled to remain neutral in the European wars, and continued to trade with both major seafaring nations, Britain and France. Unfortunately, two different views of neutrality developed. Europeans believed that neutrality was merely a phase nations went through before deciding which side to join in the hostilities. George Washington in particular knew that the United States was not ready for war, and he encouraged negotiations instead. There were several issues on the table, the most important of which was the rights of neutrals on the high seas. America and Britain had different views about this as well. The British fell back on their Rule of 1756 which stated that the final destination of goods determined whether they were neutral or contraband. In other words, any goods which were destined to end up in the hands of the French were contraband. The United States' position was that neutral ships carried neutral goods, a position it would continue to hold through World War One.

Negotiations with Britain were partially successful, resulting in Jay's Treaty. The public was unhappy, Jay was hanged in effigy, and the pro-English John Hamilton was stoned when his secret machinations were discovered. Nonetheless the treaty passed the senate, thanks to George Washington, and it delayed war with

Britain for about fifteen years. In the meantime, in 1798 America went to war with France over the same issue.

Europe's wars went on for approximately twenty-three years. It was France's folly in Russia that finally brought it to its knees and peace was restored. It was a peace that lasted a century; and it was an opportunity for American expansion that was dizzying in its speed. The United States had already bought the Louisiana territory from France, fifteen million acres in the center of North America that stretched from the Canadian border to the Gulf of Mexico. The Americans were eyeing Florida and the Pacific Northwest, Texas, and parts of Canada. Some were looking to conquer Mexico. Still others were convinced that Cuba and Puerto Rico should be the hands of the North Americans.

The thirst for dominion was unslakable. Americans believed it was their right and destiny to spread across the land. They were at the forefront of human progress, God's chosen people (American exceptionalism), and if possible they would civilize those who stood in their way—or remove them if necessary. John Quincy Adams commented in January, 1817 that "the universal feeling of Europe in witnessing the gigantic growth of the population and power [was] that we shall, if united, become a very dangerous member of the society of nations." (John Quincy Adams, January 17, 1918.

The lust to conquer, combined with a sense of moral purpose, doomed the Indians. The United States believed it was advancing Anglo-Saxon civilization among a savage people. The army fought about a thousand engagements with the Indians before crowding them into camps called "reservations." The aim was to change them into white Christian farmers. Racism was rampant.

The United States has not always acted on its principles, but has wielded its power in ways that have sometimes mirrored the tough, self-interested policies of the greatest of the great imperial powers. Americans, while expansionist, have never considered themselves to be imperialistic. After all, they argue, the conquered lands eventually became states, not colonies. Empire building and American exceptionalism are two conflicting strains in United States foreign policy, even to this day—a conflict of power and principle. And while some Europeans worried that the United States might spread its population all the way to the Pacific Ocean, before the 19th century was over, America had spread its empire *across* the Pacific.

THOMAS JEFFERSON

On Race (1785)

FROM *Notes on the State of Virginia*

Despite Thomas Jefferson's voluminous writings, he authored only one book, Notes on the State of Virginia, *which he had privately published in 1785. In the course of discussing Virginia's climate, geography, population, and history, Jefferson also commented on education, agriculture, and slavery. By far the most controversial portion of the* Notes on the State of Virginia *was Jefferson's thoughts on race.*

Jefferson, like many of his contemporaries, was both uneasy with the practice of slavery and dependent on its survival. Although in the Notes *Jefferson vaguely hoped for a "total emancipation," it was slave labor that created Jefferson's fortune and sustained his family, and it was slavery that allowed him the leisure to read and write, to participate in public affairs, and, most ironically, to contemplate human rights. Jefferson understood the contradiction, but throughout his career, his opposition to slavery in principle never translated into actual practice. One crucial reason for this inactivity was Jefferson's belief that peoples of African ancestry were naturally inferior to people of European ancestry, as the following excerpt makes abundantly clear.*

From Thomas Jefferson, *Notes on the State of Virginia* (Boston: Lilly and Wait, 1832), 144–150.

The first difference which strikes us is that of colour. Whether the black of the negro resides in the reticular membrane between the skin and scarf-skin,[1] or in the scarf-skin itself; whether it proceeds from the colour of the blood, the colour of the bile, or from that of some other secretion, the difference is fixed in nature, and is as real as if its seat and cause were better known to us. And is this difference of no importance? Is it not the foundation of a greater or less share of beauty in the two races? Are not the fine mixtures of red and white, the expressions of every passion by greater or less suffusions of colour in the one, preferable to that eternal monotony, which reigns in the countenances, that immovable veil of black which covers all the emotions of the other race? Add to these, flowing

---

1. The epidermis, the outermost layer of the skin.

hair, a more elegant symmetry of form, their own judgment in favour of the whites, declared by their preference of them, as uniformly as is the preference of the Oranootan[2] for the black women over those of his own species. The circumstance of superior beauty, is thought worthy attention in the propagation of our horses, dogs, and other domestic animals; why not in that of man? Besides those of colour, figure, and hair, there are other physical distinctions proving a difference of race. They have less hair on the face and body. They secrete less by the kidnies, and more by the glands of the skin, which gives them a very strong and disagreeable odour. This greater degree of transpiration[3] renders them more tolerant of heat, and less so of cold than the whites. Perhaps too a difference of structure in the pulmonary apparatus, which a late ingenious experimentalist[4] has discovered to be the principal regulator of animal heat, may have disabled them from extricating, in the act of inspiration, so much of that fluid from the outer air, or obliged them in expiration, to part with more of it. They seem to require less sleep. A black after hard labour through the day, will be induced by the slightest amusements to sit up till midnight, or later, though knowing he must be out with the first dawn of the morning. They are at least as brave, and more adventuresome. But this may perhaps proceed from a want of forethought, which prevents their seeing a danger till it be present. When present, they do not go through it with more coolness or steadiness than the whites. They are more ardent after their female: but love seems with them to be more an eager desire, than a tender delicate mixture of sentiment and sensation. Their griefs are transient. Those numberless afflictions, which render it doubtful whether heaven has given life to us in mercy or in wrath, are less felt, and sooner forgotten with them. In general, their existence appears to participate more of sensation than reflection. To this must be ascribed their disposition to sleep when abstracted from their diversions, and unemployed in labour. An animal whose body is at rest, and who does not reflect, must be disposed to sleep of course. Comparing them by their faculties of memory, reason, and imagination, it appears to me, that in memory they are equal to the whites; in reason much inferior, as I think one could scarcely be found capable of tracing and comprehending the investigations of Euclid; and that in imagination they are dull, tasteless, and anomalous. It would be unfair to follow them to Africa for this investigation. We will consider them here, on the same stage with the whites, and where the facts are not apocryphal on which a judgment is to be formed. It will be right to make great allowances for the difference of condition, of education, of conversation, of the sphere in which they move. Many millions of them have been brought to, and

2. Orangutan.

3. Perspiration.

4. Dr. Adair Crawford (1748–95), a physician and a professor of chemistry at Royal Military Academy, Woolwich, whose *Experiments and Observations on Animal Heat, and the Inflammation of Combustible Bodies* (1779) studied the nature and effects of human respiration.

born in America. Most of them indeed have been confined to tillage, to their own homes, and their own society: yet many have been so situated, that they might have availed themselves of the conversation of their masters; many have been brought up to the handicraft arts, and from that circumstance have always been associated with the whites. Some have been liberally educated, and all have lived in countries where the arts and sciences are cultivated to a considerable degree, and have had before their eyes samples of the best works from abroad. The Indians, with no advantages of this kind, will often carve figures on their pipes not destitute of design and merit. They will crayon out an animal, a plant, or a country, so as to prove the existence of a germ in their minds which only wants cultivation. They astonish you with strokes of the most sublime oratory; such as prove their reason and sentiment strong, their imagination glowing and elevated. But never yet could I find that a black had uttered a thought above the level of plain narration; never see even an elementary trait of painting or sculpture. In music they are more generally gifted than the whites with accurate ears for tune and time, and they have been found capable of imagining a small catch.[5] Whether they will be equal to the composition of a more extensive run of melody, or of complicated harmony, is yet to be proved. Misery is often the parent of the most affecting touches in poetry.—Among the blacks is misery enough, God knows, but no poetry. Love is the peculiar cestrum[6] of the poet. Their love is ardent, but it kindles the senses only, not the imagination. Religion indeed has produced a Phyllis Whately;[7] but it could not produce a poet. . . . The heroes of the Dunciad are to her, as Hercules to the author of that poem.[8] Ignatius Sancho[9] has approached nearer to merit in composition; yet his letters do more honour to the heart than the head. They breathe the purest effusions of friendship and general philanthropy, and shew how great a degree of the latter may be compounded with strong religious zeal. He is often happy in the turn of his compliments, and his stile is easy and familiar, except when he affects a Shandean[1] fabrication of words. But his imagination is wild and

---

5. A round for three or more unaccompanied voices.

6. A fragrant tropical flower such as night jasmine.

7. Phillis Wheatley (c. 1753–84), an African American poet and ardent Christian born in Gambia, whose *Poems on Various Subjects, Religious and Moral* (1773) was widely acclaimed and put forth as proof that persons of African descent were the intellectual and artistic equals of whites.

8. The Dunciad was an epic poem by Alexander Pope (1688–1744) that satirized a number of British authors he thought to be dull and unimaginative. Pope himself was hunchbacked and only four and a half feet tall. Thus, Jefferson is saying that the difference between the second-rate poets Pope lampooned and Wheatley is equivalent to the physical difference between the god Hercules and the disfigured and diminutive Pope.

9. (Charles) Ignatius Sancho (c. 1729–80); born on a slave ship headed for the West Indies, Sancho was taken to England, where he was educated. H is posthumously published *Letters of the Late Ignatius Sancho, an African* (1782) was hailed as further proof of the intellectual capabilities of Africans.

1. A reference to the protagonist of Laurence Sterne's comic novel *The Life and Opinions of Tristram Shandy, Gentleman* (1759–66); Sancho was known for writing in a style closely derived from Sterne's work.

extravagant, escapes incessantly from every restraint of reason and taste, and, in the course of its vagaries, leaves a tract of thought as incoherent and eccentric, as is the course of a meteor through the sky. His subjects should often have led him to a process of sober reasoning: yet we find him always substituting sentiment for demonstration. Upon the whole, though we admit him to the first place among those of his own colour who have presented themselves to the public judgment, yet when we compare him with the writers of the race among whom he lived, and particularly with the epistolary class, in which he has taken his own stand, we are compelled to enroll him at the bottom of the column. This criticism supposes the letters published under his name to be genuine, and to have received amendment from no other hand; points which would not be of easy investigation. The improvement of the blacks in body and mind, in the first instance of their mixture with the whites, has been observed by every one, and proves that their inferiority is not the effect merely of their condition of life.

* * *

The opinion, that they are inferior in the faculties of reason and imagination, must be hazarded with great diffidence. To justify a general conclusion, requires many observations, even where the subject may be submitted to the anatomical knife, to optical glasses, to analysis by fire, or by solvents. How much more then where it is a faculty, not a substance, we are examining; where it eludes the research of all the senses; where the conditions of its existence are various and variously combined; where the effects of those which are present or absent bid defiance to calculation; let me add too, as a circumstance of great tenderness, where our conclusion would degrade a whole race of men from the rank in the scale of beings which their Creator may perhaps have given them. To our reproach it must be said, that though for a century and a half we have had under our eyes the races of black and of red men, they have never yet been viewed by us as subjects of natural history, I advance it therefore as a suspicion only, that the blacks, whether originally a distinct race, or made distinct by time and circumstances, are inferior to the whites in the endowments both of body and mind.

Study Questions

1. How and why, according to Jefferson, are people of African origin distinct from people of European origin?

2. At several points, Jefferson ascribes social and cultural characteristics to genetic origins. What are some examples?

3. A decade before the publication of *Notes on the State of Virginia*, Jefferson wrote in the Declaration of Independence that "All men are created equal." Is it possible to reconcile these two documents? How do you think Jefferson would answer such a question?

4. How would you characterize the tone of Jefferson's writing in *Notes on the State of Virginia*? Who are his intended readers?

JAMES MADISON

Federalist Papers No. 10 (1787) and No. 51 (1788)

From October 1787 to August 1788, various New York newspapers published 85 essays advocating New York's ratification of the proposed Constitution of the United States. Although all of the pieces were signed "Publius"—the name of one of the founders of the Roman Republic—the essays were actually written by three men: James Madison, Alexander Hamilton, and John Jay. The Federalist Papers, *as they came to be known, were designed both to set forth reasons why America's first constitution, the Articles of Confederation, was inadequate, and also to alleviate concerns that the new constitution unnecessarily amplified the power of the national government.*

Two of the most famous Federalist Papers—*Numbers 10 and 51—were written by Madison; both discuss how the proposed constitution would prevent governmental abuse. As the essays make clear, Madison was profoundly disturbed by the actions of the state legislatures, which, in the face of a prolonged economic depression, had passed laws designed to help citizens who couldn't pay their debts and taxes. Madison despaired that such legislation demonstrated that American citizens cared only about their own interests, not the good of the whole nation—as republican theory demanded—and he desperately wished to find a federal means to regulate their behavior.*

Madison's Federalist No. 10 (today the most well-known of the essays) was directed at the prevalent fear that a republic could not exist over wide expanses of land; after all, didn't the Roman Republic collapse after spreading throughout the Mediterranean world? Yet Madison turned this concept on its head, arguing that large republics were actually more stable than small ones. In Federalist No. 51, Madison maintained that the constitution's partitioning of power—not only among the legislative, judicial, and executive branches, but between the state and federal governments—would effectively keep any one group of ambitious men from consolidating power.

Although the extent to which the essays influenced ratification debates in New York and elsewhere is unclear, it is certain that the Federalist Papers *have become essential to our understanding of the United States Constitution, serving as its most important commentary and most thorough exposition.*

From "The Federalist Papers: No. 10" and "The Federalist Papers: No. 51" (The Avalon Project, Yale Law School), http://avalon.law.yale.edu.

The Federalist Papers: No. 10

To the People of the State of New York:

Among the numerous advantages promised by a well-constructed Union, none deserves to be more accurately developed than its tendency to break and control the violence of faction. The friend of popular governments never finds himself so much alarmed for their character and fate, as when he contemplates their propensity to this dangerous vice. He will not fail, therefore, to set a due value on any plan which, without violating the principles to which he is attached, provides a proper cure for it. The instability, injustice, and confusion introduced into the public councils, have, in truth, been the mortal diseases under which popular governments have everywhere perished.

* * *

By a *faction*, I understand a number of citizens, whether amounting to a majority or a minority of the whole, who are united and actuated by some common impulse of passion, or of interest, adverse to the rights of other citizens, or to the permanent and aggregate interests of the community.

There are two methods of curing the mischiefs of faction: the one, by removing its causes; the other, by controlling its effects.

There are again two methods of removing the causes of faction: the one, by destroying the liberty which is essential to its existence, the other, by giving to every citizen the same opinions, the same passions, and the same interests.

It could never be more truly said than of the first remedy, that it was worse than the disease. Liberty is to faction what air is to fire, an aliment without which it instantly expires. But it could not be less folly to abolish liberty, which is essential to political life, because it nourishes faction, than it would be to wish the annihilation of air, which is essential to animal life, because it imparts to fire its destructive agency.

The second expedient is as impracticable as the first would be unwise. As long as the reason of man continues fallible, and he is at liberty to exercise it, different opinions will be formed.

* * *

The latent causes of faction are thus sown in the nature of man; and we see them everywhere brought into different degrees of activity, according to the different circumstances of civil society. A zeal for different opinions concerning religion, concerning government, and many other points, as well of speculation as of practice; an attachment to different leaders ambitiously contending for pre-eminence and power; or to persons of other descriptions whose fortunes have been interesting to the human passions, have, in turn, divided mankind into parties, inflamed them with mutual animosity, and rendered them much more disposed to vex and oppress each other than to co-operate for their common good. . . . The most common and durable source of factions has been the various and unequal distribution of property. Those who hold and those who are without property have ever formed distinct interests in society. Those who are creditors, and those who are debtors, fall under a like discrimination. A landed interest, a manufacturing interest, a mercantile interest, a moneyed interest, with many lesser interests, grow up of necessity in civilized nations, and divide them into different classes, actuated by different sentiments and views. The regulation of these various and interfering interests forms the principal task of modern legislation, and involves the spirit of party and faction in the necessary and ordinary operations of the government.

No man is allowed to be a judge in his own cause, because his interest would certainly bias his judgment, and, not improbably, corrupt his integrity. With equal, nay with greater reason, a body of men are unfit to be both judges and parties at the same time; yet what are many of the most important acts of legislation, but so many judicial determinations, not indeed concerning the rights of single persons, but concerning the rights of large bodies of citizens? And what are the different classes of legislators but advocates and parties to the causes which they determine? Is a law proposed concerning private debts? It is a question to which the creditors are parties on one side and the debtors on the other. Justice ought to hold the balance between them. Yet the parties are, and must be, themselves the judges; and the most numerous party, or, in other words, the most powerful faction must be expected to prevail. Shall domestic manufactures be encouraged, and in what degree, by restrictions on foreign manufactures? are questions which would be differently decided by the landed and the manufacturing classes, and probably by neither with a sole regard to justice and the public good. The apportionment of taxes on the various descriptions of property is an act which seems to require the most exact impartiality; yet there is, perhaps, no legislative act in which greater opportunity and temptation are given to a predominant party to trample on the rules of justice. Every shilling with which they overburden the inferior number, is a shilling saved to their own pockets.

It is in vain to say that enlightened statesmen will be able to adjust these clashing interests, and render them all subservient to the public good. Enlightened statesmen will not always be at the helm. Nor, in many cases, can such an adjustment be made at all without taking into view indirect and remote considerations, which will rarely prevail over the immediate interest which one party may find in disregarding the rights of another or the good of the whole.

The inference to which we are brought is, that the CAUSES of faction cannot be removed, and that relief is only to be sought in the means of controlling its EFFECTS.

If a faction consists of less than a majority, relief is supplied by the republican principle, which enables the majority to defeat its sinister views by regular vote. It may clog the administration, it may convulse the society; but it will be unable to execute and mask its violence under the forms of the Constitution. When a majority is included in a faction, the form of popular government, on the other hand, enables it to sacrifice to its ruling passion or interest both the public good and the rights of other citizens. To secure the public good and private rights against the danger of such a faction, and at the same time to preserve the spirit and the form of popular government, is then the great object to which our inquiries are directed. . . .

By what means is this object attainable? Evidently by one of two only. Either the existence of the same passion or interest in a majority at the same time must be prevented, or the majority, having such coexistent passion or interest, must be rendered, by their number and local situation, unable to concert and carry into effect schemes of oppression. If the impulse and the opportunity be suffered to coincide, we well know that neither moral nor religious motives can be relied on as an adequate control. They are not found to be such on the injustice and violence of individuals, and lose their efficacy in proportion to the number combined together, that is, in proportion as their efficacy becomes needful.

From this view of the subject it may be concluded that a pure democracy, by which I mean a society consisting of a small number of citizens, who assemble and administer the government in person, can admit of no cure for the mischiefs of faction. A common passion or interest will, in almost every case, be felt by a majority of the whole; a communication and concert result from the form of government itself; and there is nothing to check the inducements to sacrifice the weaker party or an obnoxious individual. Hence it is that such democracies have ever been spectacles of turbulence and contention; have ever been found incompatible with personal security or the rights of property; and have in general been as short in their lives as they have been violent in their deaths. Theoretic politicians, who have patronized this species of government, have erroneously supposed that by reducing mankind to a perfect equality in their political rights, they would, at the same time, be perfectly equalized and assimilated in their possessions, their opinions, and their passions.

A republic, by which I mean a government in which the scheme of representation takes place, opens a different prospect, and promises the cure for which we are seeking. Let us examine the points in which it varies from pure democracy, and we shall comprehend both the nature of the cure and the efficacy which it must derive from the Union.

The two great points of difference between a democracy and a republic are: first, the delegation of the government, in the latter, to a small number of citizens elected by the rest; secondly, the greater number of citizens, and greater sphere of country, over which the latter may be extended.

The effect of the first difference is, on the one hand, to refine and enlarge the public views, by passing them through the medium of a chosen body of citizens, whose wisdom may best discern the true interest of their country, and whose patriotism and love of justice will be least likely to sacrifice it to temporary or partial considerations. Under such a regulation, it may well happen that the public voice, pronounced by the representatives of the people, will be more consonant to the public good than if pronounced by the people themselves, convened for the purpose. On the other hand, the effect may be inverted. Men of factious tempers, of local prejudices, or of sinister designs, may, by intrigue, by corruption, or by other means, first obtain the suffrages, and then betray the interests, of the people. The question resulting is, whether small or extensive republics are more favorable to the election of proper guardians of the public weal; and it is clearly decided in favor of the latter by two obvious considerations:

In the first place, it is to be remarked that, however small the republic may be, the representatives must be raised to a certain number, in order to guard against the cabals of a few; and that, however large it may be, they must be limited to a certain number, in order to guard against the confusion of a multitude. Hence, the number of representatives in the two cases not being in proportion to that of the two constituents, and being proportionally greater in the small republic, it follows that, if the proportion of fit characters be not less in the large than in the small republic, the former will present a greater option, and consequently a greater probability of a fit choice.

In the next place, as each representative will be chosen by a greater number of citizens in the large than in the small republic, it will be more difficult for unworthy candidates to practice with success the vicious arts by which elections are too often carried; and the suffrages of the people being more free, will be more likely to centre in men who possess the most attractive merit and the most diffusive and established characters.

It must be confessed that in this, as in most other cases, there is a mean, on both sides of which inconveniences will be found to lie. By enlarging too much the number of electors, you render the representatives too little acquainted with all their local circumstances and lesser interests; as by reducing it too much, you render him unduly attached to these, and too little fit to comprehend and pursue great and national objects. The federal Constitution forms a happy combination in this respect; the great and aggregate interests being referred to the national, the local and particular to the State legislatures.

The other point of difference is, the greater number of citizens and extent of territory which may be brought within the compass of republican than of democratic government; and it is this circumstance principally which renders factious combinations less to be dreaded in the former than in the latter. The smaller the society, the fewer probably will be the distinct parties and interests composing it; the fewer the distinct parties and interests, the more frequently will a majority be found of the same party; and the smaller the number of individuals composing a majority, and the smaller the compass within which they are placed, the more easily will they concert and execute their plans of oppression. Extend the sphere, and you take in a greater variety of parties and interests; you make it less probable that a majority of the whole will have a common motive to invade the rights of other citizens; or if such a common motive exists, it will be more difficult for all who feel it to discover their own strength, and to act in unison with each other. Besides other impediments, it may be remarked that, where there is a consciousness of unjust or dishonorable purposes, communication is always checked by distrust in proportion to the number whose concurrence is necessary.

Hence, it clearly appears, that the same advantage which a republic has over a democracy, in controlling the effects of faction, is enjoyed by a large over a small republic—is enjoyed by the Union over the States composing it. Does the advantage consist in the substitution of representatives whose enlightened views and virtuous sentiments render them superior to local prejudices and schemes of injustice? It will not be denied that the representation of the Union will be most likely to possess these requisite endowments. Does it consist in the greater security afforded by a greater variety of parties, against the event of any one party being able to outnumber and oppress the rest? In an equal degree does the increased variety of parties comprised within the Union, increase this security. Does it, in fine, consist in the greater obstacles opposed to the concert and accomplishment of the secret wishes of an unjust and interested majority? Here, again, the extent of the Union gives it the most palpable advantage.

The influence of factious leaders may kindle a flame within their particular States, but will be unable to spread a general conflagration through the other States. A religious sect may degenerate into a political faction in a part of the Confederacy; but the variety of sects dispersed over the entire face of it must secure the national councils against any danger from that source. A rage for paper money, for an abolition of debts, for an equal division of property, or for any other improper or wicked project, will be less apt to pervade the whole body of the Union than a particular member of it; in the same proportion as such a malady is more likely to taint a particular county or district, than an entire State.

In the extent and proper structure of the Union, therefore, we behold a republican remedy for the diseases most incident to republican government. And according to the degree of pleasure and pride we feel in being republicans, ought to be our zeal in cherishing the spirit and supporting the character of Federalists.

PUBLIUS.

The Federalist Papers: No. 51

To the People of the State of New York:

To what expedient, then, shall we finally resort, for maintaining in practice the necessary partition of power among the several departments, as laid down in the Constitution? The only answer that can be given is, that as all these exterior provisions are found to be inadequate, the defect must be supplied, by so contriving the interior structure of the government as that its several constituent parts may, by their mutual relations, be the means of keeping each other in their proper places. Without presuming to undertake a full development of this important idea, I will hazard a few general observations, which may perhaps place it in a clearer light, and enable us to form a more correct judgment of the principles and structure of the government planned by the convention.

In order to lay a due foundation for that separate and distinct exercise of the different powers of government, which to a certain extent is admitted on all hands to be essential to the preservation of liberty, it is evident that each department should have a will of its own; and consequently should be so constituted that the members of each should have as little agency as possible in the appointment of the members of the others.

* * *

It is equally evident, that the members of each department should be as little dependent as possible on those of the others. . . . But the great security against a gradual concentration of the several powers in the same department, consists in giving to those who administer each department the necessary constitutional means and personal motives to resist encroachments of the others. The provision for defense must in this, as in all other cases, be made commensurate to the danger of attack. Ambition must be made to counteract ambition. The interest of the man must be connected with the constitutional rights of the place. It may be a reflection on human nature, that such devices should be necessary to control the abuses of government. But what is government itself, but the greatest of all reflections on human nature? If men were angels, no government would be necessary. If angels were to govern men, neither external nor internal controls on government would be necessary. In framing a government which is to be administered by men over men, the great difficulty lies in this: you must first enable the government to control the governed; and in the next place oblige it to control itself.

A dependence on the people is, no doubt, the primary control on the government; but experience has taught mankind the necessity of auxiliary precautions. This policy of supplying, by opposite and rival interests, the defect of better movies, might be traced through the whole system of human affairs, private as well as public.

We see it particularly displayed in all the subordinate distributions of power, where the constant aim is to divide and arrange the several offices in such a manner as that each may be a check on the other that the private interest of every individual may be a sentinel over the public rights. These inventions of prudence cannot be less requisite in the distribution of the supreme powers of the State. But it is not possible to give to each department an equal power of self-defense. In republican government, the legislative authority necessarily predominates. The remedy for this inconveniency is to divide the legislature into different branches; and to render them, by different modes of election and different principles of action, as little connected with each other as the nature of their common functions and their common dependence on the society will admit. It may even be necessary to guard against dangerous encroachments by still further precautions. As the weight of the legislative authority requires that it should be thus divided, the weakness of the executive may require, on the other hand, that it should be fortified.

* * *

There are two considerations particularly applicable to the federal system of America, which place that system in a very interesting point of view. First. In a single republic, all the power surrendered by the people is submitted to the administration of a single government; and the usurpations are guarded against by a division of the government into distinct and separate departments. In the compound republic of America, the power surrendered by the people is first divided between two distinct governments, and then the portion allotted to each subdivided among distinct and separate departments. Hence a double security arises to the rights of the people. The different governments will control each other, at the same time that each will be controlled by itself. Second. It is of great importance in a republic not only to guard the society against the oppression of its rulers, but to guard one part of the society against the injustice of the other part. Different interests necessarily exist in different classes of citizens. If a majority be united by a common interest, the rights of the minority will be insecure.

There are but two methods of providing against this evil: the one by creating a will in the community independent of the majority that is, of the society itself; the other, by comprehending in the society so many separate descriptions of citizens as will render an unjust combination of a majority of the whole very improbable, if not impracticable. The first method prevails in all governments possessing an hereditary or self-appointed authority. This, at best, is but a precarious security; because a power independent of the society may as well espouse the unjust views of the major, as the rightful interests of the minor party, and may possibly be turned against both parties. The second method will be exemplified in the federal republic of the United States. Whilst all authority in it will be derived from and dependent on the society, the society itself will be broken into so many parts, interests, and classes of citizens, that the rights of individuals, or of the minority, will be in little danger from interested combinations of the majority.

* * *

PUBLIUS.

Study Questions

1. What, according to Madison, was a faction? Why did factions form and why did he believe them to be so threatening?

2. What is Madison's opinion of "pure democracies"? How did he believe such a form of government was different from a republic?

3. In Federalist No. 10, what did Madison mean by insisting that America must "extend the sphere"?

4. In Federalist No. 51, Madison states that "If men were angels, no government would be necessary. If angels were to govern men, neither external nor internal controls on government would be necessary. In framing a government which is to be administered by men over men, the great difficulty lies in this: you must first enable the government to control the governed; and in the next place oblige it to control itself." What does this statement suggest about Madison's conception of human nature?

5. Are Madison's concerns about the power of government still relevant today? Why or why not?

THOMAS JEFFERSON

An Act for Establishing Religious Freedom (1786)

Throughout the colonial era, the established church of Virginia was the Anglican Church—which meant that it was, in effect, a virtual appendage of the Virginian government. During the American Revolution, however, religious establishments came under heavy criticism by a particularly unlikely alliance: secular intellectuals, who believed the state had no right to interfere with personal religious belief, and evangelicals, who resented being made to support other denominations. Among the first group was Thomas Jefferson (1743–1826), a religious skeptic who generally rejected the notion of a personal God who intervened in human affairs.

In 1779 Jefferson authored and had introduced into the Virginia assembly a bill titled "An Act for Establishing Religious Freedom," which came to be known as the Virginia Statute for Religious Freedom. Although tabled, the bill was re-introduced and shepherded through the Virginia assembly six years later by Jefferson's close friend, James Madison. The act became law in January 1786, while Jefferson was in France serving as an American ambassador.

The statute's lengthy preamble ranks among the most impassioned of Jefferson's writings. It reveals his abhorrence of forced worship, which was, he believed, just another form of tyranny over the individual, productive of little save hypocrisy and corruption. Intent that religious belief and civil rights be forever separate, Jefferson proclaimed that "no man shall be compelled to frequent or support any religious worship, place, or ministry whatsoever" and that "all men shall be free to profess, and by argument to maintain, their opinions in matters of religion." It was indeed a revolution.

Late in life, Jefferson directed that he wanted his gravestone to list only three of his many accomplishments: the establishment of the University of Virginia, the authorship of the Declaration of Independence, and the fact that he wrote the Virginia Statute of Religious Freedom.

From William Waller Hening, *The States at Large; Being a Collection of all the Laws of Virginia* (Richmond: George Cochran, 1823), 84–86.

Whereas Almighty God hath created the mind free;[1] that all attempts to influence it by temporal punishments or burdens, or by civil incapacitations, tend only to beget habits of hypocrisy and meanness, and are a departure from the plan of the Holy author of our religion,[2] who being Lord both of body and mind, yet chose not to propagate it by coercions on either, as was in his Almighty power to do;

That the impious presumption of legislators and rulers, civil as well as ecclesiastical, who, being themselves but fallible and uninspired men, have assumed dominion over the faith of others, setting up their own opinions and modes of thinking as the only true and infallible, and as such endeavouring to impose them on others, hath established and maintained false religions over the greatest part of the world, and through all time;

That to compel a man to furnish contributions of money for the propagation of opinions which he disbelieves, is sinful and tyrannical;

That even the forcing him to support this or that teacher of his own religious persuasion, is depriving him of the comfortable liberty of giving his contributions to the particular pastor whose morals he would make his pattern, and whose powers he feels most persuasive to righteousness, and is withdrawing from the Ministry those temporal rewards, which proceeding from an approbation of their personal conduct, are an additional incitement to earnest and unremitting labours for the instruction of mankind;

That our civil rights have no dependence on our religious opinions, more than our opinions in physics or geometry;

That, therefore, the proscribing any citizen as unworthy the public confidence by laying upon him an incapacity of being called to the offices of trust and emolument, unless he profess or renounce this or that religious opinion, is depriving him injuriously of those privileges and advantages to which in common with his fellow citizens he has a natural right;

That it tends also to corrupt the principles of that very Religion it is meant to encourage, by bribing, with a monopoly of worldly honours and emoluments, those who will externally profess and conform to it;

---

1. The first words of Jefferson's draft read "Well aware that the opinions and belief of men depend not on their own will, but follow involuntarily the evidence proposed in the minds. . . ." Many members of the Virginia Assembly, uneasy with such a forthright declaration of Enlightenment principles, replaced the phrase with "Whereas Almighty God hath created the mind free. . . ."
2. Here, some members of the assembly attempted to insert the words "Jesus Christ," but the motion was defeated.

That though indeed these are criminal who do not withstand such temptation, yet neither are those innocent who lay the bait in their way;

That to suffer the civil magistrate to intrude his powers into the field of opinion and to restrain the profession or propagation of principles, on the supposition of their ill tendency, is a dangerous fallacy, which at once destroys all religious liberty, because he being of course judge of that tendency, will make his opinions the rule of judgment, and approve or condemn the sentiments of others only as they shall square with or differ from his own;

That it is time enough for the rightful purposes of civil government, for its officers to interfere when principles break out into overt acts against peace and good order;

And finally, that Truth is great and will prevail if left to herself, that she is the proper and sufficient antagonist to error, and has nothing to fear from the conflict, unless by human interposition disarmed of her natural weapons, free argument and debate, errors ceasing to be dangerous when it is permitted freely to contradict them.

Be it therefore enacted by the General Assembly, that no man shall be compelled to frequent or support any religious worship, place, or ministry whatsoever, nor shall be enforced, restrained, molested, or burdened in his body or goods, nor shall otherwise suffer on account of his religious opinions or belief; but that all men shall be free to profess, and by argument to maintain, their opinions in matters of religion, and that the same shall in nowise diminish, enlarge, or affect their civil capacities.

And though we well know this Assembly, elected by the people for the ordinary purposes of legislation only, have no powers equal to our own and that therefore to declare this act irrevocable would be of no effect in law, yet we are free to declare, and do declare, that the rights hereby asserted are of the natural rights of mankind, and that if any act shall be hereafter passed to repeal the present or to narrow its operation, such act will be an infringement of natural right.

Study Questions

1. How, specifically, does Jefferson define religious freedom? What does the act explicitly forbid?

2. Why, according to Jefferson, was state-dictated worship so repugnant?

3. What is the significance of the third section that warns against the repeal or restriction of the act? Why do you think Jefferson included it?

4. Do you believe Jefferson, if he were alive, would be more pleased or alarmed at today's church-state relations?

5. Why might Jefferson have ranked the Virginia Statute of Religious Freedom as among his most significant life achievements? What does this suggest about both Jefferson's values and, more generally, the revolutionary spirit of the era?

GEORGE WASHINGTON

Farewell Address (1796)

George Washington (1732–1799) did not particularly like being president of the United States. Due to rising partisan hatreds, concern for his own reputation, and a simple desire to go home to Virginia, he dearly wanted to retire after his first term expired in 1792, but was persuaded by Thomas Jefferson, James Madison, and Alexander Hamilton to serve another four years. (As the nation's first president, he had no precedent for length of tenure—the two-term limit would not be enacted until 1951 with the passage of the Twenty-Second Amendment). In Washington's second term, political divisions between the Federalists and the Jeffersonian Republicans only worsened, and he endured a level of public criticism he had never before encountered. By 1796 he was determined to step down.

Before leaving office, however, Washington wanted to give a final message to his country, one that would summarize his hopes and fears for the fledgling republic. Although James Madison and Alexander Hamilton helped shaped the speech, the final form and content of the document reflected Washington's deeply felt sentiments. The farewell address first appeared on September 19, 1796, in David Claypoole's American Daily Advertiser *and was immediately reprinted throughout the country.*

From "George Washington's Farewell Address" (The Independent Chronicle, 1796).

Friends and Citizens:

The period for a new election of a citizen to administer the executive government of the United States being not far distant, and the time actually arrived when your thoughts must be employed in designating the person who is to be clothed with that important trust, it appears to me proper, especially as it may conduce to a more distinct expression of the public voice, that I should now apprise you of the resolution I have formed, to decline being considered among the number of those out of whom a choice is to be made.

* * *

In looking forward to the moment which is intended to terminate the career of my public life, my feelings do not permit me to suspend the deep acknowledgment of that debt of gratitude which I owe to my beloved country for the many honors it has conferred upon me; still more for the steadfast confidence with which it has supported me; and for the opportunities I have thence enjoyed of manifesting my inviolable attachment, by services faithful and persevering, though in usefulness unequal to my zeal. If benefits have resulted to our country from these services, let it always be remembered to your praise, and as an instructive example in our annals, that under circumstances in which the passions, agitated in every direction, were liable to mislead, amidst appearances sometimes dubious, vicissitudes of fortune often discouraging, in situations in which not unfrequently want of success has countenanced the spirit of criticism, the constancy of your support was the essential prop of the efforts, and a guarantee of the plans by which they were effected. Profoundly penetrated with this idea, I shall carry it with me to my grave, as a strong incitement to unceasing vows that heaven may continue to you the choicest tokens of its beneficence; that your union and brotherly affection may be perpetual; that the free Constitution, which is the work of your hands, may be sacredly maintained; that its administration in every department may be stamped with wisdom and virtue; that, in fine,[1] the happiness of the people of these States, under the auspices of liberty, may be made complete by so careful a preservation and so prudent a use of this blessing as will acquire to them the glory of recommending it to the applause, the affection, and adoption of every nation which is yet a stranger to it.

Here, perhaps, I ought to stop. But a solicitude for your welfare, which cannot end but with my life, and the apprehension of danger, natural to that solicitude, urge me, on an occasion like the present, to offer to your solemn contemplation, and to recommend to your frequent review, some sentiments which are the result of much reflection, of no inconsiderable observation.

* * *

The unity of government which constitutes you one people is also now dear to you. It is justly so, for it is a main pillar in the edifice of your real independence, the support of your tranquility at home, your peace abroad; of your safety; of your prosperity; of that very liberty which you so highly prize. But as it is easy to foresee that, from different causes and from different quarters, much pains will be taken, many artifices employed to weaken in your minds the conviction of this truth; as this is the point in your political fortress against which the batteries of internal and external enemies will be most constantly and actively (though often covertly and insidiously) directed, it is of infinite moment that you should properly estimate the immense value of your national union to your collective and individual happiness; that you should cherish a cordial, habitual, and immovable attachment to it; accustoming yourselves to think and speak of it as of the palladium of your political safety and prosperity; watching for its preservation with

---

1. In conclusion.

jealous anxiety; discountenancing whatever may suggest even a suspicion that it can in any event be abandoned; and indignantly frowning upon the first dawning of every attempt to alienate any portion of our country from the rest, or to enfeeble the sacred ties which now link together the various parts.

For this you have every inducement of sympathy and interest. Citizens, by birth or choice, of a common country, that country has a right to concentrate your affections. The name of American, which belongs to you in your national capacity, must always exalt the just pride of patriotism more than any appellation derived from local discriminations. With slight shades of difference, you have the same religion, manners, habits, and political principles. You have in a common cause fought and triumphed together; the independence and liberty you possess are the work of joint counsels, and joint efforts of common dangers, sufferings, and successes.

* * *

While, then, every part of our country thus feels an immediate and particular interest in union, all the parts combined cannot fail to find in the united mass of means and efforts greater strength, greater resource, proportionably greater security from external danger, a less frequent interruption of their peace by foreign nations; and, what is of inestimable value, they must derive from union an exemption from those broils and wars between themselves, which so frequently afflict neighboring countries not tied together by the same governments, which their own rival ships alone would be sufficient to produce, but which opposite foreign alliances, attachments, and intrigues would stimulate and embitter. Hence, likewise, they will avoid the necessity of those overgrown military establishments which, under any form of government, are inauspicious to liberty, and which are to be regarded as particularly hostile to republican liberty. In this sense it is that your union ought to be considered as a main prop of your liberty, and that the love of the one ought to endear to you the preservation of the other.

These considerations speak a persuasive language to every reflecting and virtuous mind, and exhibit the continuance of the Union as a primary object of patriotic desire. Is there a doubt whether a common government can embrace so large a sphere? Let experience solve it. To listen to mere speculation in such a case were criminal. We are authorized to hope that a proper organization of the whole with the auxiliary agency of governments for the respective subdivisions, will afford a happy issue to the experiment. It is well worth a fair and full experiment. With such powerful and obvious motives to union, affecting all parts of our country, while experience shall not have demonstrated its impracticability, there will always be reason to distrust the patriotism of those who in any quarter may endeavor to weaken its bands.

* * *

To the efficacy and permanency of your Union, a government for the whole is indispensable. No alliance, however strict, between the parts can be an adequate substitute; they must inevitably experience the infractions and interruptions which all alliances in all times have experienced. Sensible of this momentous truth, you have improved upon your first essay, by the adoption of a constitution of government better calculated than your former for an intimate union, and for the efficacious management of your common concerns. This government, the offspring of our own choice, uninfluenced and unawed, adopted upon full investigation and mature deliberation, completely free in its principles, in the distribution of its powers uniting security with energy, and containing within itself a provision for its own amendment, has a just claim to your confidence and your support. Respect for its authority, compliance with its laws, acquiescence in its measures, are duties enjoined by the fundamental maxims of true liberty. The basis of our political systems is the right of the people to make and to alter their constitutions of government. But the *Constitution* which at any time exists, till changed by an explicit and authentic act of the whole people, is sacredly obligatory upon all. The very idea of the power and the right of the people to establish government presupposes the duty of every individual to obey the established government.

All obstructions to the execution of the laws, all combinations and associations, under whatever plausible character, with the real design to direct, control, counteract, or awe the regular deliberation and action of the constituted authorities, are destructive of this fundamental principle, and of fatal tendency. They serve to organize faction, to give it an artificial and extraordinary force; to put, in the place of the delegated will of the nation the will of a party, often a small but artful and enterprising minority of the community; and, according to the alternate triumphs of different parties, to make the public administration the mirror of the ill-concerted and incongruous projects of faction, rather than the organ of consistent and wholesome plans digested by common counsels and modified by mutual interests.

However combinations or associations of the above description may now and then answer popular ends, they are likely, in the course of time and things, to become potent engines, by which cunning, ambitious, and unprincipled men will be enabled to subvert the power of the people and to usurp for themselves the reins of government, destroying afterwards the very engines which have lifted them to unjust dominion.

Towards the preservation of your government, and the permanency of your present happy state, it is requisite, not only that you steadily discountenance irregular oppositions to its acknowledged authority, but also that you resist with care the spirit of innovation upon its principles, however specious the pretexts. One method of assault may be to effect, in the forms of the *Constitution* alterations which will impair the energy of the system, and thus to undermine what cannot be directly overthrown. In all the changes to which you may be invited, remember that time and habit are at least as necessary to fix the true character of governments as of other human institutions; that experience is the surest standard by which to test the real tendency of the existing constitution of a country; that facility in changes, upon the credit of mere hypothesis and opinion, exposes to perpetual change, from the endless variety of hypothesis and opinion; and remember, especially, that for the efficient management of your common interests, in a country so extensive as ours, a government of as much vigor as is consistent with the perfect security of liberty is indispensable. Liberty itself will find in such a government, with powers properly distributed and adjusted, its surest guardian. It is, indeed, little else than a name, where the government is too feeble to withstand the enterprises of faction, to confine each member of the society within the limits prescribed by the laws, and to maintain all in the secure and tranquil enjoyment of the rights of person and property.

I have already intimated to you the danger of parties in the State, with particular reference to the founding of them on geographical discriminations. Let me now take a more comprehensive view, and warn you in the most solemn manner against the baneful effects of the spirit of party generally.

This spirit, unfortunately, is inseparable from our nature, having its root in the strongest passions of the human mind. It exists under different shapes in all governments, more or less stifled, controlled, or repressed; but, in those of the popular form, it is seen in its greatest rankness, and is truly their worst enemy.

The alternate domination of one faction over another, sharpened by the spirit of revenge, natural to party dissension, which in different ages and countries has perpetrated the most horrid enormities, is itself a frightful despotism. But this leads at length to a more formal and permanent despotism. The disorders and miseries which result gradually incline the minds of men to seek security and repose in the absolute power of an individual; and sooner or later the chief of some prevailing faction, more able or more fortunate than his competitors, turns this disposition to the purposes of his own elevation, on the ruins of public liberty.

Without looking forward to an extremity of this kind (which nevertheless ought not to be entirely out of sight), the common and continual mischiefs of the spirit of party are sufficient to make it the interest and duty of a wise people to discourage and restrain it.

It serves always to distract the public councils and enfeeble the public administration. It agitates the community with ill-founded jealousies and false alarms, kindles the animosity of one part against another, foments occasionally riot and insurrection. It opens the door to foreign influence and corruption, which finds a facilitated access to the government itself through the channels of party passions. Thus the policy and the will of one country are subjected to the policy and will of another.

* * *

It is important, likewise, that the habits of thinking in a free country should inspire caution in those entrusted with its administration, to confine themselves within their respective constitutional spheres, avoiding in the exercise of the powers of one department to encroach upon another. The spirit of encroachment tends to consolidate the powers of all the departments in one, and thus to create, whatever the form of government, a real despotism. A just estimate of that love of power, and proneness to abuse it, which predominates in the human heart, is sufficient to satisfy us of the truth of this position. The necessity of reciprocal checks in the exercise of political power, by dividing and distributing it into different depositaries, and constituting each the guardian of the public weal against invasions by the others, has been evinced by experiments ancient and modern; some of them in our country and under our own eyes. To preserve them must be as necessary as to institute them. If, in the opinion of the people, the distribution or modification of the constitutional powers be in any particular wrong, let it be corrected by an amendment in the way which the *Constitution* designates. But let there be no change by usurpation; for though this, in one instance, may be the instrument of good, it is the customary weapon by which free governments are destroyed. The precedent must always greatly overbalance in permanent evil any partial or transient benefit, which the use can at any time yield.

Of all the dispositions and habits which lead to political prosperity, religion and morality are indispensable supports. In vain would that man claim the tribute of patriotism, who should labor to subvert these great pillars of human happiness, these firmest props of the duties of men and citizens. The mere politician, equally with the pious man, ought to respect and to cherish them. A volume could not trace all their connections with private and public felicity. Let it simply be asked: Where is the security for property, for reputation, for life, if the sense of religious obligation desert the oaths which are the instruments of investigation in courts of justice? And let us with caution indulge the supposition that morality can be maintained without religion. Whatever may be conceded to the influence of refined education on minds of peculiar structure, reason and experience both forbid us to expect that national morality can prevail in exclusion of religious principle.

* * *

Promote then, as an object of primary importance, institutions for the general diffusion of knowledge. In proportion as the structure of a government gives force to public opinion, it is essential that public opinion should be enlightened.

As a very important source of strength and security, cherish public credit. One method of preserving it is to use it as sparingly as possible, avoiding occasions of expense by cultivating peace, but remembering also that timely disbursements to prepare for danger frequently prevent much greater disbursements to repel it, avoiding likewise the accumulation of debt, not only by shunning occasions of expense, but by vigorous exertion in time of peace to discharge the debts which unavoidable wars may have occasioned, not ungenerously throwing upon posterity the burden which we ourselves ought to bear. The execution of these maxims belongs to your representatives, but it is necessary that public opinion should cooperate. To facilitate to them the performance of their duty, it is essential that you should practically bear in mind that towards the payment of debts there must be revenue; that to have revenue there must be taxes; that no taxes can be devised which are not more or less inconvenient and unpleasant; that the intrinsic embarrassment, inseparable from the selection of the proper objects (which is always a choice of difficulties), ought to be a decisive motive for a candid construction of the conduct of the government in making it, and for a spirit of acquiescence in the measures for obtaining revenue, which the public exigencies may at any time dictate.

Observe good faith and justice towards all nations; cultivate peace and harmony with all. Religion and morality enjoin this conduct; and can it be, that good policy does not equally enjoin it—It will be worthy of a free, enlightened, and at no distant period, a great nation, to give to mankind the magnanimous and too novel example of a people always guided by an exalted justice and benevolence . . .

In the execution of such a plan, nothing is more essential than that permanent, inveterate antipathies against particular nations, and passionate attachments for others, should be excluded; and that, in place of them, just and amicable feelings towards all should be cultivated. The nation which indulges towards another a habitual hatred or a habitual fondness is in some degree a slave. It is a slave to its animosity or to its affection, either of which is sufficient to lead it astray from its duty and its interest. Antipathy in one nation against another disposes each more readily to offer insult and injury, to lay hold of slight causes of umbrage, and to be haughty and intractable, when accidental or trifling occasions of dispute occur. Hence, frequent collisions, obstinate, envenomed, and bloody contests. The nation, prompted by ill-will and resentment, sometimes impels to war the government, contrary to the best calculations of policy. The government sometimes participates in the national propensity, and adopts through passion what reason would reject; at other times it makes the animosity of the nation subservient to projects of hostility instigated by pride, ambition, and other sinister and pernicious motives. The peace often, sometimes perhaps the liberty, of nations, has been the victim.

So likewise, a passionate attachment of one nation for another produces a variety of evils. Sympathy for the favorite nation, facilitating the illusion of an imaginary common interest in cases where no real common interest exists, and infusing into one the enmities of the other, betrays the former into a participation in the quarrels and wars of the latter without adequate inducement or justification.

* * *

As avenues to foreign influence in innumerable ways, such attachments are particularly alarming to the truly enlightened and independent patriot. How many opportunities do they afford to tamper with domestic factions, to practice the arts of seduction, to mislead public opinion, to influence or awe the public councils. Such an attachment of a small or weak towards a great and powerful nation dooms the former to be the satellite of the latter.

Against the insidious wiles of foreign influence (I conjure you to believe me, fellow-citizens) the jealousy of a free people ought to be constantly awake, since history and experience prove that foreign influence is one of the most baneful foes of republican government. But that jealousy to be useful must be impartial; else it becomes the instrument of the very influence to be avoided, instead of a defense against it. Excessive partiality for one foreign nation and excessive dislike of another cause those whom they actuate to see danger only on one side, and serve to veil and even second the arts of influence on the other. Real patriots who may resist the intrigues of the favorite are liable to become suspected and odious, while its tools and dupes usurp the applause and confidence of the people, to surrender their interests.

The great rule of conduct for us in regard to foreign nations is in extending our commercial relations, to have with them as little political connection as possible. So far as we have already formed engagements, let them be fulfilled with perfect good faith. Here let us stop. Europe has a set of primary interests which to us have none; or a very remote relation. Hence she must be engaged in frequent controversies, the causes of which are essentially foreign to our concerns. Hence, therefore, it must be unwise in us to implicate ourselves by artificial ties in the ordinary vicissitudes of her politics, or the ordinary combinations and collisions of her friendships or enmities.

Our detached and distant situation invites and enables us to pursue a different course. If we remain one people under an efficient government, the period is not far off when we may defy material injury from external annoyance; when we may take such an attitude as will cause the neutrality we may at any time resolve upon to be scrupulously respected; when belligerent nations, under the impossibility of making acquisitions upon us, will not lightly hazard the giving us provocation; when we may choose peace or war, as our interest, guided by justice, shall counsel.

Why forego the advantages of so peculiar a situation? Why quit our own to stand upon foreign ground? Why, by interweaving our destiny with that of any part of Europe, entangle our peace and prosperity in the toils of European ambition, rivalship, interest, humor or caprice?

It is our true policy to steer clear of permanent alliances with any portion of the foreign world; so far, I mean, as we are now at liberty to do it; for let me not be understood as capable of patronizing infidelity to existing engagements. I hold the maxim no less applicable to public than to private affairs, that honesty is always the best policy. I repeat it therefore, let those engagements be observed in their genuine sense. But, in my opinion, it is unnecessary and would be unwise to extend them.

Taking care always to keep ourselves by suitable establishments on a respectable defensive posture, we may safely trust to temporary alliances for extraordinary emergencies.

Harmony, liberal intercourse with all nations, are recommended by policy, humanity, and interest. But even our commercial policy should hold an equal and impartial hand; neither seeking nor granting exclusive favors or preferences; consulting the natural course of things: diffusing and diversifying by gentle means the streams of commerce, but forcing nothing.

* * *

In offering to you, my countrymen, these counsels of an old and affectionate friend, I dare not hope they will make the strong and lasting impression I could wish; that they will control the usual current of the passions, or prevent our nation from running the course which has hitherto marked the destiny of nations. But, if I may even flatter myself that they may be productive of some partial benefit, some occasional good; that they may now and then recur to moderate the fury of party spirit, to warn against the mischiefs of foreign intrigue, to guard against the impostures of pretended patriotism; this hope will be a full recompense for the solicitude for your welfare, by which they have been dictated.

* * *

Geo. Washington

Study Questions

1. What, specifically, did Washington believe to be the greatest threats confronting America?

2. What did Washington believe to be among America's strengths and advantages?

3. Do you detect in Washington's address any indications of bitterness toward the intensifying political partisanship of his day?

4. According to Washington, what ideals and experiences bound Americans together? Do these bonds still prevail today?

5. Among other things, Washington warned against sectionalism, partisanship, "overgrown military establishments," alliances with foreign powers, embracing speculation over experience, and the disparagement of religion, morality, and public credit (that is, the government's ability to borrow money). Keeping in mind that he proclaimed "experience is the surest standard," what do you think Washington would think of America today? Does Washington's counsel still guide American leaders?

Sedition Act (1798)

In the elections of 1796, the Federalist Party took control of the presidency and both houses of Congress. Over the next year and a half, relations between the United States and France became strained over the XYZ Affair—an attempt by the French ministry to bribe American ambassadors—and the outbreak of the "Quasi-War," an undeclared naval war with France.

In this crisis atmosphere, some Federalists became convinced that French agents and their American sympathizers were plotting to discredit and even overthrow the legitimately elected government of the United States. In response, the Federalists in Congress in 1798 passed—and President John Adams signed—the Sedition Act, which made it illegal to say or write anything "false, scandalous, and malicious" against the government of the United States. (The Sedition Act is often coupled with three other bills—the Naturalization Act, the Alien Friends Act, and the Alien Enemy Act—that collectively made it harder to become an American citizen and easier for government authorities to deport resident recent immigrants.)

Today, the law seems a clear violation of First Amendment guarantees of freedom of speech and freedom of the press. Yet in the eighteenth century, the idea of absolute freedom of expression had not yet fully developed. Most Americans, including most Democratic-Republicans, still held to the common-law doctrine of seditious libel, which held that certain writings or utterances, if harsh enough, amounted to attacks upon the government and were therefore prosecutable. Freedom of the press, in fact, was not considered a license to print anything a writer chose, but as the right to publish free from prior censorship.

From 1798 to 1800, dozens of newspaper editors were indicted under the Sedition Act and ten were convicted and jailed. Others were convicted of merely speaking out against governmental policies.

By any standard, however, the Sedition Act was a disaster for the Federalist Party. Not only did it lead to the creation of dozens of new Democratic-Republican newspapers—and thereby only increased the number of outlets through which the government would be criticized—its heavy-handed enforcement alienated tens of thousands of voters. In the elections of 1800, the Democratic-Republican Party swept the presidency and both houses of Congress. To this day, the Sedition Act still stands as a stain upon the Federalists' historical reputation.

From James M. Matthews, ed., *Public laws of the Confederate States of America, passed at the first session of the first Congress* (Richmond: R. M. Smith, Printer to Congress, 1862–64), 596–97.

n Act in addition to the act, entitled "An act for the punishment of certain crimes against the United States."

SEC. 1.

Be it enacted by the Senate and House of Representatives of the United States of America, in Congress assembled, That if any persons shall unlawfully combine or conspire together, with intent to oppose any measure or measures of the government of the United States, which are or shall be directed by proper authority, or to impede the operation of any law of the United States, or to intimidate or prevent any person holding a place or office in or under the government of the United States, from undertaking, performing or executing his trust or duty; and if any person or persons, with intent as aforesaid, shall counsel, advise or attempt to procure any insurrection, riot, unlawful assembly, or combination, whether such conspiracy, threatening, counsel, advice, or attempt shall have the proposed effect or not, he or they shall be deemed guilty of a high misdemeanor, and on conviction, before any court of the United States having jurisdiction thereof, shall be punished by a fine not exceeding five thousand dollars, and by imprisonment during a term not less than six months nor exceeding five years; and further, at the discretion of the court may be holden to find sureties for his good behavior in such sum, and for such time, as the said court may direct.

SEC. 2.

And be it further enacted, That if any person shall write, print, utter or publish, or shall cause or procure to be written, printed, uttered or published, or shall knowingly and willingly assist or aid in writing, printing, uttering or publishing any false, scandalous and malicious writing or writings against the government of the United States, or either house of the Congress of the United States, or the President of the United States, with intent to defame the said government, or either house of the said Congress, or the said President, or to bring them, or either of them, into contempt or disrepute; or to excite against them, or either or any of them, the hatred of the good people of the United States, or to excite any unlawful combinations therein, for opposing or resisting any law of the United States, or any act of the President of the United States, done in pursuance of any such law, or of the powers in him vested by the Constitution of the United States, or to resist, oppose, or defeat any such law or act, or to aid, encourage or abet any hostile designs of any foreign nation against the United States, their people or government, then such person, being thereof convicted before any court of the United States having jurisdiction thereof, shall be punished by a fine not exceeding two thousand dollars, and by imprisonment not exceeding two years.

SEC. 3.

And be it further enacted, and declared, That if any person shall be prosecuted under this act, for the writing or publishing any libel aforesaid, it shall be lawful for the defendant, upon the trial of the cause, to give in evidence in his defense, the truth of the matter contained in the publication charged as a libel. And the jury who shall try the cause, shall have a right to determine the law and the fact, under the direction of the court, as in other cases.

SEC. 4.

And be it further enacted, That this act shall continue and be in force until the third day of March, one thousand eight hundred and one, and no longer: Provided, That the expiration of the act shall not prevent or defeat a prosecution and punishment of any offence against the law, during the time it shall be in force.

JONATHAN DAYTON, Speaker of the House of Representatives.

THEODORE SEDGWICK, President of the Senate, pro tempore.

APPROVED, July 14, 1798:

JOHN ADAMS, President of the United States.

Study Questions

1. How, specifically, does the act define *sedition*?

2. What actions does the legislation prohibit? What punishments are stipulated for breaking the law?

3. Why do you think the law specifically made it illegal to "defame" members of Congress and President John Adams, but not Vice President Thomas Jefferson? What is the significance of the fact that the act was set to expire on March 3, 1801?

4. Today, the American practice of allowing anyone the freedom to print or broadcast virtually anything is by far the broadest understanding of freedom of the press in the developed world. What might be the consequence if a sedition act were to be passed in America today? Do you think any contemporary legislation has intended to curtail civil liberties?

MERIWETHER LEWIS

Encountering the Shoshone (1805)

FROM *The Journals of Lewis and Clark*

The Louisiana Purchase of 1803 essentially doubled the territorial extent of the United States by acquiring the roughly 800,000 square miles drained by the Mississippi and its tributaries on the western side of that mighty stream. President Thomas Jefferson sent a small expeditionary team headed by Meriwether Lewis (1774–1809) and William Clark (1770–1838) to explore the area. Their instructions were to examine the commercial potential of the expanse in terms of its natural resources and to collect specimens of its plant and animal life to satisfy Jefferson's boundless scientific curiosity. Setting out from Missouri in 1804, Lewis and Clark followed the Missouri River to its source, crossed the Rockies, and, by way of the Columbia River, reached the Pacific Coast. By traversing that part of the Northwest, the expedition gave the United States a claim to the Oregon Country, putting the United States in contention with England, Russia, and Spain over the rights to this additional spoil.

While in Montana on the eastern slope of the Rocky Mountains, Lewis and Clark encountered the Shoshone, or Snake, Indians. This was the the tribe of their interpreter and guide, Sacagawea, who at age fifteen joined the expedition along with her husband, a French trader who lived among the Indians. Lewis assisted with the birth of Sacagawea's first child in February 1805. His journal records his impressions of the Shoshone. As you read these excerpts, consider the importance of firsthand descriptions of Plains Indian culture in this period of initial contact with white Americans.

From Gary E. Moulton, ed., *The Journals of the Lewis and Clark Expedition* (Lincoln: University of Nebraska Press, 1983–2001).

Friday August 16th 1805.

* * *

The young [Shoshone] man had come to inform us that one of the whitemen had killed a deer.   in an instant they all gave their horses the whip and I was taken

nearly a mile before I could learn what were the tidings; as I was without [S]tir-
rups and an Indian behind me the jostling was disagreeable   I therefore reigned
up my horse and forbid the indian to whip him who had given him the lash for a
mile fearing he should loose a part of the feast.   the fellow was so uneasy that he
left me the horse dismounted and ran on foot at full speed, I am confident a mile.
when they arrived where the deer was which was in view of me they dismounted
and ran in tumbling over each other like a parcel of famished dogs each seizing
and tearing away a part of the intestens which had been previously thrown out by
Drewyer[1] who killed it; the seen was such when I arrived that had I not have had
a pretty keen appetite myself I am confident I should not have taisted any part of
the venison shortly.   each one had a peice of some discription and all eating
most ravenously.   some were eating the kidnies the melt[2] and liver and the blood
runing from the corners of their mouths, others were in a similar situation with
the paunch and guts but the exuding substance in this case from their lips was of
a different discription.   one of the last who attacted my attention particularly
had been fortunate in his allotment or reather active in the division, he had provided himself with about nine feet of the small guts one end of which he was
chewing on while with his hands he was squezzing the contents out at the other.
I really did not untill now think that human nature ever presented itself in a shape
so nearly allyed to the brute creation. I viewed these poor starved divils with pity
and compassion   I directed McNeal[3] to skin the deer and reserved a quarter,
the ballance I gave the Chief to be divided among his people; they devoured the
whole of it nearly without cooking. Drewyer killed a second deer; here nearly the
same seene was encored.   a fire being kindled we cooked and eat and gave the ballance of the two deer to the Indians who eat the whole of them even to the soft
parts of the hoofs.

* * *

Monday August 19th 1805.

* * *

From what has [already] been said of the Shoshones it will be readily perceived
that they live in a wretched stait of poverty.   yet notwithstanding their extreem
poverty they are not only cheerfull but even gay, fond of gaudy dress and amusements; like most other Indians they are great egotists and frequently boast of
heroic acts which they never performed.   they are also fond of games of wrisk.
they are frank, communicative, fair in dealing, generous with the little they pos-

1. Lewis's misspelling of the surname of George Drouillard, a half-French, half-Shawnee member of the
expedition.
2. Spleen.
3. Private Hugh McNeal.

sess, extreemly honest, and by no means beggarly.   each individual is his own
sovereign master, and acts from the dictates of his own mind; the authority of the
Cheif being nothing more than mere admonition supported by the influence
which the propiety of his own exammplery conduct may have acquired him in
the minds of the individuals who composed the band.   the title of cheif is not
hereditary; . . .   in fact every man is a chief, but all have not an equal influence
on the minds of the other members of the community, and he who happens to
enjoy the greatest share of confidence is the principal Chief.

* * *

They seldom correct their children particularly the boys who soon become
masters of their own acts.   they give as a reason that it cows and breaks the Sperit
of the boy to whip him, and that he never recovers his independence of mind after
he is grown. They treat their women but with little rispect, and compel them to
perform every species of drudgery.   they collect the wild fruits and roots, attend
to the horses or assist in that duty cook dreess the skins and make all their appa-
ral, collect wood and make their fires, arrange and form their lodges, and when
they travel pack the horses and take charge of all the baggage; in short the man
dose little else except attend his horses hunt and fish, the man considers himself
degraded if he is compelled to walk any distance, and if he is so unfortunately
poor as only to possess two horses   he rides the best himself and leavs the woman
or women if he has more than one, to transport their baggage and children on the
other, and to walk if the horse is unable to carry the additional weight of their
persons—   the chastity of their women is not held in high estimation, and the
husband will for a trifle barter the companion of his bead for a night or longer if
he conceives the reward adiquate; tho' they are not so importunate that we should
caress their women as the siouxs were and some of their women appear to be held
more sacred than in any nation we have seen   I have requested the men to give
them no cause of jealousy by having connection with their women without their
knowledge, which with them strange as it may seem is considered as disgracefull
to the husband as clandestine connections of a similar kind are among civilized
nations.   to prevent this mutual exchange of good officies altogether I know it
impossible to effect, particularly on the part of our young men whom some months
abstanence have made very polite to those tawney damsels.   no evil has yet
resulted and I hope will not from these connections.

* * *

The dress of the men consists of a robe long legings, shirt, tippet and Mockersons, that of the women is also a robe, chemise, and Mockersons; sometimes they
make use of short legings.   the ornaments of both men and women are very similar, and consist of several species of sea shells, blue and white beads, bras and Iron
arm bands, plaited cords of the sweet grass, and collars of leather ornamented

with the quills of the porcupine dyed of various colours among which I observed the red, yellow, blue, and black.   the ear is purforated in the lower part to receive various ornaments but the nose is not, nor is the ear lasserated or disvigored for this purpose as among many nations.   the men never mark their skins by birning, cuting, nor puncturing and introducing a colouring matter as many nations do.   there women sometimes puncture a small circle on their forehead nose or cheeks and thus introduce a black matter usually soot and grease which leaves an indelible stane.   tho' this even is by no means common.   their arms offensive and defensive consist in the bow and arrows sheild, some lances, and a weapon called by the Cippeways who formerly used it, the pog-gar'-mag-gon'.[4]   in fishing they employ wairs, gigs, and fishing hooks.   the salmon is the principal object of their pursuit.   they snair wolves and foxes. . . .

Friday August 23rd 1805.

* * *

The metal which we found in possession of these people consited of a few indifferent knives, a few brass kettles some arm bands of iron and brass, a few buttons, woarn as ornaments in their hair, a spear or two of a foot in length and some iron and brass arrow points which they informed me they obtained in exchange for horses from the Crow or Rocky Mountain Indians on the yellowstone River.   the bridlebits and stirrips they obtained from the Spaniards, tho' these were but few.   many of them made use of flint for knives, and with this instrument, skined the animals they killed, dressed their fish and made their arrows; in short they used it for every purpose to which the knife is applyed.

* * *

Saturday August 24th 1805.

* * *

. . . these people have many names in the course of their lives, particularly if they become distinguished characters.   for it seems that every important event by which they happen to distinguish themselves intitles them to claim another name which is generally scelected by themselves and confirmed by the nation.   those distinguishing acts are the killing and scalping an enemy, the killing a white bear, leading a party to war who happen to be successfull either in destroying their enemies or robing them of their horses, or individually stealing the horses of an enemy.   these are considered acts of equal heroism among them, and that of killing an enemy without scalping him is considered of no importance; in fact the whole honour seems to be founded in the act of scalping, for if a man happens to slay a dozen of his enemies in action and others get the scalps or first lay their

4. War club with a stone head and leather binding.

hand on the dead person the honor is lost to him who killed them and devolves on those who scalp or first touch them.[5]   Among the Shoshones, as well as all the Indians of America, bravery is esteemed the primary virtue; nor can any one become eminent among them who has not at some period of his life given proofs of his possessing this virtue.   with them there can be no preferment without some warelike achievement. . .

Study Questions

1. What are Lewis's most important or striking insights into Shoshone food, clothing, child-rearing practices, and government? How would you characterize the tone in which he describes the Shoshone?

2. How did Lewis characterize the status of Shoshone women? Why was Lewis concerned about relations between Shoshone women and the men of his expedition?

3. What evidence is there in this account that the Shoshone have already had some direct or indirect contact with white men? How did the Shoshone appear to regard Lewis and his men?

4. How does Lewis characterize the warrior culture of the Shoshone? What features of their environment might have produced their warlike attributes? How would such a tribe present a barrier to American movement across the Plains?

---

5. The Plains Indian recognition of the first warrior to touch a live enemy was known as "counting coup."

HENRY CLAY

Speech on Proposed Repeal of the Non-Intercourse Act (1810)

Henry Clay, *Papers of Henry Clay, Volume 1: The Rising Statesmen, 1797–1814*, ed. James F. Hopkins (Lexington, Ky.: University Press of Kentucky, 1959), pp. 449–452. Copyright © 1959, from *The Papers of Henry Clay*, by James F. Hopkins.

No man in the nation desires peace more than I. But I prefer the troubled ocean of war, demanded by the honor and independence of the country, with all its calamities, and desolations, to the tranquil, putrescent pool of ignominious peace. If we can accommodate our differences with one of the belligerents only, I should prefer that one to be Great Britain. But if with neither, and we are forced into a selection of our enemy, then am I for war with Britain; because I believe her prior in aggression and her injuries and insults to us were atrocious in character. . . .

But we are asked for the means of carrying on War, and those who oppose it triumphantly appeal to the vacant vaults of the treasury. With the unimpaired credit of the government, invigorated by a faithful observance of public engagements, and a rapid extinction of the debt of the revolution; with the boundless territories in the west, presenting a safe pledge for reimbursement of loans to any extent—is it not astonishing that despondency itself should disparage the resources of this country?. . . .

Or, are we to be governed by the low, groveling parsimony of the counting room and to cast up the actual pence in the drawer before we assert our inestimable rights? It is said, however, that no object is attainable by war with Britain. In its fortunes we are to estimate not only the benefit to be derived to ourselves, but the injury to be done the enemy. The conquest of Canada is in your power. I trust I shall not be deemed presumptuous when I state, what I verily believe, that the militia of Kentucky are alone competent to place Montreal and Upper Canada at your feet. Is it nothing to the British nation—is it nothing to the pride of her monarch to have the last of the immense North American possessions held by him in the commencement of his reign, wrested from his dominion? Is it nothing to us to extinguish the torch that lights up savage warfare? Is it nothing to acquire the entire fur trade connected with that country, and to destroy the temptation and the opportunity of violating your revenue and other laws?. . . .

Another effect of war will be the re-production and cherishing of a martial spirit amongst us. Is there not danger that we shall become enervated by the spirit of avarice unfortunately so predominant? . . . a certain portion of military ardor (and this is what I desire) is essential to the protection of the country. The withered arm, and wrinkled brow of the illustrious founders of our freedom, are melancholy indications that they will shortly be removed from us. Their deeds of glory and renown will then be felt only through the cold medium of the historic page. We shall want the presence and living example of a new race of heroes to supply their place, and to animate us to preserve unviolated what they atchieved [sic].

TECUMSEH

Appeal to the Osages (1811)

In the early 1800s two remarkable Shawnee brothers roiled Indian relations in the Old Northwest (an area west of the Appalachian mountains now encompassed by parts of Ohio, West Virginia, Pennsylvania, and Indiana). The younger, Lala-wathika (1775–1836), was a recovering alcoholic who spurned the white man's culture and preached a message of Indian traditionalism. As a religious leader, he took the name of Tenskwatawa (The Open Door) becoming known as the Shaw-nee Prophet. As people from various tribes gathered to hear his powerful message of revitalization, the prophet's older brother, Tecumseh (1768–1813), communicated a more political vision to those assembled. Tecumseh promoted a program of unity across tribal lines to thwart the white man's westward advance and dispossession of the Native Americans. In the years preceding the War of 1812, Tecumseh trav-eled through the Mississippi Valley, recruiting a number of tribes into his alliance with the aim of creating a vast tribal confederacy. Tecumseh's interest in blocking American expansion clearly aligned with that of the British, whom he joined to fight the Americans. He was killed fighting alongside his British allies at the Battle of the Thames in 1813.

Tecumseh visited a Missouri-based tribe, the Osages, in 1811. His speech to them was witnessed by John Dunn Hunter (ca. 1796–1827), an American who claimed to have been brought up by Indians. It is Hunter's transcription that follows. Whether or not this is an exact rendering of Tecumseh's address, it surely captures the essence of his program for Indian redemption.

From John Dunn Hunter, ed., *Memoirs of a Captivity Among the Indians of North America* (London: Longman, Hurst, Bees, Orme, Brown, and Green, 1824), 45–48.

*B*rothers,—We all belong to one family; we are all children of the Great Spirit; we walk in the same path; slake our thirst at the same spring; and now affairs of the greatest concern lead us to smoke the pipe around the same council fire!

Brothers,—We are friends; we must assist each other to bear our burdens. The blood of many of our fathers and brothers has run like water on the ground, to satisfy the avarice of the white men. We, ourselves, are threatened with a great evil; nothing will pacify them but the destruction of all the red men.

Brothers,—When the white men first set foot on our grounds, they were hungry; they had no place on which to spread their blankets, or to kindle their fires. They were feeble; they could do nothing for themselves. Our fathers commiserated their distress, and shared freely with them whatever the Great Spirit had given his red children. They gave them food when hungry, medicine when sick, spread skins for them to sleep on, and gave them grounds, that they might hunt and raise corn.—Brothers, the white people are like poisonous serpents: when chilled, they are feeble and harmless; but invigorate them with warmth, and they sting their benefactors to death.

The white people came among us feeble; and now we have made them strong, they wish to kill us, or drive us back, as they would wolves and panthers.

Brothers,—The white men are not friends to the Indians: at first, they only asked for land sufficient for a wigwam; now, nothing will satisfy them but the whole of our hunting grounds, from the rising to the setting sun.

Brothers,—The white men want more than our hunting grounds; they wish to kill our warriors; they would even kill our old men, women, and little ones.

Brothers,—Many winters ago, there was no land; the sun did not rise and set: all was darkness. The Great Spirit made all things. He gave the white people a home beyond the great waters. He supplied these grounds with game, and gave them to his red children; and he gave them strength and courage to defend them.

Brothers,—My people wish for peace; the red men all wish for peace: but where the white people are, there is no peace for them, except it be on the bosom of our mother.

Brothers,—The white men despise and cheat the Indians; they abuse and insult them; they do not think the red men sufficiently good to live.

The red men have borne many and great injuries; they ought to suffer them no longer. My people will not; they are determined on vengeance; they have taken up the tomahawk; they will make it fat with blood; they will drink the blood of the white people.

Brothers,—My people are brave and numerous; but the white people are too strong for them alone. I wish you to take up the tomahawk with them. If we all unite, we will cause the rivers to stain the great waters with their blood.

Brothers,—If you do not unite with us, they will first destroy us, and then you will fall an easy prey to them. They have destroyed many nations of red men because they were not united, because they were not friends to each other.

Brothers,—The white people send runners amongst us; they wish to make us enemies, that they may sweep over and desolate our hunting grounds, like devastating winds, or rushing waters.

Brothers,—Our Great Father, over the great waters, is angry with the white people, our enemies. He will send his brave warriors against them; he will send us rifles, and whatever else we want—he is our friend, and we are his children.

Brothers,—Who are the white people that we should fear them? They cannot run fast, and are good marks to shoot at: they are only men; our fathers have killed many of them: we are not squaws, and we will stain the earth red with their blood.

Brothers,—The Great Spirit is angry with our enemies; he speaks in thunder, and the earth swallows up villages, and drinks up the Mississippi.[1] The great waters will cover their lowlands; their corn cannot grow; and the Great Spirit will sweep those who escape to the hills from the earth with his terrible breath.

Brothers,—We must be united; we must smoke the same pipe; we must fight each other's battles; and more than all, we must love the Great Spirit: he is for us; he will destroy our enemies, and make all his red children happy.

Study Questions

1. According to Tecumseh, why must Indians resist the white man? How does he argue that Indians can successfully do so? Why is he confident Indians can win?

2. What do we learn of Native American religions from this document? How might one argue that, in their spiritual teachings, Tecumseh and his brother could be viewed as religious fundamentalists?

3. What does Tecumseh's speech reveal about Indians and their relationship to nature?

4. Tecumseh is viewed by many authorities as one of the greatest Indian leaders in American history. What would earn him such an elevated status? Why do you think his program of tribal unity ultimately failed?

---

1. A series of powerful earthquakes and aftershocks centered near the juncture of the Mississippi and Ohio Rivers affected that part of the country in 1811–12, temporarily causing the Mississippi to flow backward.

SECTIONALISM

THOMAS JEFFERSON

Letter to John Holmes:
"Fire Bell in the Night" (1820)

MONTICELLO APR. 22. 20

I thank you, Dear Sir, for the copy you have been so kind as to send me of the letter to your constituents on the Missouri question. it is a perfect justification to them. I had for a long time ceased to read the newspapers or pay any attention to public affairs, confident they were in good hands, and content to be a passenger in our bark to the shore from which I am not distant. But this momentous question, like a fire bell in the night, awakened and filled me with terror. I considered it at once as the knell of the Union. it is hushed indeed for the moment. but this is a reprieve only, not a final sentence. a geographical line, coinciding with a marked principle, moral and political, once conceived and held up to the angry passions of men, will never be obliterated; and every new irritation will mark it deeper and deeper. I can say with conscious truth that there is not a man on earth who would sacrifice more than I would, to relieve us from this heavy reproach, in any *practicable* way. the cession of that kind of property, for so it is misnamed, is a bagatelle which would not cost me in a second thought, if, in that way, a general emancipation and *expatriation* could be effected: and, gradually, and with due sacrifices, I think it might be. but, as it is, we have the wolf by the ear, and we can neither hold him, nor safely let him go. justice is in one scale, and self-preservation in the other. of one thing I am certain, that as the passage of slaves from one state to another would not make a slave of a single human being who would not be so without it, so their diffusion over a greater surface would make them individually happier and proportionally facilitate the accomplishment of their emancipation, by dividing the burthen on a greater number of co-adjutors. an abstinence too from this act of power would remove the jealousy excited by the undertaking of Congress, to regulate the condition of the different descriptions of men composing a state. this certainly is the exclusive right of every state, which nothing in the constitution has taken from them and given to the general government. could congress, for example say that the Non-freemen of Connecticut, shall be freemen, or that they shall not emigrate into any other state?

I regret that I am now to die in the belief that the useless sacrifice of themselves, by the generation of $76. to acquire self government and happiness to their country, is to be thrown away by the unwise and unworthy passions of their sons, and that my only consolation is to be that I live not to weep over it. if they would but dispassionately weigh the blessings they will throw away against an abstract principle more likely to be effected by union than by scission, they would pause before they would perpetrate this act of suicide on themselves and of treason against the hopes of the world. to yourself as the faithful advocate of union I tender the offering of my high esteem and respect. Th. Jefferson

DAVID WALKER

Appeal to the Colored Citizens of the World (1829)

David Walker (1785–1830) was born to a free black mother and a slave father in North Carolina, and therefore he inherited freedom due to the legal status of his mother. As a young man he lived in Charleston, South Carolina, where he was active in the African Methodist Episcopal Church. Eventually his revulsion toward slavery drove him northward. By 1827 Walker had settled in Boston and was the owner of a used clothing store, becoming part of that city's vibrant black community.

In 1829, Walker published a militant anti-slavery pamphlet. Copies of his Appeal *were soon carried by ship into the slave states along the Atlantic Coast, where the pamphlet created a sensation. Fears of slave insurrection inspired state legislatures to crack down on slave literacy and the circulation of such seditious literature. Planters remained apprehensive about the potential for slave rebellion despite the fact that only one major one—in the New Orleans area in 1811—had yet occurred in the United States up to this point in the nineteenth century. But when Nat Turner led the bloodiest slave revolt in American history, in Virginia in 1831, many slavery apologists were convinced that Walker's* Appeal *was behind this violent outbreak—despite the lack of any evidence that Turner had ever been exposed to abolitionist material. As you read the following excerpts from the* Appeal, *consider how these writings must have shocked readers of Walker's era and whether he promoted the anti-slavery cause effectively. David Walker was found dead on his doorstep in 1830, his demise most likely the result of long-term illness.*

From David Walker, "Appeal to the Colored Citizens of the World," (Boston: David Walker, 1830).

OUR WRETCHEDNESS IN CONSEQUENCE OF SLAVERY.

My beloved brethren:—The Indians of North and of South America—the Greeks—the Irish, subjected under the king of Great—the Jews, that ancient people of the Lord—the inhabitants of the islands of the sea—in fine, all the inhabitants of the earth, (except however, the sons of Africa) are called *men*, and of course are, and ought to be free. But we, (coloured people) and our children are *brutes!!* and of course are, and *ought to be* SLAVES to the American people and their children forever!! to dig their mines and work their farms; and thus go on enriching them, from one generation to another with our *blood* and our *tears!!!!*

I promised in a preceding page to demonstrate to the satisfaction of the most incredulous, that we, (coloured people of these United States of America) are the *most wretched, degraded* and *abject* set of beings that *ever lived* since the world began, and that the white Americans having reduced us to the wretched state of *slavery*, treat us in that condition *more cruel* (they being an enlightened and Christian people,) than any heathen nation did any people whom it had reduced to our condition. These affirmations are so well confirmed in the minds of all unprejudiced men, who have taken the trouble to read histories, that they need no elucidation from me. But to put them beyond all doubt, I refer you in the first place to the children of Jacob, or of Israel in Egypt, under Pharaoh and his people.

* * *

"And Pharaoh, said unto Joseph, . . . thou shalt be over my house, and according unto thy word shall all my people be ruled: only in the throne will I be greater than thou."[1]

Now I appeal to heaven and to earth, and particularly to the American people themselves, who cease not to declare that our condition is not *hard*, and that we are comparatively satisfied to rest in wretchedness and misery, under them and their children. Not, indeed, to show me a coloured President, a Governor, a Legislator, a Senator, a Mayor, or an Attorney at the Bar.—But to show me a man of colour, who holds the low office of Constable, or one who sits in a Juror Box, even on a case of one of his wretched brethren, throughout this great Republic!!—But let us pass Joseph the son of Israel a little farther in review, as he existed with that heathen nation.

"And Pharaoh called Joseph's name Zaphnathpaaneah; and he gave him to wife Asenath the daughter of Potipherah priest of On. And Joseph went out over all the land of Egypt."

Compare the above, with the American institutions. Do they not institute laws to prohibit us from marrying among the whites? I would wish, candidly, however, before the Lord, to be understood, that I would not give a *pinch of snuff* to be married to any white person I ever saw in all the days of my life. And I do say it, that the black man, or man of colour, who will leave his own colour (provided he can get one, who is good for any thing) and marry a white woman, to be a double slave to her, just because she is *white*, ought to be treated by her as he surely will be, viz: as a NIGGER!!!! It is not, indeed, what I care about inter-marriages with the whites,

1. The story of Joseph being raised to authority in Egypt is in Genesis 41.

which induced me to pass this subject in review; for the Lord knows, that there is a day coming when they will be glad enough to get into the company of the blacks, notwithstanding, we are, in this generation, levelled by them, almost on a level with the brute creation: and some of us they treat even worse than they do the brutes that perish. I only made this extract to show how much lower we are held, and how much more cruel we are treated by the Americans, than were the children of Jacob, by the Egyptians.—We will notice the sufferings of Israel some further, under *heathen Pharaoh*, compared with ours under the *enlightened Christians of America.*

* * *

To prove farther that the condition of the Israelites was better under the Egyptians than ours is under the whites. I call upon the professing Christians, I call upon the philanthropist, I call upon the very tyrant himself, to show me a page of history, either sacred or profane, on which a verse can be found, which maintains, that the Egyptians heaped the *insupportable insult* upon the children of Israel, by telling them that they were not of the *human family.* Can the whites deny this charge? Have they not, after having reduced us to the deplorable condition of slaves under their feet, held us up as descending originally from the tribes of *Monkeys* or *Orang-Outangs?* O! my God! I appeal to every man of feeling—is not this insupportable? Is it not heaping the most gross insult upon our miseries, because they have got us under their feet and we cannot help ourselves? Oh! pity us we pray thee, Lord Jesus, Master.—Has Mr. Jefferson declared to the world, that we are inferior to the whites, both in the endowments of our bodies and our minds?[2] It is indeed surprising, that a man of such great learning, combined with such excellent natural parts, should speak so of a set of men in chains. I do not know what to compare it to, unless, like putting one wild deer in an iron cage, where it will be secured, and hold another by the side of the same, then let it go, and expect the one in the cage to run as fast as the one at liberty.

* * *

The man who would not fight under our Lord and Master Jesus Christ, in the glorious and heavenly cause of freedom and of God—to be delivered from the most wretched, abject and servile slavery, that ever a people was afflicted with since the foundation of the world, to the present day—ought to be kept with all of his children or family, in slavery, or in chains, to be butchered by his *cruel enemies.*

I saw a paragraph, a few years since, in a South Carolina paper, which, speaking of the barbarity of the Turks, it said "The Turks are the most barbarous people in the world—they treat the Greeks more like *brutes* than human beings." And in the same paper was an advertisement, which said: "Eight well built Virginia and

2. A reference to remarks in Thomas Jefferson's *Notes on the State of Virginia.*

Maryland *Negro fellows* and four *wenches* will positively be *sold* this day, *to the highest bidder!*" And what astonished me still more was, to see in this same *humane* paper!! the cuts of three men, with clubs and budgets[3] on their backs, and an advertisement offering a considerable sum of money for their apprehension and delivery. I declare, it is really so amusing to hear the Southerners and Westerners of this country talk about *barbarity*, that it is positively, enough to make a man *smile*.

* * *

I have been for years troubling the pages of historians, to find out what our fathers have done to the *white Christians of America*, to merit such condign punishment as they have inflicted on them, and do continue to inflict on us their children. But I must aver, that my researches have hitherto been to no effect. I have therefore, come to the immoveable conclusion, that they (Americans) have, and do continue to punish us for nothing else, but for enriching them and their country. For I cannot conceive of anything else. Nor will I ever believe otherwise, until the Lord shall convince me.

The world knows, that slavery as it existed among the Romans, (which was the primary cause of their destruction) was, comparatively speaking, no more than a *cypher*, when compared with ours under the Americans. Indeed I should not have noticed the Roman slaves, had not the very learned and penetrating Mr. Jefferson said, "when a master was murdered, all his slaves in the same house, or within hearing, were condemned to death."—Here let me ask Mr. Jefferson, (but he is gone to answer at the bar of God, for the deeds done in his body while living,)[4] therefore ask the whole American people, had I not rather die, or be put to death, than to be a slave to any tyrant, who takes not only my own, but my wife and children's lives by the inches? Yea, would I meet death with avidity far! far!! in preference to such *servile submission* to the murderous hands of tyrants. Mr. Jefferson's very severe remarks on us have been so extensively argued upon by men whose attainments in literature, I shall never be able to reach, that I would not have meddled with it, were it not to solicit each of my brethren, who has the spirit of a man, to buy a copy of Mr. Jefferson's "Notes on Virginia,"[5] and put it in the hand of his son. For let no one of us suppose that the refutations which have been written by our white friends are enough—they are *whites*—we are *blacks*. We, and the world wish to see the charges of Mr. Jefferson refuted by the blacks *themselves*, according to their chance; for we must remember that what the whites have written respecting this subject, is other men's labours, and did not emanate from the blacks. I know well, that there are some talents and learning among the coloured people of this country,

---

3. Bundles.
4. Thomas Jefferson had died three years earlier on July 4, 1826.
5. *Notes on the State of Virginia*, first published in 1785, contained Jefferson's most extensive writings on slaves and blacks.

which we have not a chance to develope, in consequence of oppression; but our oppression ought not to hinder us from acquiring all we can. For we will have a chance to develope them by and by. God will not suffer us, always to be oppressed. Our sufferings will come to an *end*, in spite of all the Americans this side of *eternity*. Then we will want all the learning and talents among ourselves, and perhaps more, to govern ourselves.—"Every dog must have its day," the American's is coming to an end.

* * *

It is time for me to bring this article to a close. But before I close it, I must observe to my brethren that at the close of the first Revolution in this country, with Great Britain, there were but thirteen States in the Union, now there are twenty four, most of which are slave-holding States, and the whites are dragging us around in chains and in handcuffs, to their new States and Territories to work their mines and farms, to enrich them and their children—and millions of them believing firmly that we being a little darker than they, were made by our Creator to be an inheritance to them and their children for ever—the same as a parcel of *brutes*.

Are we MEN!!—I ask you, O my brethren! are we MEN? Did our Creator make us to be slaves to dust and ashes like ourselves? Are they not dying worms as well as we? Have they not to make their appearance before the tribunal of Heaven, to answer for the deeds done in the body, as well as we? Have we any other Master but Jesus Christ alone? Is he not their Master as well as ours?—What right then, have we to obey and call any other Master, but Himself? How we could be so *submissive* to a gang of men, whom we cannot tell whether they are as good as ourselves or not, I never could conceive. However, this is shut up with the Lord, and we cannot precisely tell—but I declare, we judge men by their works.

The whites have always been an unjust, jealous, unmerciful, avaricious and blood-thirsty set of beings, always seeking after power and authority.—We view them all over the confederacy of Greece, where they were first known to be any thing, (in consequence of education) we see them there, cutting each other's throats—trying to subject each other to wretchedness and misery—to effect which, they used all kinds of deceitful, unfair, and unmerciful means. We view them next in Rome, where the spirit of tyranny and deceit raged still higher. We view them in Gaul, Spain, and in Britain.—In fine, we view them all over Europe, together with what were scattered about in Asia and Africa, as heathens, and we see them acting more like devils than accountable men. But some may ask, did not the blacks of Africa, and the mulattoes of Asia, go on in the same way as did the whites of Europe. I answer, no—they never were half so avaricious, deceitful and unmerciful as the whites, according to their knowledge.

But we will leave the whites or Europeans as heathens, and take a view of them as Christians, in which capacity we see them as cruel, if not more so than ever. In fact, take them as a body, they are ten times more cruel, avaricious and unmerciful than ever they were; for while they were heathens, they were bad enough it is true, but it is positively a fact that they were not quite so audacious as to go and take vessel loads of men, women and children, and in cold blood, and through devilishness, throw them into the sea, and murder them in all kind of ways. While they were heathens, they were too ignorant for such barbarity. But being Christians, enlightened and sensible, they are completely prepared for such hellish cruelties. Now suppose God were to give them more sense, what would they do? If it were possible, would they not *dethrone* Jehovah and seat themselves upon his throne? I therefore, in the name and fear of the Lord God of Heaven and of earth, divested of prejudice either on the side of my colour or that of the whites, advance my suspicion of them, whether they are *as good by nature* as we are or not. Their actions, since they were known as a people, have been the reverse, I do indeed suspect them, but this, as I before observed, is shut up with the Lord, we cannot exactly tell, it will be proved in succeeding generations.

Study Questions

1. What is the point of Walker's observations about ancient Egypt, Rome, and Greece? What would you conclude from these writings about Walker's level of education or sources of information?

2. Why does Walker continually attack the "white Christians of America"? What is revealed of his own religious beliefs in these writings?

3. What is Walker's view of Thomas Jefferson? What made Jefferson such an inviting target from an abolitionist perspective?

4. Comment upon the statement: " 'Every dog must have its day,' the American's is coming to an end." What would white Americans have found most threatening or disturbing about Walker's writing? How would free blacks and slaves have responded to his *Appeal?*

WILLIAM LLOYD GARRISON

Inaugural Editorial in *The Liberator* (1831)

William Lloyd Garrison (1805–1879) was born in Newburyport, Massachusetts, where he began an apprenticeship with a local newspaper in 1818. This and subsequent jobs in journalism gave him his schooling as a writer and the confidence to express himself on political matters. In April 1829, Garrison became co-editor of an anti-slavery paper published in Baltimore by the Quaker activist Benjamin Lundy. Garrison's own growing anti-slavery convictions were deepened by this opportunity to witness the evils of the institution directly in the Upper South. He soon became the publisher and editor of the abolitionist paper, The Liberator, which he launched in Boston at the beginning of 1831. This publication was the focus of Garrison's activism until its final issue appeared on December 29, 1865, shortly after the ratification of the Thirteenth Amendment abolished slavery. His had been one of the loudest and most principled voices in the abolition movement that culminated in this constitutional and moral victory.

Garrison hailed from New England, a region whose strongly anti-slavery leanings reflected the moral principles of its Puritan heritage. Like many early abolitionists, Garrison was initially drawn to colonization, the notion that the compensated emancipation of slaves would be followed by their resettlement outside the United States. By 1830, however, Garrison had rejected this strategy for its impracticality and implicit racism. As you read his opening editorial in the Liberator, consider the degree to which Garrison believed this paper would be the beginning of a new direction for the anti-slavery movement.

From *Selections from the Writings and Speeches of William Lloyd Garrison* (Boston: R. F. Wallcutt, 1852), 62–64.

During my recent tour for the purpose of exciting the minds of the people by a series of discourses on the subject of slavery, every place that I visited gave fresh evidence of the fact, that a greater revolution in public sentiment was to be effected in the free States—and particularly in New England—than at the South. I found contempt more bitter, opposition more active, detraction more relentless, prejudice more stubborn, and apathy more frozen, than among slave owners themselves. Of course, there were individual exceptions to the contrary. This state of things afflicted, but did not dishearten me. I determined, at every hazard, to lift up the standard of emancipation in the eyes of the nation, within sight of Bunker Hill, and in the birth-place of liberty. That standard is now unfurled; and long may it float, unhurt by the spoliations of time or the missiles of a desperate foe; yea, till every chain be broken, and every bondman set free! Let Southern oppressors tremble; let their secret abettors tremble; let their Northern apologists tremble; let all the enemies of the persecuted blacks tremble.

I deem the publication of my original Prospectus unnecessary, as it has obtained a wide circulation. The principles therein inculcated will be steadily pursued in this paper, excepting that I shall not array myself as the political partisan of any man. In defending the great cause of human rights, I wish to derive the assistance of all religions and of all parties.

Assenting to the 'self-evident truths' maintained in the American Declaration of Independence, 'that all men are created equal, and endowed by their Creator with certain inalienable rights—among which are life, liberty, and the pursuit of happiness,' I shall strenuously contend for the immediate enfranchisement of our slave population. In Park Street Church, on the Fourth of July, 1829, in an address on slavery, I unreflectingly assented to the popular but pernicious doctrine of gradual abolition. I seize this opportunity to make a full and unequivocal recantation, and thus publicly to ask pardon of my God, of my country, and of my brethren, the poor slaves, for having uttered a sentiment so full of timidity, injustice and absurdity. A similar recantation, from my pen, was published in the 'Genius of Universal Emancipation,'[1] at Baltimore, in September, 1829. My conscience is now satisfied.

I am aware, that many object to the severity of my language; but is there not cause for severity? I will be as harsh as truth, and as uncompromising as justice. On this subject, I do not wish to think, or speak, or write, with moderation. No! no! Tell a man, whose house is on fire, to give a moderate alarm; tell him to moderately rescue his wife from the hands of the ravisher; tell the mother to gradually extricate her babe from the fire into which it has fallen; but urge me not to use moderation in a cause like the present! I am in earnest. I will not equivocate—I will not excuse—I will not retreat a single inch—AND I WILL BE HEARD. The apathy of the people is enough to make every statue leap from its pedestal, and to hasten the resurrection of the dead.

It is pretended, that I am retarding the cause of emancipation by the coarseness of my invective, and the precipitancy of my measures. The charge is not true. On this question, my influence, humble as it is, is felt at this moment to a considerable extent, and shall be felt in coming years—not perniciously, but beneficially—not as a curse, but as a blessing; and POSTERITY WILL BEAR TESTIMONY THAT I WAS RIGHT. I desire to thank God, that he enables me to disregard 'the fear of man which bringeth a snare,' and to speak his truth in its simplicity and power. And here I close with this fresh dedication:—

---

1. The abolitionist paper published in Baltimore by Benjamin Lundy.

'Oppression! I have seen thee, face to face,
And met thy cruel eye and cloudy brow;
But thy soul-withering glance I fear not now—
For dread to prouder feelings doth give place,
Of deep abhorrence! Scorning the disgrace
Of slavish knees that at thy footstool bow,
I also kneel—but with far other vow
Do hail thee and thy herd of hirelings base:—
I swear, while life-blood warms my throbbing veins,
Still to oppose and thwart, with heart and hand,
Thy brutalizing sway—till Afric's chains
Are burst, and Freedom rules the rescued land,
Trampling Oppression and his iron rod:—
Such is the vow I take—so help me, God!'

BOSTON, *January 1, 1831.*

Study Questions

1. Why does Garrison decide to base *The Liberator* in Boston rather than in other parts of the country? What is the paper's ultimate goal? Why might some anti-slavery activists find this objectionable?

2. What insight does this editorial give regarding Garrison's religious views? Would his faith be of greater or lesser advantage in his work as an abolitionist? Explain.

3. What is most distinctive about Garrison's tone and writing style? What is his attitude toward moderation? Evaluate the merits of Garrison's journalistic approach.

4. In your view, who was *The Liberator's* primary audience? How might Garrison believe such a publication could hasten the demise of slavery?

ALEXIS DE TOCQUEVILLE

On the Negro Race in the United States (1835)

FROM *Democracy in America*

Alexis de Tocqueville, *Democracy in America* (New York, 1904), I, 383–385.

Turning my attention to the United States of our own day, I plainly see that in some parts of the country the legal barrier between the two races is tending to come down, but not that of mores: I see that slavery is in retreat, but the prejudice from which it arose is immovable.

In that part of the Union where the Negroes are no longer slaves, have they come closer to the whites? Everyone who has lived in the United States will have noticed just the opposite.

Race prejudice seems stronger in those states that have abolished slavery than in those where it still exists, and nowhere is it more into intolerant than in those states where slavery was never known.

It is true that in the North of the Union the law allows legal marriages between Negroes and whites, but public opinion would regard a white man married to a Negro woman as disgraced, and it would be very difficult to quote an example of such an event.

In almost all the states where slavery has been abolished, the Negroes have been given electoral rights, but they would come forward to vote at the risk of their lives. When oppressed, they can bring an action at law, but they will find only white men among their judges. It is true that the laws make them eligible as jurors, but prejudice wards them off. The Negro's son is excluded from the school to which the European's child goes. In the theaters he cannot for good money buy the right to sit by his former master's side; in the hospitals he lies apart. He is allowed to worship the same God as the white man but must not pray at the same altars. He has his own clergy and churches. The gates of heaven are not closed against him, but his inequality stops only just short of the boundaries of the other world. When the Negro is no more, his bones are cast aside, and some difference in condition is found even in the equality of death.

So the Negro is free, but he cannot share his rights, pleasures, labors, griefs, or even the tomb of him whose equal he has been declared; there is nowhere where he can meet him, neither in life nor in death.

In the South, where slavery still exists, less trouble is taken to keep the Negro apart: they sometimes share the labors and the pleasures of the white men; people are prepared to mix with them to some extent; legislation is more harsh against them, but customs are more tolerant and gentle.

In the South the master has no fear of lifting the slave up to his level, for he knows that when he wants to he can always throw him down into the dust. In the North the white man no longer clearly sees the barrier that separates him from the degraded race, and he keeps the Negro at a distance all the more carefully because he fears lest one day they be confounded together.

Among the Americans of the South, Nature sometimes, reclaiming her rights, does for a moment establish equality between white and black. In the North pride silences even the most imperious of human passions. Perhaps the northern American might have allowed some Negro woman to be the passing companion of his pleasures, had the legislators declared that she could not hope to share his nuptial bed; but she can become his wife, and he recoils in horror from her.

Thus it is that in the United States the prejudice rejecting the Negroes seems to increase in proportion to their emancipation, and inequality cuts deep into mores as it is effaced from the laws.

But if the relative position of the two races inhabiting the United States is as I have described it, why is it that the Americans have abolished slavery in the North of the Union, and why have they kept it in the South and aggravated its rigors?

The answer is easy. In the United States people abolish slavery for the sake not of the Negroes but of the white men.

MANIFEST DESTINY

ANDREW JACKSON

Presidential Message on Indian Removal (1829)

Andrew Jackson is commonly described as the first "popular" president. Indeed, he nearly became president in 1824, when he won a plurality of electoral votes but lost the election in the House of Representatives to John Quincy Adams, because, Jackson charged, Adams had made a "corrupt bargain" with his soon-to-be secretary of state, Henry Clay. A vicious and lengthy campaign for the 1828 election ensued, resulting in a landslide victory for Jackson. One reason for his massive popularity is that he shared many of the prejudices rampant in his era, including favoring the forcible removal of native populations from states of the union. Indeed, by the 1820s much of his national renown stemmed from his having commanded troops against such tribes as the Creeks and the Seminoles.

By the time Jackson became president in 1829, popular pressure was building to take action against the Indians who still lived east of the Mississippi, in particular the Five Civilized Tribes—Cherokees, Creeks, Choctaws, Chickasaws, and Seminoles—who populated the southeast. Jackson articulated his policy recommendations in his first annual message to Congress on December 8, 1829. The end result was the passage of the Indian Removal Act of 1830, one of the hallmarks (for better or for worse) of Jackson's presidency. As you read Jackson's address, consider what it reveals about his true feelings toward Native Americans and their ultimate place in American society.

From James D. Richardson, *A Compilation of the Messages and Papers of the Presidents*, vol. 2 (Bureau of National Literature, 1897), 1019–1022.

The condition and ulterior destiny of the Indian tribes within the limits of some of our States have become objects of much interest and importance. It has long been the policy of Government to introduce among them the arts of civilization, in the hope of gradually reclaiming them from a wandering life. This policy has, however, been coupled with another wholly incompatible with its success. Professing a desire to civilize and settle them, we have at the same time lost no opportunity to purchase their lands and thrust them farther into the wilderness. By this means they have not only been kept in a wandering state, but been led to look upon us as unjust and indifferent to their fate. Thus, though lavish in its expenditures upon the subject, Government has constantly defeated its own policy, and the Indians in general, receding farther and farther to the west, have retained their savage habits. A portion, however, of the Southern tribes, having mingled much with the whites and made some progress in the arts of civilized life, have lately attempted to erect an independent government within the limits of Georgia and Alabama.[1] These States, claiming to be the only sovereigns within their territories, extended their laws over the Indians, which induced the latter to call upon the United States for protection.

Under these circumstances the question presented was whether the General Government had a right to sustain those people in their pretensions. The Constitution declares that "no new State shall be formed or erected within the jurisdiction of any other State" without the consent of its legislature. If the General Government is not permitted to tolerate the erection of a confederate State within the territory of one of the members of this Union against her consent, much less could it allow a foreign and independent government to establish itself there. Georgia became a member of the Confederacy which eventuated in our Federal Union as a sovereign State, always asserting her claim to certain limits, which, having been originally defined in her colonial charter and subsequently recognized in the treaty of peace, she has ever since continued to enjoy. . . . Alabama was admitted into the Union on the same footing with the original States, with boundaries which were prescribed by Congress. There is no constitutional, conventional, or legal provision which allows them less power over the Indians within their borders than is possessed by Maine or New York.

* * *

If the principle involved . . . be abandoned, it will follow that the objects of this Government are reversed, and that it has become a part of its duty to aid in destroying the States which it was established to protect.

Actuated by this view of the subject, I informed the Indians inhabiting parts of Georgia and Alabama that their attempt to establish an independent government would not be countenanced by the Executive of the United States, and advised them to emigrate beyond the Mississippi or submit to the laws of those States.

Our conduct toward these people is deeply interesting to our national character. Their present condition, contrasted with what they once were, makes a most powerful appeal to our sympathies. Our ancestors found them the uncontrolled possessors of these vast regions. By persuasion and force they have been made to retire from river to river and from mountain to mountain, until some of the tribes have become extinct and others have left but remnants to preserve for awhile

---

1. In 1827 the Cherokee Nation East adopted a constitution modeled largely on the U.S. Constitution, establishing a three-branch goverment with a bicameral legislature and an independent judiciary.

their once terrible names. Surrounded by the whites with their arts of civilization, which by destroying the resources of the savage doom him to weakness and decay, the fate of the Mohegan, the Narragansett, and the Delaware is fast overtaking the Choctaw, the Cherokee, and the Creek. That this fate surely awaits them if they remain within the limits of the States does not admit of a doubt. Humanity and national honor demand that every effort should be made to avert so great a calamity. It is too late to inquire whether it was just in the United States to include them and their territory within the bounds of new States, whose limits they could control. That step can not be retraced. A State can not be dismembered by Congress or restricted in the exercise of her constitutional power. But the people of those States and of every State, actuated by feelings of justice and a regard for our national honor, submit to you the interesting question whether something can not be done, consistently with the rights of the States, to preserve this much-injured race.

As a means of effecting this end I suggest for your consideration the propriety of setting apart an ample district west of the Mississippi, and without the limits of any State or Territory now formed, to be guaranteed to the Indian tribes as long as they shall occupy it, each tribe having a distinct control over the portion designated for its use. There they may be secured in the enjoyment of governments of their own choice, subject to no other control from the United States than such as may be necessary to preserve peace on the frontier and between the several tribes. There the benevolent may endeavor to teach them the arts of civilization, and, by promoting union and harmony among them, to raise up an interesting commonwealth, destined to perpetuate the race and to attest the humanity and justice of this Government.

This emigration should be voluntary, for it would be as cruel as unjust to compel the aborigines to abandon the graves of their fathers and seek a home in a distant land. But they should be distinctly informed that if they remain within the limits of the States they must be subject to their laws. In return for their obedience as individuals they will without doubt be protected in the enjoyment of those possessions which they have improved by their industry. . . . Submitting to the laws of the States, and receiving, like other citizens, protection in their persons and property, they will ere long become merged in the mass of our population.

Study Questions

1. What is the immediate problem in Indian relations that Jackson is addressing? How does he propose to solve it? What choices does he give Indians in regard to their future?

2. In what sense would Jackson view Indians as being "savage"? In his mind, how had certain tribes in Alabama and Georgia become more "civilized"? To what degree would this earn more favorable treatment from the federal and state governments?

3. How might Jackson's outlook be seen as sympathetic toward Indians? Was it so in reality? Would relocation west of the Mississippi ultimately be beneficial to the Indians in the way Jackson suggests? Why or why not?

4. Recent presidential ranking surveys indicate that current-day Americans (including historians) are less admiring of Jackson than those of prior generations. To what degree do you think his Indian policy is responsible? What other factors might account for Jackson's diminished standing? How permissible is it to judge him by standards of the present?

JOHN ROSS

Appeal of the Cherokee Nation (1830)

One of the ugliest aspects of Andrew Jackson's presidency was his willingness to appeal to the racism and land hunger of many of the common white men who supported him. Jackson's experience as an Indian fighter and expansionist make unsurprising his strongly held view that the Indian tribes which continued to occupy lands east of the Mississippi should be compelled to relocate west of the river. The state of Georgia, emboldened by Jackson's election to the presidency in 1828, announced soon afterward that it was extending its authority over the Cherokees within its borders, a move which would strip the Indians of rights and lands guaranteed by federal treaty. The Cherokees had made great advances in prior years as they practiced extensive agriculture, established permanent towns, adopted a written constitution, and created a distinctive written language. None of this would save them. Congress passed the Indian Removal Act, which President Jackson signed on May 28, 1830. Despite a favorable Supreme Court ruling in 1832, the Cherokees were forced to yield to relentless state and federal pressure and relocate to Oklahoma in 1838–1839. Thousands died en route along the notorious Trail of Tears.

The following document is an appeal to Congress authored primarily by Cherokee principal chief John Ross (1790–1866), a man of mixed Scottish and Cherokee descent. As you read it, consider its effect upon Congress and the broader public audience. At the time of its writing, Ross remained hopeful the Cherokees might be allowed to remain on their ancestral lands. In 1838, with all options now exhausted, Ross accompanied his people on the long and dreadful march to their new domicile in the West.

From Lewis Ross et, al., "Address of the Committee and Council of the Cherokee Nation," in *General Council convened, to the people of the United States* (July 17, 1803).

Soon after the war of the revolution, as we have learned from our fathers, the Cherokees looked upon the promises of the whites with great distrust and suspicion; but the frank and magnanimous conduct of General Washington did much to allay these feelings. The perseverance of successive presidents, and especially of Mr. Jefferson, in the same course of policy, and in the constant assurance that our country should remain inviolate, except so far as we voluntarily ceded it, nearly banished anxiety in regard to encroachments from the whites. To this result the aid which we received from the United States in the attempts of our people to become civilized, and the kind efforts of benevolent societies, have greatly contributed. Of late years, however, much solicitude was occasioned among our people by the claims of Georgia. This solicitude arose from the apprehension, that by extreme importunity, threats, and other undue influence, a treaty would be made, which should cede the territory, and thus compel the inhabitants to remove. But it never occurred to us for a moment that without any new treaty, without any assent of our rulers and people, without even a pretended compact, and against our vehement and unanimous protestations, we should be delivered over to the discretion of those, who had declared by a legislative act, that they wanted the Cherokee lands and would have them.

Finding that relief could not be obtained from the chief magistrate, and not doubting that our claim to protection was just, we made our application to congress. During four long months our delegation waited, at the doors of the national legislature of the United States, and the people at home, in the most painful suspense, to learn in what manner our application would be answered; and, now that congress has adjourned, on the very day before the date fixed by Georgia for the extension of her oppressive laws over the greater part of our country, the distressing intelligence has been received that we have received no answer at all; and no department of the government has assured us, that we are to receive the desired protection. But just at the close of the session, an act was passed, by which an half a million of dollars was appropriated towards effecting a removal of Indians; and we have great reason to fear that the influence of this act will be brought to bear most injuriously upon us. The passage of this act was certainly understood by the representatives of Georgia as abandoning us to the oppressive and cruel measures of the state, and as sanctioning the opinion that treaties with Indians do not restrain state legislation. We are informed by those, who are competent to judge, that the recent act does not admit of such construction; but that the passage of it, under the actual circumstances of the controversy, will be considered as sanctioning the pretensions of Georgia, there is too much reason to fear.

Thus have we realized, with heavy hearts, that our supplication has not been heard; that the protection heretofore experienced is now to be withheld; that the guaranty, in consequence of which our fathers laid aside their arms and ceded the best portions of their country, means nothing; and that we must either emigrate to an unknown region and leave the pleasant land to which we have the strongest attachment, or submit to the legislation of a state, which has already made our people outlaws, and enacted that any Cherokee, who shall endeavor to prevent the selling of his country, shall be imprisoned in the penitentiary of Georgia not less than four years. To our countrymen this has been melancholy intelligence, and with the most bitter disappointment has it been received.

But in the midst of our sorrows, we do not forget our obligations to our friends and benefactors. It was with sensations of inexpressible joy that we have learned that the voice of thousands, in many parts of the United States, has been raised in our behalf, and numerous memorials offered in our favor, in both houses of congress. To those numerous friends, who have thus sympathized with us in our low estate, we tender our grateful acknowledgements. In pleading our cause, they have pleaded the cause of the poor and defenceless throughout the world. Our special thanks are due, however, to those honorable men, who so ably and eloquently asserted our rights, in both branches of the national legislature. Their efforts will be appreciated wherever the merits of this question shall be known; and we cannot but think, that they have secured for themselves a permanent reputation among the disinterested advocates of humanity, equal rights, justice, and good faith. We even cherish the hope, that these efforts, seconded and followed by others of a similar character, will yet be available, so far as to mitigate our sufferings, if not to effect our entire deliverance.

* * *

We are aware, that some persons suppose it will be for our advantage to remove beyond the Mississippi. We think otherwise. Our people universally think otherwise. Thinking that it would be fatal to their interests, they have almost to a man sent their memorial to congress deprecating the necessity of a removal. This question was distinctly before their minds when they signed their memorial. Not an adult person can be found, who has not an opinion on the subject, and if the people were to understand distinctly, that they could be protected against the laws of the neighboring states, there is probably not an adult person in the nation, who would think it best to remove; though possibly a few might emigrate individually. There are doubtless many, who would flee to an unknown country, however beset with dangers, privations and sufferings, rather than be sentenced to spend six years in a Georgia prison for advising one of their neighbors not to betray his country. And there are others who could not think of living as outlaws in their native land, exposed to numberless vexations, and excluded from being parties or witnesses in a court of justice. It is incredible that Georgia should ever have enacted the oppressive laws to which reference is here made, unless she had supposed that something extremely terrific in its character was necessary in order to make the Cherokees willing to remove. We are not willing to remove; and if we could be brought to this extremity, it would be not by argument, not because our judgment was satisfied, not because our condition will be improved; but only because we cannot endure to be deprived of our national and individual rights and subjected to a process of intolerable oppression.

We wish to remain on the land of our fathers. We have a perfect and original right to remain without interruption or molestation. The treaties with us, and laws of the United States made in pursuance of treaties, guaranty our residence and our privileges, and secure us against intruders. Our only request is, that these treaties may be fulfilled, and these laws executed.

But if we are compelled to leave our country, we see nothing but ruin before us. The country west of the Arkansas territory[1] is unknown to us. From what we can learn of it, we have no prepossessions in its favor. All the inviting parts of it, as we believe, are preoccupied by various Indian nations, to which it has been assigned. They would regard us as intruders, and look upon us with an evil eye. The far greater part of that region is, beyond all controversy, badly supplied with wood and water; and no Indian tribe can live as agriculturists without these articles. All our neighbors, in case of our removal, though crowded into our near vicinity, would speak a language totally different from ours, and practice different customs. The original possessors of that region are now wandering savages lurking for prey in the neighborhood. They have always been at war, and would be easily tempted to turn their arms against peaceful emigrants. Were the country to which we are urged much better than it is represented to be, and were it free from the objections which we have made to it, still it is not the land of our birth, nor of our affections. It contains neither the scenes of our childhood, nor the graves of our fathers.

The removal of families to a new country, even under the most favorable auspices, and when the spirits are sustained by pleasing visions of the future, is attended with much depression of mind and sinking of heart. This is the case, when the removal is a matter of decided preference, and when the persons concerned are in early youth or vigorous manhood. Judge, then, what must be the circumstances of a removal, when a whole community, embracing persons of all classes and every description, from the infant to the man of extreme old age, the sick, the blind, the lame, the improvident, the reckless, the desperate, as well as the prudent, the considerate, the industrious, are compelled to remove by odious and intolerable vexations and persecutions, brought upon them in the forms of law, when all will agree only in this, that they have been cruelly robbed of their country, in violation of the most solemn compacts, which it is possible for communities to form with each other; and that, if they should make themselves comfortable in their new residence, they have nothing to expect hereafter but to be the victims of a future legalized robbery!

Such we deem, and are absolutely certain, will be the feelings of the whole Cherokee people, if they are forcibly compelled, by the laws of Georgia, to remove; and with these feelings, how is it possible that we should pursue our present course of improvement, or avoid sinking into utter despondency? We have been called a poor, ignorant, and degraded people. We certainly are not rich; nor have we ever boasted of our knowledge, or our moral or intellectual elevation. But there is not a man within our limits so ignorant as not to know that he has the right to live on the land of his fathers, in the possession of his immemorial privileges, and that this right has been acknowledged and guaranteed by the United

1. The capital of the Cherokee Nation today is located just west of Arkansas in Tahlequah, Oklahoma.

States; nor is there a man so degraded as not to feel a keen sense of injury, on being deprived of this right and driven into exile.

* * *

We entreat those to whom the foregoing paragraphs are addressed, to remember the great law of love. "Do to others as ye would that others should do to you"— Let them remember that of all nations on the earth, they are under the greatest obligation to obey this law. We pray them to remember that, for the sake of principle, their forefathers were compelled to leave, therefore driven from the old world, and that the winds of persecution wafted them over the great waters and landed them on the shores of the new world, when the Indian was the sole lord and proprietor of these extensive domains—Let them remember in what way they were received by the savage of America, when power was in his hand, and his ferocity could not be restrained by any human arm. We urge them to bear in mind, that those who would now ask of them a cup of cold water, and a spot of earth, a portion of their own patrimonial possessions, on which to live and die in peace, are the descendants of those, whose origin, as inhabitants of North America, history and tradition are alike insufficient to reveal. Let them bring to remembrance all these facts, and they cannot, and we are sure, they will not fail to remember, and sympathize with us in these our trials and sufferings.

Study Questions

1. Why do the Cherokees object to the actions taken by Georgia? Upon what rights do they insist? What are their primary arguments against removal?

2. The Cherokee appeal refers to "our friends and benefactors." Who might these have been? What sections of the United States might have contained the greatest number of Indian sympathizers?

3. What does this document reveal of Cherokee relations with other Indians? What might have caused them to have tense relations with other tribes? Who were the "wandering savages" that lived west of the Mississippi and why were they especially to be feared?

4. Evaluate the appeal made by the Cherokees in the final paragraph of this document. Why was it ultimately ineffective at preventing their expulsion? What does this document predict or imply about the future well-being of the Cherokee people?

JOHN L. O'SULLIVAN

Annexation (1845)

Nineteenth-century American expansionism entered a new phase in 1844 with the election of James K. Polk; by the end of his term the United States had grown by more than a third. Polk, a Tennessee Democrat and protégé of Andrew Jackson, campaigned on a bold expansionist platform, pledging himself to the annexation of Texas and promising settlement of the Oregon question with Britain by acquiring the Pacific Northwest. Polk's victory over Henry Clay in November provided lame-duck president John Tyler with a mandate for action regarding Texas: just before he departed the White House in March 1845, Tyler pushed through Congress a joint resolution in favor of annexation. Texas would enter the Union as the twenty-eighth state just before the end of the year.

It was in this context that John L. O'Sullivan (1813–1895), ardent expansionist and editor of the United States Democratic Review *(a journal founded in 1837 to promote Jacksonian ideals and candidates like Polk), penned the article in the summer of 1845 that introduced the phrase "manifest destiny." While appearing for the first time in print at this juncture, "manifest destiny" would ultimately enter the American lexicon as the shorthand for the deeply rooted belief that the United States had a divinely sanctioned mission to spread its values and institutions over as wide an expanse of territory as possible. This would become one of the most crucial concepts for understanding American conduct in regard to other nations and peoples from the mid-nineteenth century onward.*

From *The United States Magazine and Democratic Review*, vol. 17 (New York: J. L. O'Sullivan & O. C. Gardiner, 1846), 5, 7, 9.

Texas is now ours. Already, before these words are written, her Convention has undoubtedly ratified the acceptance, by her Congress, of our proffered invitation into the Union; and made the requisite changes in her already republican form of constitution to adopt it to its future federal relations. Her star and her stripe may already be said to have taken their place in the glorious blazon of our common nationality; and the sweep of our eagle's wing already includes within its circuit the wide extent of her fair and fertile land.[1] She

---

1. Texas at that time would have been about one-third larger than its current size, as its western boundary ran the entire length of the Rio Grande from present-day Colorado to the Gulf of Mexico.

is no longer to us a mere geographical space—a certain combination of coast, plain, mountain, valley, forest and stream. She is no longer to us a mere country on the map. She comes within the dear and sacred designation of Our Country; no longer a "*pays*," she is a part of "*la patrie;*"[2] and that which is at once a sentiment and a virtue, Patriotism, already begins to thrill for her too within the national heart.

* * *

Why, were other reasoning wanting, in favor of now elevating this question of the reception of Texas into the Union, out of the lower region of our past party dissensions, up to its proper level of a high and broad nationality, it surely is to be found, found abundantly, in the manner in which other nations have undertaken to intrude themselves into it, between us and the proper parties to the case, in a spirit of hostile interference against us, for the avowed object of thwarting our policy and hampering our power, limiting our greatness and checking the fulfilment of our manifest[3] destiny to overspread the continent allotted by Providence for the free development of our yearly multiplying millions.

* * *

Mr. Clay was right when he declared that Annexation was a question with which slavery had nothing to do. The country which was the subject of Annexation in this case, from its geographical position and relations, happens to be—or rather the portion of it now actually settled, happens to be—a slave country. But a similar process might have taken place in proximity to a different section of our Union; and indeed there is a great deal of Annexation yet to take place, within the life of the present generation, along the whole line of our northern border. Texas has been absorbed into the Union in the inevitable fulfilment of the general law which is rolling our population westward ; the connexion of which with that ratio of growth in population which is destined within a hundred years to swell our numbers to the enormous population of *two hundred and fifty millions* (if not more), is too evident to leave us in doubt of the manifest design of Providence in regard to the occupation of this continent. It was disintegrated from Mexico in the natural course of events, by a process perfectly legitimate on its own part, blameless on ours; and in which all the censures due to wrong, perfidy and folly, rest on Mexico alone.

* * *

California will, probably, next fall away from the loose adhesion which, in such a country as Mexico, holds a remote province in a slight equivocal kind of depen-

2. That is, Texas is no longer a separate nation, but is now part of the American fatherland itself. (*Pays* and *patrie* are French for "nation" and "fatherland," respectively.)

3. Obvious or made evident.

dence on the metropolis. Imbecile and distracted, Mexico never can exert any real governmental authority over such a country.

* * *

The Anglo-Saxon foot is already on its borders. Already the advance guard of the irresistible army of Anglo-Saxon emigration has begun to pour down upon it, armed with the plough and the rifle, and marking its trail with schools and colleges, courts and representative halls, mills and meeting-houses. A population will soon be in actual occupation of California, over which it will be idle for Mexico to dream of dominion. They will necessarily become independent. All this without agency of our government, without responsibility of our people— in the natural flow of events, the spontaneous working of principles, and the adaptation of the tendencies and wants of the human race to the elemental circumstances in the midst of which they find themselves placed.

* * *

Whether they will then attach themselves to our Union or not, is not to be predicted with any certainty. Unless the projected rail-road across the continent to the Pacific be carried into effect, perhaps they may not; though even in that case, the day is not distant when the Empires of the Atlantic and Pacific would again flow together into one, as soon as their inland border should approach each other. But that great work, colossal as appears the plan on its first suggestion, cannot remain lung unbuilt. Its necessity for this very purpose of binding and holding together in its iron clasp our fast settling Pacific region with that of the Mississippi valley—the natural facility of the route—the ease with which any amount of labor for the construction can be drawn in from the overcrowded populations of Europe, to be paid in the lands made valuable by the progress of the work itself—and its immense utility to the commerce of the world with the whole eastern coast of Asia, alone almost sufficient for the support of such a road—these considerations give assurance that the day cannot be distant which shall witness the conveyance of the representatives from Oregon and California to Washington within less time than a few years ago was devoted to a similar journey by those from Ohio; while the magnetic telegraph will enable the editors of the "San Francisco Union," the "Astoria[4] Evening Post," or the "Nootka[5] Morning News" to set up in type the first half of the President's inaugural, before the echoes of the latter half shall have died away beneath the lofty porch of the Capitol, as spoken from his lips.

Away, then, with all idle French talk of *balances of power* on the American Continent. There is no growth in Spanish America! Whatever progress of population there may be in the British Canadas, is only for their own early severance of their

4. A settlement on the coast of Oregon.
5. An island off the coast of British Columbia.

present colonial relation to the little island three thousand miles across the Atlantic; soon to be followed by Annexation, and destined to swell the still accumulating momentum of our progress.

Study Questions

1. What exactly does the writer mean by "manifest destiny"? To what degree is it a religious concept? Why must the United States inevitably expand? According to O'Sullivan, how far will U.S. territorial expansion ultimately extend?

2. O'Sullivan refers to "other nations" that had inserted themselves into the Texas controversy in an effort to block U.S. acquisition of that territory. What nations might he have been referring to? Why might certain world powers have seen it in their strategic interest to block further American westward expansion?

3. How were advances in transportation and communication revolutionizing American life in this period? How does O'Sullivan see the railroad and telegraph as agents of continental expansion?

4. What was O'Sullivan's view of Mexico and by extension, Mexicans? When he writes that "a population will soon be in actual occupation of California, over which it will be idle for Mexico to dream of dominion," what ironies might we find in light of contemporary demographic trends?

JAMES K. POLK

War Message to Congress (1846)

On March 1, 1845, three days before the inauguration of James K. Polk, President John Tyler signed the Texas annexation resolution, which would add Texas as the twenty-eighth state. Polk's electoral victory the prior November on an expansionist platform had made Congress's approval of Texas annexation possible. Mexico, which had never recognized Texas independence, regarded this as an act of aggression and severed diplomatic relations with the United States. Soon afterward, President Polk added to his expansionist agenda U.S. acquisition of the northern Mexican states of New Mexico and California. The president sent John Slidell as his envoy to Mexico City to see if Mexico were willing to sell the coveted territories. When Mexican president Mariano Paredes instead expelled Slidell and put the Mexican army on a war footing in early 1846, the two nations stood at the brink of official hostilities.

Meanwhile, Polk exploited a boundary dispute—over whether the Rio Grande or a shorter and more northerly stream, the Nueces, marked the southwestern limits of Texas—in order to push for war with Mexico. In January 1846 he ordered General Zachary Taylor to move his force stationed at Corpus Christi, at the mouth of the Nueces, deeply through the disputed territory south of that river, to the north bank of the Rio Grande. It could have been predicted that Mexico would respond forcefully to what it regarded as such a provocative gesture. When Mexican dragoons attacked a contingent of American soldiers north of the Rio Grande on April 25, 1846, Polk had his cause for war. The House and Senate approved his request by overwhelming numbers and the Mexican-American War officially commenced. As you read Polk's words, evaluate the effectiveness of his case for hostilities with Mexico.

From *The Congressional Globe*, May 11, 1846.

In my message at the commencement of the present session, I informed you that, upon the earnest appeal both of the Congress and convention of Texas, I had ordered an efficient military force to take a position "between the Nueces and the Del Norte."[1] This had become necessary to meet a threatened invasion of Texas by the Mexican forces, for which extensive military preparations had been

---

1. The Del Norte or the Rio del Norte is the Rio Grande.

made. The invasion was threatened solely because Texas had determined, in accordance with a solemn resolution of the Congress of the United States, to annex herself to our Union; and, under these circumstances, it was plainly our duty to extend our protection over her citizens and soil.

This force was concentrated at Corpus Christi, and remained there until after I had received such information from Mexico as rendered it probable, if not certain, that the Mexican Government would refuse to receive our Envoy.

Meantime Texas, by the final action of our Congress, had become an integral part of our Union. The Congress of Texas by its act of December 19th, 1836, had declared the Rio del Norte to be the boundary of that Republic. Its jurisdiction had been extended and exercised beyond the Nueces. The country between that river and the Del Norte had been represented in the Congress and in the Convention of Texas, had thus taken part in the act of annexation itself, and is now included within one of our Congressional districts. Our own Congress had, moreover, with great unanimity, by the act approved December 31st, 1845, recognised the country beyond the Nueces as a part of our territory by including it within our own revenue system; and a revenue officer, to reside within that district, has been appointed by and with the advice and consent of the Senate. It became, therefore, of urgent necessity to provide for the defence of that portion of our country. Accordingly, on the thirteenth of January last, instructions were issued to the general in command of these troops to occupy the left bank of the Del Norte. This river—which is the southwestern boundary of the State of Texas—is an exposed frontier. From this quarter invasion was threatened; upon it and in its immediate vicinity, in the judgment of high military experience, are the proper stations for the protecting forces of the Government.

* * *

The movement of the troops to the Del Norte was made by the Commanding General, under positive instructions to abstain from all aggressive acts towards Mexico, or Mexican citizens, and to regard the relations between that Republic and the United States as peaceful, unless she should declare war, or commit acts of hostility indicative of a state of war. He was specially directed to protect private property and respect personal rights.

The army moved from Corpus Christi on the 11th of March, and on the 28th of that month arrived on the left bank of the Del Norte, opposite to Matamoras, where it encamped on a commanding position,[2] which has since been strengthened by the erection of field works. A depôt has also been established at Point Isabel, near the Brasos Santiago, thirty miles in rear of the encampment. The selection of his position was necessarily confided to the judgment of the general in command.

---

2. This is now the site of Brownsville, Texas.

The Mexican forces at Matamoras assumed a belligerent attitude, and on the 12th of April, General Ampudia, then in command, notified General Taylor to break up his camp within twenty-four hours, and to retire beyond the Nueces river; and in the event of his failure to comply with these demands, announced that arms, and arms alone, must decide the question. But no open act of hostility was committed until the 24th of April. On that day, General Arista, who had succeeded to the command of the Mexican forces, communicated to General Taylor that "he considered hostilities commenced, and should prosecute them." A party of dragoons of sixty-three men and officers were on the same day despatched from the American camp up the Rio del Norte, on its left bank, to ascertain whether the Mexican troops had crossed, or were preparing to cross, the river, "became engaged with a large body of these troops, and after a short affair, in which some sixteen were killed and wounded, appear to have been surrounded and compelled to surrender."

The grievous wrongs perpetrated by Mexico upon our citizens throughout a long period of years, remain unredressed; and solemn treaties, pledging her public faith for this redress, have been disregarded. A Government either unable or unwilling to enforce the execution of such treaties, fails to perform one of its plainest duties.

Our commerce with Mexico has been almost annihilated. It was formerly highly beneficial to both nations; but our merchants have been deterred from prosecuting it, by the system of outrage and extortion which the Mexican authorities have pursued against them; whilst their appeals through their own Government for indemnity have been made in vain. Our forbearance has gone to such an extreme as to be mistaken in its character. Had we acted with vigor in repelling the insults and redressing the injuries inflicted by Mexico at the commencement, we should doubtless have escaped all the difficulties in which we are now involved.

Instead of this, however, we have been exerting our best efforts to propitiate her good will. Upon the pretext that Texas, a nation as independent as herself, thought proper to unite its destinies with our own, she has affected to believe that we have severed her rightful territory, and, in official proclamations and manifestoes, has repeatedly threatened to make war upon us, for the purpose of reconquering Texas. In the meantime, we have tried every effort at reconciliation. The cup of forbearance had been exhausted, even before the recent information from the frontier of the Del Norte. But now, after reiterated menaces, Mexico has passed the boundary of the United States, has invaded our territory, and shed American blood upon the American soil. She has proclaimed that hostilities have commenced, and that the two nations are now at war.

As war exists, and, notwithstanding all our efforts to avoid it, exists by the act of Mexico herself, we are called upon, by every consideration of duty and patriotism, to vindicate, with decision, the honor, the rights, and the interests of our country.

* * *

In further vindication of our rights and defence of our territory, I invoke the prompt action of Congress to recognise the existence of the war, and to place at the disposition of the Executive the means of prosecuting the war with vigor, and thus hastening the restoration of peace. To this end I recommend that authority should be given to call into the public service a large body of volunteers to serve for not less than six or twelve months unless sooner discharged. A volunteer force is, beyond question, more efficient than any other description of citizen soldiers; and it is not to be doubted that a number far beyond that required would readily rush to the field upon the call of their country. I further recommend that a liberal provision be made for sustaining our entire military force, and furnishing it with supplies and munitions of war.

The most energetic and prompt measures, and the immediate appearance in arms of a large and overpowering force, are recommended to Congress as the most certain and efficient means of bringing the existing collision with Mexico to a speedy and successful termination.

WASHINGTON, *May 11th*, 1846.

Study Questions

1. According to Polk, what was the root cause of the war? Why did he send American troops to the north ("left") bank of the Rio Grande? Fully evaluate his statement that "Mexico has . . . invaded our territory, and shed American blood upon the American soil."

2. Based upon Polk's war address, what would you say were the chief war objectives of the United States? To what degree does Polk address the question of U.S. acquisition of additional Mexican territory? How might this be explained?

3. Polk calls for volunteers to come forward to fight. What region do you think would have supplied the greatest number? Why? Do you think Polk convinced the majority of Americans to support the war? Explain fully.

4. Imagine yourself an American in 1846 opposed to war on moral grounds. What alternatives to war might have peacefully resolved the tensions between the United States and Mexico? How successfully might the case for such alternatives have been made to President Polk?

ABRAHAM LINCOLN

On the Mexican War (1847)

R.W. Emerson, "Lectures on the Times," *The Dial, III* (July, 1842), 6–13.

Whereas the President of the United States in his message of May 11, 1846, has declared that the "Mexican Government not only refused to receive him, [the envoy of the United States,] or listen to his propositions, but, after a long-continued series of menaces, have at last invaded *our territory* and shed the blood of our fellow-citizens on *our own soil:*"

And again, in his message of December 8, 1846, that "we had ample cause of war against Mexico long before the breaking out of hostilities; but even then we forbore to take redress into our own hands until Mexico herself became the aggressor, by invading our soil in hostile array, and shedding the blood of our citizens";

And yet again, in his message of December 7, 1847, that "the Mexican Government refused even to hear the terms of adjustment which he [our minister of peace] was authorized to propose, and finally, under wholly unjustifiable pretexts, involved the two countries in war, by invading the territory of the State of Texas, striking the first blow, and shedding the blood of our citizens on our own soil";

And whereas, This House is desirous to obtain a full knowledge of all the facts which go to establish whether the particular spot on which the blood of our citizens was so shed was or was not at that time our own soil: therefore,

Resolved, By the House of Representatives, that the President of the United States be respectfully requested to inform this House—

First. Whether the spot on which the blood of our citizens was shed, as in his message declared, was or was not within the territory of Spain, at least after the treaty of 1819, until the Mexican revolution.

Second. Whether that spot is or is not within the territory which was wrested from Spain by the revolutionary government of Mexico.

Third. Whether that spot is or is not within a settlement of people, which settlement has existed ever since long before the Texas revolution, and until its inhabitants fled before the approach of the United States army.

Fourth. Whether that settlement is or is not isolated from any and all other settlements by the Gulf and the Rio Grande on the south and west, and by wide uninhabited regions on the north and east.

Fifth. Whether the people of that settlement, or a majority of them, or any of them, have ever submitted themselves to the government or laws of Texas or of the United States, by consent or by compulsion, either by accepting office, or voting at elections, or paying tax, or serving on juries, or having process served upon them, or in any other way.

Sixth. Whether the people of that settlement did or did not flee from the approach of the United States army, leaving unprotected their homes and their growing crops, *before* the blood was shed, as in the message stated; and whether the first blood, so shed, was or was not shed within the inclosure of one of the people who had thus fled from it.

Seventh. Whether our citizens, whose blood was shed, as in his message declared, were or were not, at that time, armed officers and soldiers, sent into that settlement by the military order of the President, through the Secretary of War.

Eighth. Whether the military force of the United States was or was not so sent into that settlement after General Taylor had more than once intimated to the War Department that, in his opinion, no such movement was necessary to the defence or protection of Texas.

ANTEBELLUM PERIOD

HENRY DAVID THOREAU

Resistance to Civil Government (1849)

Henry David Thoreau (1817–1862) was born in Concord, Massachusetts, and lived there most of his life. He received his education from Harvard University. As a follower of the Transcendentalist philosophy made famous by his neighbor, Ralph Waldo Emerson, Thoreau believed in the equality of all men. Much of his writing and his life reflected his adherence to Transcendentalism. For instance, he refused to pay his poll tax because he believed it would help fund the Mexican War, a war that many considered illegal because President Polk had failed to get Congress to approve it. Consequently, Thoreau spent one night in jail. Thoreau is remembered for this act and for his environmental and philosophical masterpiece Walden *(1854).*

"Resistance to Civil Government," also known as "Civil Disobedience," was written for a lecture delivered at the Concord Lyceum. In it, Thoreau argues systematically against the government's right to compel individual citizens to violate their consciences. He advocates that citizens should disobey unjust laws and be willing to accept the consequences of their actions—in his case, he refused to pay his poll tax and so spent a night in jail, an event that he describes as liberating and enlightening. A classic statement of the philosophy behind civil disobedience, this essay helped to inspire Mahatma Gandhi's campaign to win independence for India in the 1940s and the struggle of Martin Luther King Jr. for civil rights in the 1960s.

I heartily accept the motto,—"That government is best which governs least;[1] and I should like to see it acted up to more rapidly and systematically. Carried out, it finally amounts to this, which also I believe,—"That government is best which governs not at all"; and when men are prepared for it, that will be the kind of government which they will have. Government is at best but an expedient; but most governments are usually, and all governments are sometimes, inexpedient. The objections which have been brought against a standing army, and they are many and weighty, and deserve to prevail, may also at last be brought against a standing government. The standing army is only an arm of the standing

---

1. The *Democratic Review*, a New York magazine that had published two pieces by Thoreau in 1843, used these words on its masthead.

government. The government itself, which is only the mode which the people have chosen to execute their will, is equally liable to be abused and perverted before the people can act through it. Witness the present Mexican war, the work of comparatively a few individuals using the standing government as their tool; for, in the outset, the people would not have consented to this measure.[2]

This American government,—what is it but a tradition, though a recent one, endeavoring to transmit itself unimpaired to posterity, but each instant losing some of its integrity? It has not the vitality and force of a single living man; for a single man can bend it to his will. It is a sort of wooden gun to the people themselves; and, if ever they should use it in earnest as a real one against each other, it will surely split. But it is not the less necessary for this; for the people must have some complicated machinery or other, and hear its din, to satisfy that idea of government which they have. Governments show thus how successfully men can be imposed on, even impose on themselves, for their own advantage. It is excellent, we must all allow; yet this government never of itself furthered any enterprise, but by the alacrity with which it got out of its way. *It* does not keep the country free. *It* does not settle the West. *It* does not educate. The character inherent in the American people has done all that has been accomplished; and it would have done somewhat more, if the government had not sometimes got in its way. For government is an expedient by which men would fain succeed in letting one another alone; and, as has been said, when it is most expedient, the governed are most let alone by it. Trade and commerce, if they were not made of India rubber, would never manage to bounce over the obstacles which legislators are continually putting in their way; and, if one were to judge these men wholly by the effects of their actions, and not partly by their intentions, they would deserve to be classed and punished with those mischievous persons who put obstructions on the railroads.

But, to speak practically and as a citizen, unlike those who call themselves no-government men, I ask for, not at once no government, but *at once* a better government. Let every man make known what kind of government would command his respect, and that will be one step toward obtaining it.

After all, the practical reason why, when the power is once in the hands of the people, a majority are permitted, and for a long period continue, to rule, is not because they are most likely to be in the right, nor because this seems fairest to the minority, but because they are physically the strongest. But a government in which the majority rule in all cases cannot be based on justice, even as far as men understand it. Can there not be a government in which majorities do not virtually decide right and wrong, but conscience?—in which majorities decide only those

2. The Mexican War (1846–48) was considered illegal by many because President Polk declared war on Mexico without Congressional approval. Many opposed the war because, besides extending the territory of the United States, it was also intended to spread slavery into Texas.

questions to which the rule of expediency is applicable? Must the citizen ever for a moment, or in the least degree, resign his conscience to the legislator? Why has every man a conscience, then? I think that we should be men first, and subjects afterward. It is not desirable to cultivate a respect for the law, so much as for the right. The only obligation which I have a right to assume, is to do at any time what I think right. It is truly enough said, that a corporation has no conscience; but a corporation of conscientious men is a corporation *with* a conscience. Law never made men a whit more just; and, by means of their respect for it, even the well-disposed are daily made the agents of injustice. A common and natural result of an undue respect for law is, that you may see a file of soldiers, colonel, captain, corporal, privates, powder-monkeys and all, marching in admirable order over hill and dale to the wars, against their wills, aye, against their common sense and consciences, which makes it very steep marching indeed, and produces a palpitation of the heart. They have no doubt that it is a damnable business in which they are concerned; they are all peaceably inclined. Now, what are they? Men at all? or small moveable forts and magazines, at the service of some unscrupulous man in power? Visit the Navy Yard, and behold a marine, such a man as an American government can make, or such as it can make a man with its black arts, a mere shadow and reminiscence of humanity, a man laid out alive and standing, and already, as one may say, buried under arms with funeral accompaniments, though it may be

> Not a drum was heard, nor a funeral note,
> As his corse to the ramparts we hurried;
> Not a soldier discharged his farewell shot
> O'er the grave where our hero we buried.[3]

The mass of men serve the State thus, not as men mainly, but as machines, with their bodies. They are the standing army, and the militia, jailers, constables, *posse comitatus*, &c.[4] In most cases there is no free exercise whatever of the judgment or of the moral sense; but they put themselves on a level with wood and earth and stones; and wooden men can perhaps be manufactured that will serve the purpose as well. Such command no more respect than men of straw, or a lump of dirt. They have the same sort of worth only as horses and dogs. Yet such as these even are commonly esteemed good citizens. Others, as most legislators, politicians, lawyers, ministers, and office-holders, serve the State chiefly with their heads; and, as they rarely make any moral distinctions, they are as likely to serve the devil, without intending it, as God. A very few, as heroes, patriots, martyrs, reformers in the great sense, and *men*, serve the State with their consciences

---

3. Irish poet Charles Wolfe (1791–1823), "Burial of Sir John Moore at Corunna."
4. "&c." is an abbreviated form of *et cetera*, "and so forth" (Latin); *posse comitatus*: Sheriff's posse (Latin).

also, and so necessarily resist it for the most part; and they are commonly treated by it as enemies. A wise man will only be useful as a man, and will not submit to be "clay," and "stop a hole to keep the wind away,"[5] but leave that office to his dust at least:—

> I am too high-born to be propertied,
> To be a secondary at control,
> Or useful serving-man and instrument
> To any sovereign state throughout the world.[6]

He who gives himself entirely to his fellow-men appears to them useless and selfish; but he who gives himself partially to them is pronounced a benefactor and philanthropist.

How does it become a man to behave toward this American government today? I answer that he cannot without disgrace be associated with it. I cannot for an instant recognize that political organization as *my* government which is the *slave's* government also.

All men recognize the right of revolution; that is, the right to refuse allegiance to and to resist the government, when its tyranny or its inefficiency are great and unendurable. But almost all say that such is not the case now. But such was the case, they think, in the Revolution of '75. If one were to tell me that this was a bad government because it taxed certain foreign commodities brought to its ports, it is most probable that I should not make an ado about it, for I can do without them: all machines have their friction; and possibly this does enough good to counterbalance the evil. At any rate, it is a great evil to make a stir about it. But when the friction comes to have its machine, and oppression and robbery are organized, I say, let us not have such a machine any longer. In other words, when a sixth of the population of a nation which has undertaken to be the refuge of liberty are slaves, and a whole country is unjustly overrun and conquered by a foreign army, and subjected to military law, I think that it is not too soon for honest men to rebel and revolutionize. What makes this duty the more urgent is the fact, that the country so overrun is not our own, but ours is the invading army.

Paley, a common authority with many on moral questions, in his chapter on the "Duty of Submission to Civil Government,"[7] resolves all civil obligation into expediency; and he proceeds to say, "that so long as the interest of the whole society requires it, that is, so long as the established government cannot be resisted or changed without public inconveniency, it is the will of God that the established

---

5. William Shakespeare (1558–1616), *Hamlet*, 5.1.196–7.

6. William Shakespeare, *King John*, 5.2.79–82.

7. English theologian and essayist William Paley (1743–1805), *Principles of Moral and Political Philosophy*.

government be obeyed, and no longer."—"This principle being admitted, the justice of every particular case of resistance is reduced to a computation of the quantity of the danger and grievance on the one side, and of the probability and expense of redressing it on the other." Of this, he says, every man shall judge for himself. But Paley appears never to have contemplated those cases to which the rule of expediency does not apply, in which a people, as well as an individual, must do justice, cost what it may. If I have unjustly wrested a plank from a drowning man, I must restore it to him though I drown myself.[8] This, according to Paley, would be inconvenient. But he that would save his life, in such a case, shall lose it.[9] This people must cease to hold slaves, and to make war on Mexico, though it cost them their existence as a people.

In their practice, nations agree with Paley; but does any one think that Massachusetts does exactly what is right at the present crisis?

> A drab of state, a cloth-o'-silver slut,
> To have her train borne up, and her soul trial in the dirt.[1]

Practically speaking, the opponents to a reform in Massachusetts are not a hundred thousand politicians at the South, but a hundred thousand merchants and farmers here, who are more interested in commerce and agriculture than they are in humanity, and are not prepared to do justice to the slave and to Mexico, *cost what it may*. I quarrel not with far-off foes, but with those who, near at home, co-operate with, and do the bidding of those far away, and without whom the latter would be harmless. We are accustomed to say, that the mass of men are unprepared; but improvement is slow, because the few are not materially wiser or better than the many. It is not so important that many should be as good as you, as that there be some absolute goodness somewhere; for that will leaven the whole lump.[2] There are thousands who are *in opinion* opposed to slavery and to the war, who yet in effect do nothing to put an end to them; who, esteeming themselves children of Washington and Franklin, sit down with their hands in their pockets, and say that they know not what to do, and do nothing; who even postpone the question of freedom to the question of free-trade, and quietly read the prices-current along with the latest advices from Mexico, after dinner, and, it may be, fall asleep over them both. What is the price-current of an honest man and patriot to-day? They hesitate, and they regret, and sometimes they petition; but they do nothing in earnest and with effect. They will wait, well disposed, for others to remedy the evil, that they may no longer have it to regret. At most, they give only a cheap vote, and a feeble countenance and God-speed, to the right, as it goes by

---

8. Roman statesman and philosopher Marcus Tullius Cicero (106–43 BCE), *De Officiis*.
9. Matthew 10:39 and Luke 9:24.
1. Cyril Tourneur (1575?–1626), *The Revenger's Tragedy*.
2. "Know ye not that a little leaven leaveneth the whole lump?" (1 Corinthians 5:6).

them. There are nine hundred and ninety-nine patrons of virtue to one virtuous man; but it is easier to deal with the real possessor of a thing than with the temporary guardian of it.

All voting is a sort of gaming, like chequers or backgammon, with a slight moral tinge to it, a playing with right and wrong, with moral questions; and betting naturally accompanies it. The character of the voters is not staked. I cast my vote, perchance, as I think right; but I am not vitally concerned that that right should prevail. I am willing to leave it to the majority. Its obligation, therefore, never exceeds that of expediency. Even voting *for the right* is *doing* nothing for it. It is only expressing to men feebly your desire that it should prevail. A wise man will not leave the right to the mercy of chance, nor wish it to prevail through the power of the majority. There is but little virtue in the action of masses of men. When the majority shall at length vote for the abolition of slavery, it will be because they are indifferent to slavery, or because there is but little slavery left to be abolished by their vote. *They* will then be the only slaves. Only *his* vote can hasten the abolition of slavery who asserts his own freedom by his vote.

I hear of a convention to be held at Baltimore, or elsewhere, for the selection of a candidate for the Presidency, made up chiefly of editors, and men who are politicians by profession; but I think, what is it to any independent, intelligent, and respectable man what decision they may come to, shall we not have the advantage of his wisdom and honesty, nevertheless? Can we not count upon some independent votes? Are there not many individuals in the country who do not attend conventions? But no: I find that the respectable man, so called, has immediately drifted from his position, and despairs of his country, when his country has more reason to despair of him. He forthwith adopts one of the candidates thus selected as the only *available* one, thus proving that he is himself *available* for any purposes of the demagogue. His vote is of no more worth than that of any unprincipled foreigner or hireling native, who may have been bought. Oh for a man who is a *man*, and, as my neighbor says, has a bone in his back which you cannot pass your hand through! Our statistics are at fault: the population has been returned too large. How many *men* are there to a square thousand miles in this country? Hardly one. Does not America offer any inducement for men to settle here? The American has dwindled into an Odd Fellow,—one who may be known by the development of his organ of gregariousness, and a manifest lack of intellect and cheerful self-reliance; whose first and chief concern, on coming into the world, is to see that the alms-houses are in good repair; and, before yet he has lawfully donned the virile garb,[3] to collect a fund for the support of the widows and orphans that may be; who, in short, ventures to live only by the aid of the mutual insurance company, which has promised to bury him decently.

---

3. Reference to "toga virilis," a white toga symbolizing manhood that teenaged Roman boys were allowed to wear.

It is not a man's duty, as a matter of course, to devote himself to the eradication of any, even the most enormous wrong; he may still properly have other concerns to engage him; but it is his duty, at least, to wash his hands of it, and, if he gives it no thought longer, not to give it practically his support. If I devote myself to other pursuits and contemplations, I must first see, at least, that I do not pursue them sitting upon another man's shoulders. I must get off him first, that he may pursue his contemplations too. See what gross inconsistency is tolerated. I have heard some of my townsmen say, "I should like to have them order me out to help put down an insurrection of the slaves, or to march to Mexico,—see if I would go"; and yet these very men have each, directly by their allegiance, and so indirectly, at least, by their money, furnished a substitute. The soldier is applauded who refuses to serve in an unjust war by those who do not refuse to sustain the unjust government which makes the war; is applauded by those whose own act and authority he disregards and sets as nought; as if the State were penitent to that degree that it hired one to scourge it while it sinned, but not to that degree that it left off sinning for a moment. Thus, under the name of order and civil government, we are all made at last to pay homage to and support our own meanness. After the first blush of sin, comes its indifference; and from immoral it becomes, as it were, *un*moral, and not quite unnecessary to that life which we have made.

The broadest and most prevalent error requires the most disinterested virtue to sustain it. The slight reproach to which the virtue of patriotism is commonly liable, the noble are most likely to incur. Those who, while they disapprove of the character and measures of a government, yield to it their allegiance and support, are undoubtedly its most conscientious supporters, and so frequently the most serious obstacles to reform. Some are petitioning the State to dissolve the Union, to disregard the requisitions of the President. Why do they not dissolve it themselves,—the union between themselves and the State,—and refuse to pay their quota into its treasury? Do not they stand in the same relation to the State, that the State does to the Union? And have not the same reasons prevented the State from resisting the Union, which have prevented them from resisting the State?

How can a man be satisfied to entertain an opinion merely, and enjoy *it?* Is there any enjoyment in it, if his opinion is that he is aggrieved? If you are cheated out of a single dollar by your neighbor, you do not rest satisfied with knowing that you are cheated, or with saying that you are cheated, or even with petitioning him to pay you your due; but you take effectual steps at once to obtain the full amount, and see that you are never cheated again. Action from principle,—the perception and the performance of right,—changes things and relations; it is essentially revolutionary, and does not consist wholly with any thing which was. It not only divides states and churches, it divides families; aye, it divides the *individual*, separating the diabolical in him from the divine.

Unjust laws exist: shall we be content to obey them, or shall we endeavor to amend them, and obey them until we have succeeded, or shall we transgress them at once? Men generally, under such a government as this, think that they ought to wait until they have persuaded the majority to alter them. They think that, if they should resist, the remedy would be worse than the evil. But it is the fault of the government itself that the remedy *is* worse than the evil. *It* makes it worse. Why is it not more apt to anticipate and provide for reform? Why does it not cherish its wise minority? Why does it cry and resist before it is hurt? Why does it not encourage its citizens to be on the alert to point out its faults, and *do* better than it would have them? Why does it always crucify Christ, and excommunicate Copernicus and Luther,[4] and pronounce Washington and Franklin rebels?

One would think, that a deliberate and practical denial of its authority was the only offence never contemplated by government; else, why has it not assigned its definite, its suitable and proportionate penalty? If a man who has no property refuses but once to earn nine shillings[5] for the State, he is put in prison for a period unlimited by any law that I know, and determined only by the discretion of those who placed him there; but if he should steal ninety times nine shillings from the State, he is soon permitted to go at large again.

If the injustice is part of the necessary friction of the machine of government, let it go, let it go: perchance it will wear smooth,—certainly the machine will wear out. If the injustice has a spring, or a pulley, or a rope, or a crank, exclusively for itself, then perhaps you may consider whether the remedy will not be worse than the evil; but if it is of such a nature that it requires you to be the agent of injustice to another, then, I say, break the law. Let your life be a counter friction to stop the machine. What I have to do is to see, at any rate, that I do not lend myself to the wrong which I condemn.

As for adopting the ways which the State has provided for remedying the evil, I know not of such ways. They take too much time, and a man's life will be gone. I have other affairs to attend to. I came into this world, not chiefly to make this a good place to live in, but to live in it, be it good or bad. A man has not every thing to do, but something; and because he cannot do *every thing*, it is not necessary that he should do *something* wrong. It is not my business to be petitioning the governor or the legislature any more than it is theirs to petition me; and, if they should not hear my petition, what should I do then? But in this case the State has provided no way: its very Constitution is the evil. This may seem to be harsh and stubborn and unconciliatory; but it is to treat with the utmost kindness and consideration the only spirit that can appreciate or deserves it. So is all change for the better, like birth and death which convulse the body.

---

4. Polish astronomer Nicolaus Copernicus (1473–1543) was excommunicated from the Catholic Church for his arguments that the earth revolved around the sun rather than the earth being the unmoving center of the universe. German monk Martin Luther (1483–1546) was excommunicated for the publication of his rejection of the selling of indulgences and other common practices of the Catholic Church.

5. Approximately $1.50, the poll tax Thoreau refused to pay (worth about $40 in today's U.S. currency).

I do not hesitate to say, that those who call themselves abolitionists should at once effectually withdraw their support, both in person and property, from the government of Massachusetts, and not wait till they constitute a majority of one, before they suffer the right to prevail through them. I think that it is enough if they have God on their side, without waiting for that other one. Moreover, any man more right than his neighbors, constitutes a majority of one already.[6]

I meet this American government, or its representative the State government, directly, and face to face, once a year, no more, in the person of its tax-gatherer; this is the only mode in which a man situated as I am necessarily meets it; and it then says distinctly, Recognize me; and the simplest, the most effectual, and, in the present posture of affairs, the indispensablest mode of treating with it on this head, of expressing your little satisfaction with and love for it, is to deny it then. My civil neighbor, the tax-gatherer,[7] is the very man I have to deal with,—for it is, after all, with men and not with parchment that I quarrel,—and he has voluntarily chosen to be an agent of the government. How shall he ever know well what he is and does as an officer of the government, or as a man, until he is obliged to consider whether he shall treat me, his neighbor, for whom he has respect, as a neighbor and well-disposed man, or as a maniac and disturber of the peace, and see if he can get over this obstruction to his neighborliness without a ruder and more impetuous thought or speech corresponding with his action? I know this well, that if one thousand, if one hundred, if ten men whom I could name,—if ten honest men only,—aye, if one HONEST man, in this State of Massachusetts, ceasing to hold slaves, were actually to withdraw from this copartnership, and be locked up in the county jail therefore, it would be the abolition of slavery in America. For it matters not how small the beginning may seem to be: what is once well done is done for ever. But we love better to talk about it: that we say is our mission. Reform keeps many scores of newspapers in its service, but not one man. If my esteemed neighbor, the State's ambassador,[8] who will devote his days to the settlement of the question of human rights in the Council Chamber, instead of being threatened with the prisons of Carolina, were to sit down the prisoner of Massachusetts, that State which is so anxious to foist the sin of slavery upon her sister,—though at present she can discover only an act of inhospitality to be the ground of a quarrel with her,—the Legislature would not wholly waive the subject the following winter.

Under a government which imprisons any unjustly, the true place for a just man is also a prison. The proper place to-day, the only place which Massachusetts has provided for her freer and less desponding spirits, is in her prisons, to be put

6. John Knox (1505–72), a Protestant philosopher and reformer in Scotland, said that "a man with God is always in the majority."

7. Sam Staples, who occasionally assisted Thoreau's surveying work.

8. Samuel Hoar (1778–1856), who had once been expelled from Charleston, South Carolina, for protesting the treatment of black sailors from Massachusetts.

out and locked out of the State by her own act, as they have already put themselves out by their principles. It is there that the fugitive slave, and the Mexican prisoner on parole, and the Indian come to plead the wrongs of his race, should find them; on that separate, but more free and honorable ground, where the State places those who are not *with* her but *against* her,—the only house in a slave-state in which a free man can abide with honor. If any think that their influence would be lost there, and their voices no longer afflict the ear of the State, that they would not be as an enemy within its walls, they do not know by how much truth is stronger than error, nor how much more eloquently and effectively he can combat injustice who has experienced a little in his own person. Cast your whole vote, not a strip of paper merely, but your whole influence. A minority is powerless while it conforms to the majority; it is not even a minority then; but it is irresistible when it clogs by its whole weight. If the alternative is to keep all just men in prison, or give up war and slavery, the State will not hesitate which to choose. If a thousand men were not to pay their tax-bills this year, that would not be a violent and bloody measure, as it would be to pay them, and enable the State to commit violence and shed innocent blood. This is, in fact, the definition of a peaceable revolution, if any such is possible. If the tax-gatherer, or any other public officer, asks me, as one has done, "But what shall I do?" my answer is, "If you really wish to do anything, resign your office." When the subject has refused allegiance, and the officer has resigned his office, then the revolution is accomplished. But even suppose blood should flow. Is there not a sort of blood shed when the conscience is wounded? Through this wound a man's real manhood and immortality flow out, and he bleeds to an everlasting death. I see this blood flowing now.

I have contemplated the imprisonment of the offender, rather than the seizure of his goods,—though both will serve the same purpose,—because they who assert the purest right, and consequently are most dangerous to a corrupt State, commonly have not spent much time in accumulating property. To such the State renders comparatively small service, and a slight tax is wont to appear exorbitant, particularly if they are obliged to earn it by special labor with their hands. If there were one who lived wholly without the use of money, the State itself would hesitate to demand it of him. But the rich man—not to make any invidious comparison—is always sold to the institution which makes him rich. Absolutely speaking, the more money, the less virtue; for money comes between a man and his objects, and obtains them for him; and it was certainly no great virtue to obtain it. It puts to rest many questions which he would otherwise be taxed to answer; while the only new question which it puts is the hard but superfluous one, how to spend it. Thus his moral ground is taken from under his feet. The opportunities of living are diminished in proportion as what are called the "means" are increased. The best thing a man can do for his culture when he is rich is to endeavour to carry out those schemes which he entertained when he was poor. Christ answered the Herodians according to their condition. "Show me the tribute-money," said he;—and one took a penny out of his pocket;—If you use money which has the image of Caesar on it, and which he has made current and valuable, that is, *if you are men of the State,* and gladly enjoy the advantages of Caesar's government, then pay him back some of his own when he demands it: "Render therefore to Caesar that which is Caesar's, and to God those things which are God's,"[9]—leaving them no wiser than before as to which was which; for they did not wish to know.

When I converse with the freest of my neighbors, I perceive that, whatever they may say about the magnitude and seriousness of the question, and their regard for the public tranquility, the long and the short of the matter is, that they cannot spare the protection of the existing government, and they dread the consequences of disobedience to it to their property and families. For my own part, I should not like to think that I ever rely on the protection of the State. But, if I deny the authority of the State when it presents its tax-bill, it will soon take and waste all my property, and so harass me and my children without end. This is hard. This makes it impossible for a man to live honestly and at the same time comfortably in outward respects. It will not be worth the while to accumulate property; that would be sure to go again. You must hire or squat somewhere, and raise but a small crop, and eat that soon. You must live within yourself, and depend upon yourself, always tucked up and ready for a start, and not have many affairs. A man may grow rich in Turkey even, if he will be in all respects a good subject of the Turkish government. Confucious said,—"If a State is governed by the principles of reason, poverty and misery are subjects of shame; if a State is not governed by the principles of reason, riches and honors are the subjects of shame."[1] No: until I want the protection of Massachusetts to be extended to me in some distant southern port, where my liberty is endangered, or until I am bent solely on building up an estate at home by peaceful enterprise, I can afford to refuse allegiance to Massachusetts, and her right to my property and life. It costs me less in every sense to incur the penalty of disobedience to the State, than it would to obey. I should feel as if I were worth less in that case.

Some years ago, the State met me in behalf of the church, and commanded me to pay a certain sum toward the support of a clergyman whose preaching my father attended, but never I myself. "Pay," it said, "or be locked up in the jail." I declined to pay. But, unfortunately, another man saw fit to pay it. I did not see why the schoolmaster should be taxed to support the priest, and not the priest the schoolmaster; for I was not the State's schoolmaster, but I supported myself by voluntary subscription. I did not see why the lyceum should not present its tax-bill, and have the State to back its demand, as well as the church. However, at the request of the selectmen, I condescended to make some such statement as this in

9. Matthew 22:16–21.
1. Chinese philosopher Confucius (551–479 BCE), *Analects,* 8:13.

writing:—"Know all men by these presents, that I, Henry Thoreau, do not wish to be regarded as a member of any incorporated society which I have not joined." This I gave to the town-clerk; and he has it. The State, having thus learned that I did not wish to be regarded as a member of that church, has never made a like demand on me since; though it said that it must adhere to its original presumption that time. If I had known how to name them, I should then have signed off in detail from all the societies which I never signed on to; but I did not know where to find a complete list.

I have paid no poll-tax for six years. I was put into a jail[2] once on this account, for one night; and, as I stood considering the walls of solid stone, two or three feet thick, the door of wood and iron, a foot thick, and the iron grating which strained the light, I could not help being struck with the foolishness of that institution which treated me as if I were mere flesh and blood and bones, to be locked up. I wondered that it should have concluded at length that this was the best use it could put me to, and had never thought to avail itself of my services in some way. I saw that, if there was a wall of stone between me and my townsmen, there was a still more difficult one to climb or break through, before they could get to be as free as I was. I did not for a moment feel confined, and the walls seemed a great waste of stone and mortar. I felt as if I alone of all my townsmen had paid my tax. They plainly did not know how to treat me, but behaved like persons who are underbred. In every threat and in every compliment there was a blunder; for they thought that my chief desire was to stand the other side of that stone wall. I could not but smile to see how industriously they locked the door on my meditations, which followed them out again without let or hindrance, and *they* were really all that was dangerous. As they could not reach me, they had resolved to punish my body; just as boys, if they cannot come at some person against whom they have a spite, will abuse his dog. I saw that the State was half-witted, that it was timid as a lone woman with her silver spoons, and that it did not know its friends from its foes, and I lost all my remaining respect for it, and pitied it.

Thus the State never intentionally confronts a man's sense, intellectual or moral, but only his body, his senses. It is not armed with superior wit or honesty, but with superior physical strength. I was not born to be forced. I will breathe after my own fashion. Let us see who is the strongest. What force has a multitude? They only can force me who obey a higher law than I. They force me to become like themselves. I do not hear of *men* being *forced* to live this way or that by masses of men. What sort of life were that to live? When I meet a government which says to me, "Your money or your life," why should I be in haste to give it my money? It may be in a great strait, and not know what to do: I cannot help that. It must help itself; do as I do. It is not worth the while to snivel about it. I am not responsible for the successful working of the machinery of society. I am not the son of the engineer. I perceive that, when an

2. In Concord.

acorn and a chestnut fall side by side, the one does not remain inert to make way for
the other, but both obey their own laws, and spring and grow and flourish as best
they can, till one, perchance, overshadows and destroys the other. If a plant cannot
live according to its nature, it dies; and so a man.

The night in prison was novel and interesting enough. The prisoners in their
shirt-sleeves were enjoying a chat and the evening air in the doorway, when I
entered. But the jailer said, "Come, boys, it is time to lock up"; and so they dispersed, and I heard the sound of their steps returning into the hollow apartments. My room-mate was introduced to me by the jailer, as "a first-rate fellow
and a clever man." When the door was locked, he showed me where to hang my
hat, and how he managed matters there. The rooms were whitewashed once a
month; and this one, at least, was the whitest, most simply furnished, and probably the neatest apartment in the town. He naturally wanted to know where I
came from, and what brought me there; and, when I had told him, I asked him
in my turn how he came there, presuming him to be an honest man, of course;
and, as the world goes, I believe he was. "Why," said he, "they accuse me of
burning a barn; but I never did it." As near as I could discover, he had probably
gone to bed in a barn when drunk, and smoked his pipe there; and so a barn was
burnt. He had the reputation of being a clever man, had been there some three
months waiting for his trial to come on, and would have to wait as much longer;
but he was quite domesticated and contented since he got his board for nothing,
and thought that he was well treated.

He occupied one window, and I the other; and I saw, that, if one stayed there
long, his principal business would be to look out the window. I had soon read all
the tracts that were left there, and examined where former prisoners had broken out, and where a grate had been sawed off, and heard the history of the various occupants of that room; for I found that even here there was a history and
a gossip which never circulated beyond the walls of the jail. Probably this is the
only house in the town where verses are composed, which are afterward printed
in a circular form, but not published. I was shown quite a long list of verses
which were composed by some young men who had been detected in an attempt
to escape, who avenged themselves by singing them.

I pumped my fellow-prisoner as dry as I could, for fear I should never see
him again; but at length he showed me which was my bed, and left me to blow
out the lamp.

It was like travelling into a far country, such as I had never expected to
behold, to lie there for one night. It seemed to me that I never had heard the
town-clock strike before, nor the evening sounds of the village; for we slept with
the windows open, which were inside the grating. It was to see my native village
in the light of the middle ages, and our Concord was turned into a Rhine
stream, and visions of knights and castles passed before me. They were the
voices of old burghers that I heard in the streets. I was an involuntary spectator
and auditor of whatever was done and said in the kitchen of the adjacent village-
inn,—a wholly new and rare experience to me. It was a closer view of my native

town. I was fairly inside of it. I never had seen its institutions before. This is one of its peculiar institutions; for it is a shire town. I began to comprehend what its inhabitants were about.

In the morning, our breakfasts were put through the hole in the door, in small oblong-square tin pans, made to fit, and holding a pint of chocolate, with brown bread, and an iron spoon. When they called for the vessels again, I was green enough to return what bread I had left; but my comrade seized it, and said that I should lay that up for lunch or dinner. Soon after, he was let out to work at haying in a neighboring field, whither he went every day, and would not be back till noon; so he bade me good-day, saying that he doubted if he should see me again.

When I came out of prison,—for some one interfered, and paid the tax,—I did not perceive that great changes had taken place on the common, such as he observed who went in a youth, and emerged a tottering and gray-headed man; and yet a change had to my eyes come over the scene,—the town, and State, and country,—greater than any that mere time could effect. I saw yet more distinctly the State in which I lived. I saw to what extent the people among whom I lived could be trusted as good neighbors and friends; that their friendship was for summer weather only; that they did not greatly purpose to do right; that they were a distinct race from me by their prejudices and superstitions, as the Chinamen and Malays are; that, in their sacrifices to humanity, they ran no risks, not even to their property; that, after all, they were not so noble but they treated the thief as he had treated them, and hoped, by a certain outward observance and a few prayers, and by walking in a particular straight though useless path from time to time, to save their souls. This may be to judge my neighbors harshly; for I believe that most of them are not aware that they have such an institution as the jail in their village.

It was formerly the custom in our village, when a poor debtor came out of jail, for his acquaintances to salute him, looking through their fingers, which were crossed to represent the grating of a jail window, "How do ye do?" My neighbors did not thus salute me, but first looked at me, and then at one another, as if I had returned from a long journey. I was put into jail as I was going to the shoemaker's to get a shoe which was mended. When I was let out the next morning, I proceeded to finish my errand, and, having put on my mended shoe, joined a huckleberry party, who were impatient to put themselves under my conduct; and in half an hour,—for the horse was soon tackled,[3]—was in the midst of a huckleberry field, on one of our highest hills, two miles off; and then the State was nowhere to be seen.

This is the whole history of "My Prisons."[4]

I have never declined paying the highway tax, because I am as desirous of being a good neighbor as I am of being a bad subject; and, as for supporting

---

3. Harnessed.
4. Also a title of a memoir by Italian poet by Silvio Pellico (1789–1854).

schools, I am doing my part to educate my fellow-countrymen now. It is for no particular item in the tax-bill that I refuse to pay it. I simply wish to refuse allegiance to the State, to withdraw and stand aloof from it effectually. I do not care to trace the course of my dollar, if I could, till it buys a man, or a musket to shoot one with,—the dollar is innocent,—but I am concerned to trace the effects of my allegiance. In fact, I quietly declare war with the State, after my fashion, though I will still make what use and get what advantage of her I can, as is usual in such cases.

If others pay the tax which is demanded of me, from a sympathy with the State, they do but what they have already done in their own case, or rather they abet injustice to a greater extent than the State requires. If they pay the tax from a mistaken interest in the individual taxed, to save his property or prevent his going to jail, it is because they have not considered wisely how far they let their private feelings interfere with the public good.

This, then, is my position at present. But one cannot be too much on his guard in such a case, lest his action be biassed by obstinacy, or an undue regard for the opinions of men. Let him see that he does only what belongs to himself and to the hour.

I think sometimes, Why, this people mean well; they are only ignorant; they would do better if they knew how; why give your neighbors this pain to treat you as they are not inclined to? But I think, again, this is no reason why I should do as they do, or permit others to suffer much greater pain of a different kind. Again, I sometimes say to myself, When many millions of men, without heat, without ill-will, without personal feeling of any kind, demand of you a few shillings only, without the possibility, such is their constitution, of retracting or altering their present demand, and without the possibility, on your side, of appeal to any other millions, why expose yourself to this overwhelming brute force? You do not resist cold and hunger, the winds and the waves, thus obstinately; you quietly submit to a thousand similar necessities. You do not put your head into the fire. But just in proportion as I regard this as not wholly a brute force, but partly a human force, and consider that I have relations to those millions as to so many millions of men, and not of mere brute or inanimate things, I see that appeal is possible, first and instantaneously, from them to the Maker of them, and, secondly, from them to themselves. But, if I put my head deliberately into the fire, there is no appeal to fire or to the Maker of fire, and I have only myself to blame. If I could convince myself that I have any right to be satisfied with men as they are, and to treat them accordingly, and not according, in some respects, to my requisitions and expectations of what they and I ought to be, then, like a good Mussulman[5] and fatalist, I should endeavor to be satisfied with things as they are, and say it is the will of God. And, above all, there is this difference between resisting this and a purely

5. Muslim.

brute or natural force, that I can resist this with some effect; but I cannot expect, like Orpheus,[6] to change the nature of the rocks and trees and beasts.

I do not wish to quarrel with any man or nation. I do not wish to split hairs, to make fine distinctions, or set myself up as better than my neighbors. I seek rather, I may say, even an excuse for conforming to the laws of the land. I am but too ready to conform to them. Indeed I have reason to suspect myself on this head; and each year, as the tax-gatherer comes round, I find myself disposed to review the acts and position of the general and State governments, and the spirit of the people, to discover a pretext for conformity.

> We must affect our country as our parents;
> And if at any lime we alienate
> Our love or industry from doing it honor,
> We must respect effects and teach the soul
> Matter of conscience and religion,[7]
> And not desire of rule or benefit.

I believe that the State will soon be able to take all my work of this sort out of my hands, and then I shall be no better a patriot than my fellow-countrymen. Seen from a lower point of view, the Constitution, with all its faults, is very good; the law and the courts are very respectable; even this State and this American government are, in many respects, very admirable and rare things, to be thankful for, such as a great many have described them; but seen from a point of view a little higher, they are what I have described them; seen from a higher still, and the highest, who shall say what they are, or that they are worth looking at or thinking of at all?

However, the government does not concern me much, and I shall bestow the fewest possible thoughts on it. It is not many moments that I live under a government, even in this world. If a man is thought-free, fancy-free, imagination-free, that which *is not* never for a long time appearing *to be* to him, unwise rulers or reformers cannot fatally interrupt him.

I know that most men think differently from myself; but those whose lives are by profession devoted to the study of these or kindred subjects, content me as little as any. Statesmen and legislators, standing so completely within the institution, never distinctly and nakedly behold it. They speak of moving society, but have no resting-place without it. They may be men of a certain experience and discrimination, and have no doubt invented ingenious and even useful systems, for which we sincerely thank them; but all their wit and usefulness lie within certain not very wide limits. They are wont to forget that the world is

6. In Greek mythology, poet and musician, son of the Muse Calliope; his songs were said to charm animals and even trees and rocks into dancing.

7. English playwright George Peele (1556–96), The Battle of Alcazar.

not governed by policy and expediency. Webster[8] never goes behind government, and so cannot speak with authority about it. His words are wisdom to those legislators who contemplate no essential reform in the existing government; but for thinkers, and those who legislate for all time, he never once glances at the subject. I know of those whose serene and wise speculations on this theme would soon reveal the limits of his mind's range and hospitality. Yet, compared with the cheap professions of most reformers, and the still cheaper wisdom and eloquence of politicians in general, his are almost the only sensible and valuable words, and we thank Heaven for him. Comparatively, he is always strong, original, and, above all, practical. Still his quality is not wisdom, but prudence. The lawyer's truth is not Truth, but consistency, or a consistent expediency. Truth is always in harmony with herself, and is not concerned chiefly to reveal the justice that may consist with wrongdoing. He well deserves to be called, as he has been called, the Defender of the Constitution. There are really no blows to be given by him but defensive ones. He is not a leader, but a follower. His leaders are the men of '87.[9] "I have never made an effort," he says, "and never propose to make an effort; I have never countenanced an effort, and never mean to countenance an effort, to disturb the arrangement as originally made, by which the various States came into the Union."[1] Still thinking of the sanction which the Constitution gives to slavery, he says, "Because it was a part of the original compact,—let it stand." Notwithstanding his special acuteness and ability, he is unable to take a fact out of its merely political relations, and behold it as it lies absolutely to be disposed of by the intellect,—what, for instance, it behooves a man to do here in America to-day with regard to slavery, but ventures, or is driven, to make some such desperate answer as the following, while professing to speak absolutely, and as a private man,—from which what new and singular code of social duties might be inferred?—"The manner," says he, "in which the government of those States where slavery exists are to regulate it, is for their own consideration, under their responsibility to their constituents, to the general laws of propriety, humanity, and justice, and to God. Associations formed elsewhere, springing from a feeling of humanity, or any other cause, having nothing whatever to do with it. They have never received any encouragment from me, and they never will."

They who know of no purer sources of truth, who have traced up its stream no higher, stand, and wisely stand, by the Bible and the Constitution, and drink at it there with reverence and humility; but they who behold where it comes trickling into this lake or that pool, gird up their loins once more, and continue their pilgrimage toward its fountain-head.

8. U.S. statesman and orator Daniel Webster (1782–1852).
9. That is, the writers of the Constitution in 1787.
1. Daniel Webster, "The Admission of Texas," a speech delievered in 1845.

No man with a genius for legislation has appeared in America. They are rare in the history of the world. There are orators, politicians, and eloquent men, by the thousand; but the speaker has not yet opened his mouth to speak, who is capable of settling the much-vexed questions of the day. We love eloquence for its own sake, and not for any truth which it may utter, or any heroism it may inspire. Our legislators have not yet learned the comparative value of free-trade and of freedom, of union, and of rectitude, to a nation. They have no genius or talent for comparatively humble questions of taxation and finance, commerce and manufactures and agriculture. If we were left solely to the wordy wit of legislators in Congress for our guidance, uncorrected by the seasonable experience and the effectual complaints of the people, America would not long retain her rank among the nations. For eighteen hundred years, though perchance I have no right to say it, the New Testament has been written; yet where is the legislator who has wisdom and practical talent enough to avail himself of the light which it sheds on the science of legislation?

The authority of government, even such as I am willing to submit to,—for I will cheerfully obey those who know and can do better than I, and in many things even those who neither know nor can do so well,—is still an impure one: to be strictly just, it must have the sanction and consent of the governed. It can have no pure right over my person and property but what I concede to it. The progress from an absolute to a limited monarchy, from a limited monarchy to a democracy, is a progress toward a true respect for the individual. Is a democracy, such as we know it, the last improvement possible in government? Is it not possible to take a step further towards recognizing and organizing the rights of man? There will never be a really free and enlightened State, until the State comes to recognize the individual as a higher and independent power, from which all its own power and authority are derived, and treats him accordingly. I please myself with imagining a State at last which can afford to be just to all men, and to treat the individual with respect as a neighbor; which even would not think it inconsistent with its own repose, if a few were to live aloof from it, not meddling with it, nor embraced by it, who fulfilled all the duties of neighbors and fellowmen. A State which bore this kind of fruit, and suffered it to drop off as fast as it ripened, would prepare the way for a still more perfect and glorious State, which also I have imagined, but not yet anywhere seen.

Declaration of Sentiments (1848)

The American women's rights movement arguably began in 1848 when a handful of activists called a convention to assemble in a Methodist church in Seneca Falls, New York. Lucretia Mott (1793–1880), a Quaker minister, and Elizabeth Cady Stanton (1815–1902), an abolitionist, were the foremost leaders in this effort. Both were representative of educated, middle-class women who had been prepared in church and the antislavery movement to take leading roles in additional antebellum reform causes. Women from such backgrounds were increasingly likely to push against the constraints imposed upon them in a male-dominated society.

About three hundred people showed up for the two-day conference that opened on July 19; since men were present, in deference to established tradition Lucretia Mott's husband chaired the proceedings. Delegates debated and approved a dozen women's rights resolutions. At the conference's conclusion, sixty-eight women and thirty-two men signed the Declaration of Sentiments, which was authored primarily by Elizabeth Cady Stanton. As you read this document, ponder the wisdom and effectiveness of Stanton's modeling it on Thomas Jefferson's Declaration of Independence. The Seneca Falls meeting enjoyed national press coverage and inspired subsequent feminist efforts. Not until 1920 would one of its major demands—full voting equality for women—reach fruition with the adoption of the Nineteenth Amendment.

From Elizabeth Cady Stanton, Susan B. Anthony, and Matilda Joslyn Gage, eds., "Seneca Falls Declaration of Sentiments," in *History of Woman Suffrage* (New York: Fowler & Wells, 1881).

When, in the course of human events, it becomes necessary for one portion of the family of man to assume among the people of the earth a position different from that which they have hitherto occupied, but one to which the laws of nature and of nature's God entitle them, a decent respect to the opinions of mankind requires that they should declare the causes that impel them to such a course.

We hold these truths to be self-evident: that all men and women are created equal; that they are endowed by their Creator with certain inalienable rights; that among these are life, liberty, and the pursuit of happiness; that to secure these rights governments are instituted, deriving their just powers from the consent of the governed. Whenever any form of government becomes destructive of these ends, it is the right of those who suffer from it to refuse allegiance to it, and to insist upon the institution of a new government, laying its foundation on such principles, and organizing its powers in such form, as to them shall seem most likely to effect their safety and happiness. Prudence indeed, will dictate that governments long established should not be changed for light and transient causes; and accordingly all experience hath shown that mankind are more disposed to suffer, while evils are sufferable, than to right themselves by abolishing the forms to which they were accustomed. But when a long train of abuses and usurpations, pursuing invariably the same object evinces a design to reduce them under absolute despotism, it is their duty to throw off such government, and to provide new guards for their future security. Such has been the patient sufferance of the women under this government, and such is now the necessity which constrains them to demand the equal station to which they are entitled.

The history of mankind is a history of repeated injuries and usurpations on the part of man toward woman, having in direct object the establishment of an absolute tyranny over her. To prove this, let facts be submitted to a candid world.

He has never permitted her to exercise her inalienable right to the elective franchise.

He has compelled her to submit to laws, in the formation of which she had no voice.

He has withheld from her rights which are given to the most ignorant and degraded men—both natives and foreigners.

Having deprived her of this first right of a citizen, the elective franchise, thereby leaving her without representation in the halls of legislation, he has oppressed her on all sides.

He has made her, if married, in the eye of the law, civilly dead.

He has taken from her all right in property, even to the wages she earns.

He has made her, morally, an irresponsible being, as she can commit many crimes with impunity, provided they can be done in the presence of her husband. In the covenant of marriage, she is compelled to promise obedience to her husband, he becoming, to all intents and purposes, her master—the law giving him power to deprive her of her liberty and to administer chastisement.

He has so framed the laws of divorce, as to what shall be the proper causes, and in case of separation, to whom the guardianship of the children shall be given, as to be wholly regardless of the happiness of women—the law, in all cases, going upon a false supposition of the supremacy of man, giving all power into his hands.

After depriving her of all rights as a married woman, if single, and the owner of property, he has taxed her to support a government which recognizes her only when her property can be made profitable to it.

He has monopolized nearly all the profitable employments, and from those she is permitted to follow, she receives but a scanty remuneration. He closes against her all the avenues to wealth and distinction which he considers most honorable to himself. As a teacher of theology, medicine, or law, she is not known.

He has denied her the facilities for obtaining a thorough education, all colleges being closed against her.

He allows her in Church, as well as State, but a subordinate position, claiming Apostolic authority[1] for her exclusion from the ministry, and, with some exceptions, from any public participation in the affairs of the Church.

He has created a false public sentiment by giving to the world a different code of morals for men and women, by which moral delinquencies which exclude women from society, are not only tolerated, but deemed of little account in man.

He has usurped the prerogative of Jehovah himself, claiming it as his right to assign for her a sphere of action, when that belongs to her conscience and to her God.

He has endeavored, in every way that he could, to destroy her confidence in her own powers, to lessen her self-respect, and to make her willing to lead a dependent and abject life.

Now, in view of this entire disfranchisement of one-half the people of this country, their social and religious degradation—in view of the unjust laws above mentioned, and because women do feel themselves aggrieved, oppressed, and fraudulently deprived of their most sacred rights, we insist that they have immediate admission to all the rights and privileges which belong to them as citizens of the United States.

In entering upon the great work before us, we anticipate no small amount of misconception, misrepresentation, and ridicule; but we shall use every instrumentality within our power to effect our object. We shall employ agents, circulate tracts, petition the State and National legislatures, and endeavor to enlist the pulpit and the press in our behalf. We hope this Convention will be followed by a series of Conventions embracing every part of the county.

Whereas, The great precept of nature is conceded to be, that "man shall pursue his own true and substantial happiness." Blackstone in his Commentaries[2] remarks, that this law of Nature being coeval with mankind, and dictated by God himself, is of course superior in obligation to any other. It is binding over all the globe, in all countries and at all times; no human laws are of any validity if contrary

---

1. Authority derived from that of the original twelve apostles of Jesus.
2. Sir William Blackstone published his seminal commentaries on English common law between 1765 and 1769.

to this, and such of them as are valid, derive all their force, and all their validity, and all their authority, mediately and immediately, from this original; therefore,

Resolved, That such laws as conflict, in any way, with the true and substantial happiness of woman, are contrary to the great precept of nature and of no validity, for this is "superior in obligation to any other."

Resolved, That all laws which prevent woman from occupying such a station in society as her conscience shall dictate, or which place her in a position inferior to that of man, are contrary to the great precept of nature, and therefore of no force or authority.

Resolved, That woman is man's equal—was intended to be so by the Creator, and the highest good of the race demands that she should be recognized as such.

Resolved, That the women of this country ought to be enlightened in regard to the laws under which they live, that they may no longer publish their degradation by declaring themselves satisfied with their present position, nor their ignorance, by asserting that they have all the rights they want.

Resolved, That inasmuch as man, while claiming for himself intellectual superiority, does accord to woman moral superiority, it is pre-eminently his duty to encourage her to speak and teach, as she has an opportunity, in all religious assemblies.

Resolved, That the same amount of virtue, delicacy, and refinement of behavior that is required of woman in the social state, should also be required of man, and the same transgressions should be visited with equal severity on both man and woman.

Resolved, That the objection of indelicacy and impropriety, which is so often brought against woman when she addresses a public audience, comes with a very ill-grace from those who encourage, by their attendance, her appearance on the stage, in the concert, or in feats of the circus.

Resolved, That woman has too long rested satisfied in the circumscribed limits which corrupt customs and a perverted application of the Scriptures have marked out for her, and that it is time she should move in the enlarged sphere which her great Creator has assigned her.

Resolved, That it is the duty of the women of this country to secure to themselves their sacred right to the elective franchise.

Resolved, That the equality of human rights results necessarily from the fact of the identity of the race in capabilities and responsibilities.

Resolved, therefore, That, being invested by the Creator with the same capabilities, and the same consciousness of responsibility for their exercise, it is demonstrably the right and duty of woman, equally with man, to promote every righteous cause by every righteous means; and especially in regard to the great subjects of morals and religion, it is self-evidently her right to participate with her brother in teaching them, both in private and in public, by writing and by speaking, by any instrumentalities proper to be used, and in any assemblies proper to be held; and this being a self-evident truth growing out of the divinely implanted principles of human nature, any custom or authority adverse to it, whether modern or wearing the hoary sanction of antiquity, is to be regarded as a self-evident falsehood, and at war with mankind.

———————

R esolved, That the speedy success of our cause depends upon the zealous and untiring efforts of both men and women, for the overthrow of the monopoly of the pulpit, and for the securing to woman an equal participation with men in the various trades, professions, and commerce.

Study Questions

1. What are the most significant departures from the Declaration of Independence in the opening sections of this document? While Jefferson's document contains a whole series of sentences in which "he" refers to King George III, who is the "he" whose offenses are cited in the Declaration of Sentiments? How much difference does it make?

2. What is the evidence in this document that many of women's grievances in this era were church-related? How might churchgoing women have encountered discrimination in religious settings?

3. Why does this Declaration place so much emphasis on the right to vote? Who could or could not vote in 1848? What other forms of equality were women demanding?

4. Analyze the use of the term "sentiments" in the title of the statement. How would you imagine the Declaration of Sentiments was received by the press and general public upon its adoption?

ROGER B. TANEY

Dred Scott v. Sanford (1857)

Dred Scott (1795–1858) was a Missouri slave who in 1834 traveled with his owner, an Army surgeon named John Emerson, into the free state of Illinois. Scott then resided with his master for several years in the Wisconsin Territory, an area then entirely off-limits to slavery under the terms of the Missouri Compromise of 1820. After Emerson's death in 1843, Scott (now back in the South and working as a slave for Emerson's widow) sued for his freedom on the grounds that his extended residence on free soil should have made him free.

Scott's original Missouri suit took eleven years to reach the Supreme Court, which issued its ruling in 1857. The defendant by this stage was John Sanford, a New York resident who had become executor of John Emerson's estate. The Court ruled 7–2 against Scott, with Chief Justice Roger Taney's opinion being the most definitive for the majority. Taney (1777–1864), a Marylander who had owned slaves himself, had been appointed to the Court in 1835 by Andrew Jackson. His ruling on the Scott case came at a time when a veritable war over slavery was raging in Kansas. As you read the following excerpts from Taney's opinion, think about the potential effects on already tense North-South relations. Current-day historians and constitutional scholars frequently select the Dred Scott ruling as one of the worst in the Supreme Court's history. As you follow Taney's argument, look for the passages that are most problematic from a twenty-first-century perspective.

From *Dred Scott v. Sanford*, 60 U.S. 393, 1857.

Mr. Chief Justice TANEY delivered the opinion of the court.

* * *

The question is simply this: Can a negro whose ancestors were imported into this country, and sold as slaves, become a member of the political community formed and brought into existence by the Constitution of the United States, and as such become entitled to all the rights and privileges and immunities guaranteed to the citizen? One of which rights is the privilege of suing in a court of the United States in the cases specified in the Constitution.

* * *

In the opinion of the court, the legislation and histories of the times, and the language used in the Declaration of Independence, show, that neither the class of persons who had been imported as slaves, nor their descendants, whether they had become free or not, were then acknowledged as a part of the people, nor intended to be included in the general words used in that memorable instrument.

It is difficult at this day to realize the state of public opinion in relation to that unfortunate race, which prevailed in the civilized and enlightened portions of the world at the time of the Declaration of Independence, and when the Constitution of the United States was framed and adopted. But the public history of every European nation displays it in a manner too plain to be mistaken.

They had for more than a century before been regarded as beings of an inferior order, and altogether unfit to associate with the white race, either in social or political relations; and so far inferior, that they had no rights which the white man was bound to respect; and that the negro might justly and lawfully be reduced to slavery for his benefit. He was bought and sold, and treated as an ordinary article of merchandise and traffic, whenever a profit could be made by it. This opinion was at that time fixed and universal in the civilized portion of the white race. It was regarded as an axiom in morals as well as in politics, which no one thought of disputing, or supposed to be open to dispute; and men in every grade and position in society daily and habitually acted upon it in their private pursuits, as well as in matters of public concern; without doubting for a moment the correctness of this opinion.

* * *

It proceeds to say: "We hold these truths to be self-evident: that all men are created equal; that they are endowed by their Creator with certain unalienable rights; that among them is life, liberty, and the pursuit of happiness; that to secure these rights, Governments are instituted, deriving their just powers from the consent of the governed."

The general words above quoted would seem to embrace the whole human family, and if they were used in a similar instrument at this day would be so understood. But it is too clear for dispute, that the enslaved African race were not intended to be included, and formed no part of the people who framed and adopted this declaration; for if the language, as understood in that day, would embrace them, the conduct of the distinguished men who framed the Declaration of Independence would have been utterly and flagrantly inconsistent with the principles they asserted; and instead of the sympathy of mankind, to which they so confidently appealed, they would have deserved and received universal rebuke and reprobation.

Yet the men who framed this declaration were great men—high in literary acquirements—high in their sense of honor, and incapable of asserting principles inconsistent with those on which they were acting. They perfectly understood the meaning of the language they used, and how it would be understood by others; and they knew that it would not in any part of the civilized world be supposed to embrace the negro race, which by common consent, had been excluded from civilized Governments and the family of nations, and doomed to slavery. They spoke and acted according to the then established doctrines and principles, and in the ordinary language of the day, and no one misunderstood them. The unhappy black race were separated from the white by indelible marks, and laws long before established, and were never thought of or spoken of except as property, and when the claims of the owner or the profit of the trader were supposed to need protection.

This state of public opinion had undergone no change when the Constitution was adopted, as is equally evident from its provisions and language.

* * *

But there are two clauses in the Constitution which point directly and specifically to the negro race as a separate class of persons, and show clearly that they were not regarded as a portion of the people or citizens of the Government then formed.

One of these clauses reserves to each of the thirteen States the right to import slaves until the year 1808,[1] if it thinks proper. And the importation which it thus sanctions was unquestionably of persons of the race of which we are speaking, as the traffic in slaves in the United States had always been confined to them. And by the other provision the States pledge themselves to each other to maintain the right of property of the master, by delivering up to him any slave who may have escaped from his service, and be found within their respective territories.[2] By the first above-mentioned clause, therefore, the right to purchase and hold this property is directly sanctioned and authorized for twenty years by the people who framed the Constitution. And by the second, they pledge themselves to maintain and uphold the right of the master in the manner specified, as long as the Government they then formed should endure. And these two provisions show, conclusively, that neither the description of persons therein referred to, nor their descendants, were embraced in any of the other provisions of the Constitution; for certainly these two clauses were not intended to confer on them or their posterity the blessings of liberty, or any of the personal rights so carefully provided for the citizen.

1. See Article I, Section 9, of the Constitution.
2. See Article IV, Section 2, of the Constitution.

* * *

And upon a full and careful consideration of the subject, the court is of opinion, that, upon the facts stated in the plea in abatement, Dred Scott was not a citizen of Missouri within the meaning of the Constitution of the United States, and not entitled as such to sue in its courts; and, consequently, that the Circuit Court had no jurisdiction of the case, and that the judgment on the plea in abatement is erroneous.

* * *

We proceed, therefore, to inquire whether the facts relied, on by the plaintiff entitled him to his freedom.

* * *

The act of Congress, upon which the plaintiff relies, declares that slavery and involuntary servitude, except as a punishment for crime, shall be forever prohibited in all that part of the territory ceded by France, under the name of Louisiana, which lies north of thirty-six degrees thirty minutes north latitude, and not included within the limits of Missouri. And the difficulty which meets us at the threshold of this part of the inquiry is, whether Congress was authorised to pass this law under any of the powers granted to it by the Constitution; for if the authority is not given by that instrument, it is the duty of this court to declare it void and inoperative, and incapable of conferring freedom upon anyone who is held as a slave under the laws of anyone of the States.

* * *

The power of Congress over the person or property of a citizen can never be a more discretionary power under our Constitution and form of Government. The powers of the Government and the rights and privileges of the citizen are regulated and plainly defined by the Constitution itself. And when the Territory becomes a part of the United States, the Federal Government enters into possession in the character impressed upon it by those who created it. It enters upon it with its powers over the citizen strictly defined, and limited by the Constitution, from which it derives its own existence, and by virtue of which alone it continues to exist and act as a Government and sovereignty. It has no power of any kind beyond it; and it cannot, when it enters a Territory of the United States, put off its character, and assume discretionary or despotic powers which the Constitution has denied to it. It cannot create for itself a new character separated from the citizens of the United States, and the duties it owes them under the provisions of the Constitution. The Territory being a part of the United States, the Government and the citizen both enter it under the authority of the Constitution, with their respective rights defined and marked out; and the Federal Government can exercise no power over his person or property, beyond what that instrument confers, nor lawfully deny any right which it has reserved.

A reference to a few of the provisions of the Constitution will illustrate this proposition.

For example, no one, we presume, will contend that Congress can make any law in a Territory respecting the establishment of religion, or the free exercise thereof, or abridging the freedom of speech or of the press, or the right of the people of the Territory peaceably to assemble, and to petition the Government for the redress of grievances.

Nor can Congress deny to the people the right to keep and bear arms, nor the right to trial by jury, nor compel anyone to be a witness against himself in a criminal proceeding.

These powers, and others, in relation to rights of person, which it is not necessary here to enumerate, are, in express and positive terms, denied to the General Government; and the rights of private property have been guarded with equal care. Thus the rights of property are united with the rights of person, and placed on the same ground by the fifth amendment to the Constitution, which provides that no person shall be deprived of life, liberty, and property, without due process of law. And an act of Congress which deprives a citizen of the United States of his liberty or property, merely because he came himself or brought his property into a particular Territory of the United States, and who had committed no offence against the laws, could hardly be dignified with the name of due process of law.

* * *

Now, as we have already said in an earlier part of this opinion, upon a different point, the right of property in a slave is distinctly and expressly affirmed in the Constitution. The right to traffic in it, like an ordinary article of merchandise and property, was guarantied to the citizens of the United States, in every State that might desire it, for twenty years. And the Government in express terms is pledged to protect it in all future time, if the slave escapes from his owner. This is done in plain words—too plain to be misunderstood. And no word can be found in the Constitution which gives Congress a greater power over slave property, or which entitles property of that kind to less protection than property of any other description. The only power conferred is the power coupled with the duty of guarding and protecting the owner in his rights.

Upon these considerations, it is the opinion of the court that the act of Congress which prohibited a citizen from holding and owning property of this kind in the territory of the United States north of the line therein mentioned, is not warranted by the Constitution, and is therefore void; and that neither Dred Scott himself, nor any of his family, were made free by being carried into this territory; even if they had been carried there by the owner, with the intention of becoming a permanent resident.

* * *

Upon the whole, therefore, it is the judgment of this court, that it appears by the record before us that the plaintiff in error is not a citizen of Missouri, in the sense in which that word is used in the Constitution; and that the Circuit Court of the United States, for that reason, had no jurisdiction in the case, and could give no judgment in it. Its judgment for the defendant must, consequently, be reversed, and a mandate issued, directing the suit to be dismissed for want of jurisdiction.

Study Questions

1. According to Taney, did Dred Scott have the right to sue in a federal court? Why or why not?

2. How does Taney interpret the passage in the Declaration of Independence that "all men are created equal" in regard to blacks? What does he believe to have been the racial views of the Founders? Why was Taney convinced the Constitution was clear on the question of black citizenship or equality? Was he right?

3. Why did Taney rule the Missouri Compromise unconstitutional? What were the implications of this ruling for keeping slavery out of the Western territories? What if anything could free-soil advocates do about the *Dred Scott* ruling?

4. The *Dred Scott* case is frequently cited as the worst Supreme Court decision in history. What earns it this stigma? To what degree is it justified?

MARTIN DELANY

To the Mayor of Allegheny City on the Fugitive Slave Law of 1850 (1850)

Honorable mayor, whatever ideas of liberty I may have, have been received from reading the lives of your revolutionary fathers. I have therein learned that a man has a right to defend his castle with his life, even unto the taking of life. Sir, my house is my castle; in that castle are none but my wife and my children, as free as the angels of heaven, and whose liberty is as sacred as the pillars of God. If any man approaches that house in search of a slave,—I care not who he may be, whether constable or sheriff, magistrate or even judge of the Supreme Court—nay, let it be he who sanctioned this act to become a law [President Millard Fillmore], surrounded by his cabinet as his body-guard, with the Declaration of Independence waving above his head as his banner, and the constitution of his country upon his breast as his shield,—if he crosses the threshold of my door, and I do not lay him a lifeless corpse at my feet, I hope the grave may refuse my body a resting-place, and righteous Heaven my spirit a home. O, no! he cannot enter that house and we both live.

SOJOURNER TRUTH

Ar'n't I a Woman? (1851)

Sojourner Truth (1797–1883) was born into slavery as Isabella Baumfree in upstate New York; she was separated from her family at age nine and was resold several times in the next decade. In 1817, her owner, John Dumont, arranged her marriage to a fellow slave, and the couple added four more children to the daughter she had from a previous relationship (she had thirteen children in all). After Dumont reneged on his promise to free her in 1826, she escaped with her youngest daughter and was sheltered by a sympathetic couple until emancipation took effect in New York State in 1827. For a short time, she was part of a cooperative religious community; when it disbanded, she moved to New York City. In 1843, she changed her name to Sojourner Truth and became a traveling preacher. She joined another cooperative, this one founded by abolitionists, and dictated her autobiography, The Narrative of Sojourner Truth (1850), to a fellow community member. The book's publication won her popularity as a speaker in both the abolitionist and women's suffrage movements. In 1857 Truth relocated her family to Michigan, which remained her home base for the rest of her life even as she continued to travel widely, meeting with presidents and speaking in favor of many moral and progressive causes.

Truth delivered "Ar'n't I a Woman?" her most famous speech, in 1851 at a women's rights convention in Ohio where she was the only African American woman in attendance. Truth felt moved to share her opinion with the assembled crowd. Think about her rhetorical situation as you read the text of her speech, transcribed by Frances D. Gage, the president of the convention, who attempted to record Truth's distinctive dialect. As you read, think about the effect of reading the speech in dialect. How would it have been different if it were written in standard English?

Well, chilern, whar dar is so much racket dar must be something out o'kilter. I tink dat 'twixt de niggers of de Souf and de women at de Norf[1] all a talkin' 'bout rights, de white men will be in a fix pretty soon. But what's all dis here talkin' 'bout? Dat man ober dar say dat women needs to be helped into carriages, and lifted ober ditches, and to have de best place

---

1. "Souf" is South and "Norf" is North; this transcription of Truth's dialect was made by the president of the convention, Frances D. Gage; what she renders as "ar'n't," contemporary writers would probably spell "ain't."

every whar. Nobody eber help me into carriages, or ober mud puddles, or gives me any best place, and ar'n't I a woman? Look at me! Look at my arm! I have plowed, and planted, and gathered into barns, and no man could head me—and ar'n't I a woman? I could work as much and eat as much as a man (when I could get it), and bear de lash as well—and ar'n't I a woman? I have borne thirteen chil-ern and seen 'em mos' all sold off into slavery, and when I cried out with a mother's grief, none but Jesus heard—and ar'n't I a woman? Den dey talks 'bout dis ting in de head—what dis dey call it? ["Intellect," whispered some one near.] Dat's it honey. What's dat got to do with women's rights or niggers' rights? If my cup won't hold but a pint and yourn holds a quart, would n't ye be mean not to let me have my little half-measure full?

Den dat little man in black dar, he say women can't have as much rights as man, cause Christ wa'n't a woman. Whar did your Christ come from? From God and a woman. Man had nothing to do with him. . . . If de fust woman God ever made was strong enough to turn the world upside down, all 'lone, dese togedder ought to be able to turn it back and get it right side up again, and now dey is ask-ing to do it, de men better let em. 'Bleeged to ye for hearin' on me, and now ole Sojourner ha'n't got nothing more to say.

FREDERICK DOUGLASS

Fourth of July Speech (1852)

Frederick Douglass (1818–1895) was one of the most remarkable Americans ever to live, and certainly the most prominent leader among African Americans through the second half of the nineteenth century. Douglass was born a slave on a large Maryland plantation in 1818, suspected to be the son of his master. He learned to read at an early age and later testified that his literacy had given him an absolute determination to be free. After becoming a skilled shipyard worker in Baltimore, Douglass escaped to the North in 1838. Douglass met prominent white abolitionists such as William Lloyd Garrison and Wendell Phillips and, by the early 1840s, was drawing large audiences across the Northeast as an antislavery speaker. His autobiography, published in Boston in 1843, secured his fame and remains one of the classic narratives of the slave experience.

The following speech was delivered on Independence Day of 1852 before an antislavery audience of 600 in Rochester, New York. As you read this excerpt, evaluate Douglass's oratorical skill and imagine his credibility, as a former slave, in the minds of his listeners. Douglass went on to serve the Union cause during the Civil War as a military recruiter and a principled critic of Lincoln's war leadership, continually pushing the president for bolder policies in regard to emancipation and black equality. After the war, Douglass served in a number of diplomatic and government positions and ceaselessly advocated for the rights and uplift of African Americans.

From Frederick Douglass, *Oration, Delivered in Corinthian Hall* (Rochester: Lee, Mann & Co., 1852), 3–4, 14–21.

He who could address this audience without a quailing sensation, has stronger nerves than I have. I do not remember ever to have appeared as a speaker before any assembly more shrinkingly, nor with greater distrust of my ability, than I do this day. A feeling has crept over me, quite unfavorable to the exercise of my limited powers of speech. The task before me is one which requires much previous thought and study for its proper performance. I know that apologies of this sort are generally considered flat and unmeaning. I trust, however, that mine will not be so considered. Should I seem at ease, my appearance would much misrepresent me. The little experience I have had in addressing public meetings, in country school houses, avails me nothing on the present occasion.

The papers and placards say, that I am to deliver a 4th July oration. This certainly, sounds large, and out of the common way, for me. It is true that I have often had the privilege to speak in this beautiful Hall, and to address many who now honor me with their presence. But neither their familiar faces, nor the perfect gage I think I have of Corinthian Hall, seems to free me from embarrassment.

The fact is, ladies and gentlemen, the distance between this platform and the slave plantation, from which I escaped, is considerable—and the difficulties to be overcome in getting from the latter to the former, are by no means slight. That I am here to-day, is, to me, a matter of astonishment as well as of gratitude. You will not, therefore, be surprised, if in what I have to say, I evince no elaborate preparation, nor grace my speech with any high sounding exordium. With little experience and with less learning, I have been able to throw my thoughts hastily and imperfectly together; and trusting to your patient and generous indulgence, I will proceed to lay them before you.

* * *

Fellow-citizens, pardon me, allow me to ask, why am I called upon to speak here to-day? What have I, or those I represent, to do with your national independence? Are the great principles of political freedom and of natural justice, embodied in that Declaration of Independence, extended to us? and am I, therefore, called upon to bring our humble offering to the national altar, and to confess the benefits and express devout gratitude for the blessings resulting from your independence to us?

Would to God, both for your sakes and ours, that an affirmative answer could be truthfully returned to these questions! Then would my task be light, and my burden easy and delightful. For *who* is there so cold, that a nation's sympathy could not warm him? Who so obdurate and dead to the claims of gratitude, that would not thankfully acknowledge such priceless benefits? Who so stolid and selfish, that would not give his voice to swell the hallelujahs of a nation's jubilee, when the chains of servitude had been torn from his limbs? I am not that man. In a case like that, the dumb might eloquently speak, and the "lame man leap as an hart."[1]

But, such is not the state of the case. I say it with a sad sense of the disparity between us. I am not included within the pale[2] of this glorious anniversary! Your high independence only reveals the immeasurable distance between us. The blessings in which you, this day, rejoice, are not enjoyed in common. The rich

---

1. "Then shall the lame man leap as an hart, and the tongue of the dumb sing" (Isaiah 35:6).
2. Douglass here employs "pale" in the sense of an area enclosed by a fence or a boundary.

inheritance of justice, liberty, prosperity and independence, bequeathed by your fathers, is shared by you, not by me. The sunlight that brought life and healing to you, has brought stripes and death to me. This Fourth July is *yours*, not *mine*. *You* may rejoice, *I* must mourn. To drag a man in fetters into the grand illuminated temple of liberty, and call upon him to join you in joyous anthems, were inhuman mockery and sacrilegious irony. Do you mean, citizens, to mock me, by asking me to speak to-day? If so, there is a parallel to your conduct. And let me warn you that it is dangerous to copy the example of a nation whose crimes, towering up to heaven, were thrown down by the breath of the Almighty, burying that nation in irrecoverable ruin! I can to-day take up the plaintive lament of a peeled and woe-smitten people!

"By the rivers of Babylon, there we sat down. Yea! we wept when we remembered Zion. We hanged our harps upon the willows in the midst thereof. For there, they that carried us away captive, required of us a song; and they who wasted us required of us mirth, saying, Sing us one of the songs of Zion. How can we sing the Lord's song in a strange land? If I forget thee, O Jerusalem, let my right hand forget her cunning. If I do not remember thee, let my tongue cleave to the roof of my mouth."[3]

Fellow-citizens; above your national, tumultuous joy, I hear the mournful wail of millions! whose chains, heavy and grievous yesterday, are, to-day, rendered more intolerable by the jubilee shouts[4] that reach them. If I do forget, if I do not faithfully remember those bleeding children of sorrow this day, "may my right hand forget her cunning, and may my tongue cleave to the roof of my mouth!" To forget them, to pass lightly over their wrongs, and to chime in with the popular theme, would be treason most scandalous and shocking, and would make me a reproach before God and the world. My subject, then, fellow-citizens, is AMERICAN SLAVERY. I shall see, this day, and its popular characteristics, from the slave's point of view. Standing, there, identified with the American bondman, making his wrongs mine, I do not hesitate to declare, with all my soul, that the character and conduct of this nation never looked blacker to me than on this 4th of July! Whether we turn to the declarations of the past, or to the professions of the present, the conduct of the nation seems equally hideous and revolting. America is false to the past, false to the present, and solemnly binds herself to be false to the future. Standing with God and the crushed and bleeding slave on this occasion, I will, in the name of humanity which is outraged, in the name of liberty which is fettered, in the name of the constitution and the Bible, which are disregarded and trampled upon, dare to call in question and to denounce, with all the emphasis I can command, everything that serves to perpetuate slavery—the great sin and

---

3. Psalm 137:1–6.

4. In ancient Hebrew law, Jubilee was the year every fifty years when all slaves were freed.

shame of America! "I will not equivocate; I will not excuse;"[5] I will use the sever-est language I can command; and yet not one word, shall escape me that any man, whose judgment is not blinded by prejudice, or who is not at heart a slave-holder, shall not confess to be right and just.

But I fancy I hear some one of my audience say, it is just in this circumstance that you and your brother abolitionists fail to make a favorable impression on the public mind. Would you argue more, and denounce less, would you persuade more, and rebuke less, your cause would be much more likely to succeed. But, I submit, where all is plain there is nothing to be argued. What point in the anti-slavery creed would you have me argue? On what branch of the subject do the people of this country need light? Must I undertake to prove that the slave is a man? That point is conceded already. Nobody doubts it. The slaveholders themselves acknowledge it in the enactment of laws for their government. They acknowledge it when they punish disobedience on the part of the slave. There are seventy-two crimes in the State of Virginia, which, if committed by a black man, (no matter how ignorant he be,) subject him to the punishment of death; while only two of the same crimes will subject a white man to the like punishment.—What is this but the acknowledgement that the slave is a moral, intellectual and responsible being. The manhood of the slave is conceded. It is admitted in the fact that South-ern statute books are covered with enactments forbidding, under severe fines and penalties, the teaching of the slave to read or to write.—When you can point to any such laws, in reference to the beasts of the field, then I may consent to argue the manhood of the slave. When the dogs in your streets, when the fowls of the air, when the cattle on your hills, when the fish of the sea, and the reptiles that crawl, shall be unable to distinguish the slave from a brute, *then* will I argue with you that the slave is a man!

For the present, it is enough to affirm the equal manhood of the negro race. Is it not astonishing that, while we are ploughing, planting and reaping, using all kinds of mechanical tools; erecting houses, constructing bridges, building ships, working in metals of brass, iron, copper, silver and gold; that, while we are read-ing, writing and cyphering, acting as clerks, merchants and secretaries, having among us lawyers, doctors, ministers, poets, authors, editors, orators and teach-ers; that, while we are engaged in all manner of enterprises common to other men, digging gold in California, capturing the whale in the Pacific, feeding sheep and cattle on the hill-side, living, moving, acting, thinking, planning, living in families as husbands, wives and children, and, above all, confessing and worship-ping the Christian's God, and looking hopefully for life and immortality beyond the grave, we are called upon to prove that we are men!

---

5. William Lloyd Garrison's words from the first issue of his abolitionist paper, *The Liberator*, upon its appear-ance in 1831; Douglass became an avid subscriber in New Bedford, Massachusetts, soon after his escape from slavery.

Would you have me argue that man is entitled to liberty? that he is the rightful owner of his own body? You have already declared it. Must I argue the wrongfulness of slavery? Is that a question for republicans? Is it to be settled by the rules of logic and argumentation, as a matter beset with great difficulty, involving a doubtful application of the principle of justice, hard to be understood? How should I look to-day, in the presence of Americans, dividing, and subdividing a discourse, to show that men have a natural right to freedom? speaking of it relatively, and positively, negatively, and affirmatively. To do so, would be to make myself ridiculous, and to offer an insult to your understanding.—There is not a man beneath the canopy of heaven, that does not know that slavery is wrong *for him.*

What, am I to argue that it is wrong to make men brutes, to rob them of their liberty, to work them without wages, to keep them ignorant of their relations to their fellow men, to beat them with stick, to flay their flesh with the lash, to load their limbs with irons, to hunt them with dogs, to sell them at auction, to sunder their families, to knock out their teeth, to burn their flesh, to starve them into obedience and submission to their masters? Must I argue that a system thus marked with blood, and stained with pollution, is *wrong*? No I will not. I have better employment for my time and strength, than such arguments would imply.

What, then, remains to be argued? Is it that slavery is not divine; that God did not establish it; that our doctors of divinity are mistaken? There is blasphemy in the thought. That which is inhuman, cannot be divine! *Who* can reason on such a proposition? They that can, may; I cannot. The time for such argument is past.

At a time like this, scorching irony, not convincing argument, is needed. O! had I the ability, and could I reach the nation's ear, I would, to-day, pour out a fiery stream of biting ridicule, blasting reproach, withering sarcasm, and stern rebuke. For it is not light that is needed, but fire; it is not the gentle shower, but thunder. We need the storm, the whirlwind, and the earthquake. The feeling of the nation must be quickened; the conscience of the nation must be roused; the propriety of the nation must be startled; the hypocrisy of the nation must be exposed; and its crimes against God and man must be proclaimed and denounced.

What, to the American slave, is your 4th of July? I answer; a day that reveals to him, more than all other days in the year, the gross injustice and cruelty to which he is the constant victim. To him, your celebration is a sham; your boasted liberty, an unholy license; your national greatness, swelling vanity; your sounds of rejoicing are empty and heartless; your denunciations of tyrants, brass fronted impudence; your shouts of liberty and equality, hollow mockery; your prayers and hymns, your sermons and thanksgivings, with all your religious parade, and solemnity, are, to him, mere bombast, fraud, deception, impiety, and hypocrisy—a thin veil to cover up crimes which would disgrace a nation of savages. There is not a nation on the earth guilty of practices, more shocking and bloody, than are the people of these United States, at this very hour.

Go where you may, search where you will, roam through all the monarchies and despotisms of the old world, travel through South America, search out every abuse, and when you have found the last, lay your facts by the side of the every day practices of this nation, and you will say with me, that, for revolting barbarity and shameless hypocrisy, America reigns without a rival.

Study Questions

1. What tone did Douglass employ at the very beginning of his speech? In what way was this part of a conscious oratorical strategy? Which parts of the speech might have been most uncomfortable or even offensive to his audience?

2. What were Douglass's feelings toward the Declaration of Independence? To what degree was he or was he not an American patriot?

3. Fully explain why Douglass cites the scriptural passage on the "rivers of Babylon." What was his criticism of American Christians in the 1850s? What can you surmise about his own religious beliefs?

4. Analyze this speech in terms of its literary quality. How did a former slave develop such power and eloquence as a writer? What can you imagine of Frederick Douglass's ability as a public speaker?

ABRAHAM LINCOLN AND STEPHEN DOUGLAS

FROM The Lincoln-Douglas Debates (1858)

The Illinois U.S. Senate race of 1858 pitted two superb politicians against one another. Stephen Douglas (1813–1861), the Democratic incumbent, was already an established figure on the national stage, known for his role in passing the Compromise of 1850 and the Kansas-Nebraska Act of 1854. The latter bill, of which Douglas was the prime author, canceled the Missouri Compromise of 1820 when it opened the Kansas and Nebraska territories to the possibility of slavery on the basis of popular sovereignty. The resulting uproar among those determined to stop slavery's extension made Douglas a political target and jeopardized his obvious presidential ambitions.

Abraham Lincoln (1809–1865) was the candidate of the new Republican party, which was founded in opposition to the Kansas-Nebraska Act and pledged itself to resist any further expansion of slavery. Lincoln was a successful lawyer but, having served one term in Congress in the mid-1840s, was relatively inexperienced as a politician on the national level. Douglas and Lincoln met in a series of three-hour debates in towns around Illinois. These exchanges took place in the aftermath of the Supreme Court's 1857 pro-slavery ruling in the Dred Scott v. Sanford case. The following excerpts are from the seventh and final debate of the series, which took place in Alton, a town notorious for the mob killing of abolitionist editor Elijah Lovejoy in 1837. As you read these exchanges, weigh how well they illuminate the core issues before the country in this period, and consider why the Lincoln-Douglas debates have become so legendary in American history.

From "The Lincoln-Douglas Debates 7th Debate," (Ashbrook Center at Ashland University, TeachingAmericanHistory.org), http://teachingamerican history.org/library/index.asp?document=1055.

SENATOR DOUGLAS' SPEECH.

Ladies and gentlemen: It is now nearly four months since the canvass between Mr. Lincoln and myself commenced. On the 16th of June the Republican Convention assembled at Springfield and nominated Mr. Lincoln as their candidate for the United States Senate, and he, on that occasion, delivered a speech in which he laid down what he understood to be the

Republican creed and the platform on which he proposed to stand during the contest. The principal points in that speech of Mr. Lincoln's were: First, that this Government could not endure permanently divided into free and slave States, as our fathers made it; that they must all become free or all become slave; all become one thing or all become the other, otherwise this Union could not continue to exist. I give you his opinions almost in the identical language he used. His second proposition was a crusade against the Supreme Court of the United States because of the *Dred Scott* decision; urging as an especial reason for his opposition to that decision that it deprived the negroes of the rights and benefits of that clause in the Constitution of the United States which guaranties to the citizens of each State all the rights, privileges, and immunities of the citizens of the several States.[1] On the 10th of July I returned home, and delivered a speech to the people of Chicago, in which I announced it to be my purpose to appeal to the people of Illinois to sustain the course I had pursued in Congress. In that speech I joined issue with Mr. Lincoln on the points which he had presented. Thus there was an issue clear and distinct made up between us on these two propositions laid down in the speech of Mr. Lincoln at Springfield, and controverted by me in my reply to him at Chicago. On the next day, the 11th of July, Mr. Lincoln replied to me at Chicago, explaining at some length, and reaffirming the positions which he had taken in his Springfield speech. In that Chicago speech he even went further than he had before and uttered sentiments in regard to the negro being on an equality with the white man. ["That's so."][2] He adopted in support of this position the argument which Lovejoy and Codding, and other Abolition lecturers had made familiar in the northern and central portions of the State, to wit: that the Declaration of Independence having declared all men free and equal, by Divine law, also that negro equality was an inalienable right, of which they could not be deprived. He insisted, in that speech, that the Declaration of Independence included the negro in the clause, asserting that all men were created equal, and went so far as to say that if one man was allowed to take the position, that it did not include the negro, others might take the position that it did not include other men. He said that all these distinctions between this man and that man, this race and the other race, must be discarded, and we must all stand by the Declaration of Independence, declaring that all men were created equal.

The issue thus being made up between Mr. Lincoln and myself on three points, we went before the people of the State. During the following seven weeks, between the Chicago speeches and our first meeting at Ottawa, he and I addressed large assemblages of the people in many of the central counties. In my speeches I confined myself closely to those three positions which he had taken, controvert-

---

1. Article IV, Section 2, of the Constitution, which also contains a fugitive slave clause.
2. Remarks in brackets indicate the comments and reaction of the audience.

ing his proposition that this Union could not exist as our fathers made it, divided into free and slave States, controverting his proposition of a crusade against the Supreme Court because of the *Dred Scott* decision, and controverting his proposition that the Declaration of Independence included and meant the negroes as well as the white men, when it declared all men to be created equal. [Cheers for Douglas.] I supposed at that time that these propositions constituted a distinct issue between us, and that the opposite positions we had taken upon them we would be willing to be held to in every part of the State. I never intended to waver one hair's breadth from that issue either in the North or the South, or wherever I should address the people of Illinois. I hold that when the time arrives that I cannot proclaim my political creed in the same terms not only in the northern but the southern part of Illinois, not only in the Northern but the Southern States, and wherever the American flag waves over American soil, that then there must be something wrong in that creed. ["Good, good," and cheers.] So long as we live under a common Constitution, so long as we live in a confederacy of sovereign and equal States, joined together as one for certain purposes, that any political creed is radically wrong which cannot be proclaimed in every State, and every section of that Union, alike. I took up Mr. Lincoln's three propositions in my several speeches, analyzed them, and pointed out what I believed to be the radical errors contained in them. First, in regard to his doctrine that this Government was in violation of the law of God, which says that a house divided against itself cannot stand, I repudiated it as a slander upon the immortal framers of our Constitution. I then said, I have often repeated, and now again assert, that in my opinion our Government can endure forever, ["good"] divided into free and slave States as our fathers made it,—each State having the right to prohibit, abolish or sustain slavery, just as it pleases. ["Good," "right," and cheers.] This Government was made upon the great basis of the sovereignty of the States, the right of each State to regulate its own domestic institutions to suit itself, and that right was conferred with the understanding and expectation that inasmuch as each locality had separate interests, each locality must have different and distinct local and domestic institutions, corresponding to its wants and interests. Our fathers knew when they made the Government, that the laws and institutions which were well adapted to the green mountains of Vermont, were unsuited to the rice plantations of South Carolina. They knew then, as well as we know now, that the laws and institutions which would be well adapted to the beautiful prairies of Illinois would not be suited to the mining regions of California. They knew that in a Republic as broad as this, having such a variety of soil, climate and interest, there must necessarily be a corresponding variety of local laws—the policy and institutions of each State adapted to its condition and wants. For this reason this Union was established on the right of each State to do as it pleased on the question of slavery, and every other question; and the various States were not allowed to complain of, much less interfere with, the policy, of their neighbors. ["That's good doctrine," "that's the doctrine," and cheers.]

* * *

But the Abolition party really think that under the Declaration of Independence the negro is equal to the white man, and that negro equality is an inalienable right conferred by the Almighty, and hence that all human laws in violation of it are null and void. With such men it is no use for me to argue. I hold that the signers of the Declaration of Independence had no reference to negroes at all when they declared all men to be created equal. They did not mean negro, nor the savage Indians, nor the Fejee Islanders,[3] nor any other barbarous race. They were speaking of white men. ["It's so," "it's so," and cheers.] They alluded to men of European birth and European descent—to white men, and to none others, when they declared that doctrine. ["That's the truth."] I hold that this Government was established on the white basis. It was established by white men for the benefit of white men and their posterity forever, and should be administered by white men, and none others. But it does not follow, by any means, that merely because the negro is not a citizen, and merely because he is not our equal, that, therefore, he should be a slave. On the contrary, it does follow that we ought to extend to the negro race, and to all other dependent races all the rights, all the privileges, and all the immunities which they can exercise consistently with the safety of society. Humanity requires that we should give them all these privileges; Christianity commands that we should extend those privileges to them. The question then arises what are those privileges, and what is the nature and extent of them. My answer is that that is a question which each State must answer for itself. We in Illinois have decided it for ourselves. We tried slavery, kept it up for twelve years, and finding that it was not profitable, we abolished it for that reason, and became a free State. We adopted in its stead the policy that a negro in this State shall not be a slave and shall not be a citizen. We have a right to adopt that policy. For my part I think it is a wise and sound policy for us. You in Missouri must judge for yourselves whether it is a wise policy for you. If you choose to follow our example, very good; if you reject it, still well, it is your business, not ours. So with Kentucky. Let Kentucky adopt a policy to suit herself. If we do not like it we will keep away from it, and if she does not like ours let her stay at home, mind her own business and let us alone. If the people of all the States will act on that great principle, and each State mind its own business, attend to its own affairs, take care of its own negroes and not meddle with its neighbors, then there will be peace between the North and the South, the East and the West, throughout the whole Union. [Cheers.]

* * *

3. Douglas means inhabitants of the Fiji island chain in the South Pacific.

MR. LINCOLN'S REPLY.

Ladies and gentlemen . . .

You have heard him frequently allude to my controversy with him in regard to the Declaration of Independence. I confess that I have had a struggle with Judge Douglas on that matter, and I will try briefly to place myself right in regard to it on this occasion.

* * *

At Galesburgh the other day, I said in answer to Judge Douglas, that three years ago there never had been a man, so far as I knew or believed, in the whole world, who had said that the Declaration of Independence did not include negroes in the term "all men." I reassert it to-day. I assert that Judge Douglas and all his friends may search the whole records of the country, and it will be a matter of great astonishment to me if they shall be able to find that one human being three years ago had ever uttered the astounding sentiment that the term "all men" in the Declaration did not include the negro. Do not let me be misunderstood. I know that more than three years ago there were men who, finding this assertion constantly in the way of their schemes to bring about the ascendancy and perpetuation of slavery, *denied the truth of it.* I know that Mr. Calhoun[4] and all the politicians of his school denied the truth of the Declaration. I know that it ran along in the mouth of some Southern men for a period of years, ending at last in that shameful though rather forcible declaration of Pettit of Indiana,[5] upon the floor of the United States Senate, that the Declaration of Independence was in that respect "a self-evident lie," rather than a self-evident truth. But I say, with a perfect knowledge of all this hawking at the Declaration without directly attacking it, that three years ago there never had lived a man who had ventured to assail it in the sneaking way of pretending to believe it and then asserting it did not include the negro. I believe the first man who ever said it was Chief Justice Taney in the *Dred Scott* case, and the next to him was our friend, Stephen A. Douglas. And now it has become the catch-word of the entire party. I would like to call upon his friends every where to consider how they have come in so short a time to view this matter in a way so entirely different from their former belief? to ask whether they are not being borne along by an irresistible current—whither, they know not? [Great applause.]

* * *

And when this new principle—this new proposition that no human being ever thought of three years ago—is brought forward, I *combat* it as having an evil tendency, if not an evil design. I combat it as having a tendency to dehumanize the negro—to take away from him the right of ever striving to be a man. I combat it as being one of the thousand things constantly done in these days to prepare the public mind to make property, and nothing but property, of the *negro in all the States of this Union.* [Tremendous applause. "Hurrah for Lincoln."

* * *

Now irrespective of the moral aspect of this question as to whether there is a right or wrong in enslaving a negro, I am still in favor of our new Territories being in such a condition that white men may find a home—may find some spot where they can better their condition—where they can settle upon new soil and better their condition in life. [Great and continued cheering.] I am in favor of this not merely, (I must say it here as I have elsewhere,) for our own people who are born amongst us, but as an outlet for *free white people every where,* the world over—in which Hans and Baptiste and Patrick,[6] and all other men from all the world, may find new homes and better their conditions in life. [Loud and long continued applause.]

I have stated upon former occasions, and I may as well state again, what I understand to be the real issue in this controversy between Judge Douglas and myself. On the point of my wanting to make war between the free and the slave States, there has been no issue between us. So, too, when he assumes that I am in favor of introducing a perfect social and political equality between the white and black races. These are false issues, upon which Judge Douglas has tried to force the controversy. There is no foundation in truth for the charge that I maintain either of these propositions. The real issue in this controversy—the one pressing upon every mind—is the sentiment on the part of one class that looks upon the institution of slavery *as a wrong,* and of another class that *does not* look upon it as a wrong. The sentiment that contemplates the institution of slavery in this country as a wrong is the sentiment of the Republican party. It is the sentiment around which all their actions—all their arguments circle—from which all their propositions radiate. They look upon it as being a moral, social and political wrong; and while they contemplate it as such, they nevertheless have due regard for its actual existence among us, and the difficulties of getting rid of it in any satisfactory way and to all the constitutional obligations thrown about it. Yet having a due regard for these, they desire a policy in regard to it that looks to its not creating any more danger. They insist that it should as far as may be, *be treated* as a wrong, and one of the methods of treating it as a wrong is to *make provision that it shall grow no*

---

6. Here, Lincoln alludes to large numbers of Germans, French, Irish, and other Europeans entering the United States in the 1850s.

larger. [Loud applause.] They also desire a policy that looks to a peaceful end of slavery at sometime, as being wrong. These are the views they entertain in regard to it as I understand them; and all their sentiments—all their arguments and propositions are brought within this range. I have said and I repeat it here, that if there be a man amongst us who does not think that the institution of slavery is wrong in any one of the aspects of which I have spoken, he is misplaced and ought not to be with us. And if there be a man amongst us who is so impatient of it as a wrong as to disregard its actual presence among us and the difficulty of getting rid of it suddenly in a satisfactory way, and to disregard the constitutional obligations thrown about it, that man is misplaced if he is on our platform. We disclaim sympathy with him in practical action. He is not placed properly with us.

On this subject of treating it as a wrong, and limiting its spread, let me say a word. Has any thing ever threatened the existence of this Union save and except this very institution of Slavery? What is it that we hold most dear amongst us? Our own liberty and prosperity. What has ever threatened our liberty and prosperity save and except this institution of Slavery? If this is true, how do you propose to improve the condition of things by enlarging Slavery—by spreading it out and making it bigger? You may have a wen or cancer upon your person and not be able to cut it out lest you bleed to death; but surely it is no way to cure it, to engraft it and spread it over your whole body. That is no proper way of treating what you regard a wrong. You see this peaceful way of dealing with it as a wrong—restricting the spread of it, and not allowing it to go into new countries where it has not already existed. That is the peaceful way, the old-fashioned way, the way in which the fathers themselves set us the example.

On the other hand, I have said there is a sentiment which treats it as *not* being wrong. That is the Democratic sentiment of this day. I do not mean to say that every man who stands within that range positively asserts that it is right. That class will include all who positively assert that it is right, and all who like Judge Douglas treat it as indifferent and do not say it is either right or wrong. These two classes of men fall within the general class of those who do not look upon it as a wrong.

* * *

That is the real issue. That is the issue that will continue in this country when these poor tongues of Judge Douglas and myself shall be silent. It is the eternal struggle between these two principles—right and wrong—throughout the world. They are the two principles that have stood face to face from the beginning of time; and will ever continue to struggle. The one is the common right of humanity and the other the divine right of kings. It is the same principle in whatever shape it develops itself. It is the same spirit that says, "You work and toil and earn bread, and I'll eat it," No matter in what shape it comes, whether from the mouth of a king who seeks to bestride the people of his own nation and live by the fruit of their labor, or from one race of men as an apology for enslaving another race it is the same tyrannical principle. I was glad to express my gratitude at Quincy, and I re-express it here to Judge Douglas—*that he looks to no end of the institution of slavery.* That will help the people to see where the struggle really is. It will hereafter place with us all men who really do wish the wrong may have an end.

Study Questions

1. What was the fundamental difference between Douglas and Lincoln in regard to slavery? Why was Lincoln determined to keep slavery from spreading further? Would Douglas support additional slave states in the Union?

2. What was Douglas's primary contention about blacks and the Declaration of Independence? How did Lincoln respond? Why did it matter what the Declaration really means on this topic?

3. How and why did Lincoln and Douglas make racist appeals in these speeches? Had blacks been allowed to vote in Illinois in 1858, which candidate would they most likely have supported? Why?

4. How do these Lincoln-Douglas exchanges compare with typical debates of candidates today? What accounts for the differences in how politics is conducted?

JOHN BROWN

Aftermath of the Raid on Harpers Ferry: Final Speech and Prison Communications (1859)

John Brown's September 1859 raid on the federal armory in Harpers Ferry, Virginia, polarized North and South at the end of a tumultuous decade of contention over the future of slavery. Brown (1800–1859), a native of Connecticut and lifelong abolitionist, intended to seize weapons that he would then distribute to local slaves. Brown and his small army then planned to retreat into the surrounding mountains and wage guerilla warfare against slavery. The incursion into Harpers Ferry resulted in military calamity, however, as almost all of his force of twenty-two men were killed or taken prisoner by federal soldiers.

    Brown himself was taken alive and soon tried in a Virginia court for treason, murder, and inciting slave insurrection. Upon being convicted and sentenced to hang, Brown made a last address to the court on November 2. His remarks profoundly affected many readers who read them in the northern press. The documents that follow are the text of that speech, a final letter written to his family, and a note he handed to a jailer just before he departed for the gallows. As you read them, consider how they would have influenced northern and southern readers (Brown's prison correspondence was aimed at a wide public audience) and why John Brown's Raid thereby became one of the key events that led to civil war.

From F. B. Sanborn, ed., *The Life and Letters of John Brown* (Boston: Roberts Brothers, 1891), 584–585, 613–615, 620.

FINAL SPEECH

I have, may it please the Court, a few words to say.

    "In the first place, I deny everything but what I have all along admitted,— the design on my part to free the slaves. I intended certainly to have made a clean thing of that matter, as I did last winter, when I went into Missouri and there took slaves without the snapping of a gun on either side, moved them through the country, and finally left them in Canada.[1] I designed to have done the same thing again, on a larger scale. That was all I intended. I never did intend murder, or treason, or the destruction of property, or to excite or incite slaves to rebellion, or to make insurrection.

"I have another objection: and that is, it is unjust that I should suffer such a penalty. Had I interfered in the manner which I admit, and which I admit has been fairly proved (for I admire the truthfulness and candor of the greater portion of the witnesses who have testified in this case),—had I so interfered in behalf of the rich, the powerful, the intelligent, the so-called great, or in behalf of any of their friends,—either father, mother, brother, sister, wife, or children, or any of that class,—and suffered and sacrificed what I have in this interference, it would have been all right; and every man in this court would have deemed it an act worthy of reward rather than punishment.

"This court acknowledges, as I suppose, the validity of the law of God. I see a book kissed here which I suppose to be the Bible, or at least the New Testament. That teaches me that all things whatsoever I would that men should do to me, I should do even so to them. It teaches me, further, to 'remember them that are in bonds, as bound with them.' I endeavored to act up to that instruction. I say, I am yet too young to understand that God is any respecter of persons. I believe that to have interfered as I have done—as I have always freely admitted I have done—in behalf of His despised poor, was not wrong, but right. Now, if it is deemed necessary that I should forfeit my life for the furtherance of the ends of justice, and mingle my blood further with the blood of my children[2] and with the blood of millions in this slave country whose rights are disregarded by wicked, cruel, and unjust enactments,—I submit; so let it be done!

"Let me say one word further.

"I feel entirely satisfied with the treatment I have received on my trial. Considering all the circumstances, it has been more generous than I expected. But I feel no consciousness of guilt. I have stated from the first what was my intention, and what was not. I never had any design against the life of any person, nor any disposition to commit treason, or excite slaves to rebel, or make any general insurrection. I never encouraged any man to do so, but always discouraged any idea of that kind.

"Let me say, also, a word in regard to the statements made by some of those connected with me. I hear it has been stated by some of them that I have induced them to join me. But the contrary is true. I do not say this to injure them, but as regretting their weakness. There is not one of them but joined me of his own accord, and the greater part of them at their own expense. A number of them I never saw, and

1. In December 1858, Brown led a raiding party of twenty men into Missouri, where he took eleven slaves from their plantations and accompanied them to freedom in Canada. Contrary to what Brown says, one slaveowner was shot and killed in the process.
2. Brown's sons Watson and Oliver were killed in the raid on Harpers Ferry. Brown had already lost his son Frederick during a battle with pro-slavery men at Osawatomie, Kansas in August 1856.

never had a word of conversation with, till the day they came to me; and that was for the purpose I have stated.

"Now I have done."

LAST LETTERS

Charlestown Prison, Jefferson County, Va.,
Nov. 30, 1859.

My dearly beloved Wife, Sons, and Daughters, every one,—As I now begin probably what is the last letter I shall ever write to any of yon, I conclude to write to all at the same time. I will mention some little matters particularly applicable to little property concerns in another place.

I recently received a letter from my wife, from near Philadelphia, dated November 22, by which it would seem that she was about giving up the idea of seeing me again. I had written her to come on if she felt equal to the undertaking, but I do not know that she will get my letter in time. It was on her own account, chiefly, that I asked her to stay back. At first I had a most strong desire to see her again, but there appeared to be very serious objections; and should we never meet in this life, I trust that she will in the end be satisfied it was for the best at least, if not most for her comfort.

I am waiting the hour of my public murder with great composure of mind and cheerfulness; feeling the strong assurance that in no other possible way could I be used to so much advantage to the cause of God and of humanity, and that nothing that either I or all my family have sacrificed or suffered will he lost. The reflection that a wise and merciful as well as just and holy God rules not only the affairs of this world but of all worlds, is a rock to set our feet upon under all circumstances,—even those more severely trying ones in which our own feelings and wrongs have placed us. I have now no doubt but that our seeming disaster will ultimately result in the most glorious success. So, my dear shattered and broken family, be of good cheer, and believe and trust in God with all your heart and with all your soul; for He doeth all things well. Do not feel ashamed on my account, nor for one moment despair of the cause or grow weary of well-doing. I bless God I never felt stronger confidence in the certain and near approach of a bright morning and glorious day than I have felt, and do now feel, since my confinement here. I am endeavoring to return, like a poor prodigal as I am, to my Father, against whom I have always sinned, in the hope that he may kindly and forgivingly meet me, though a very great way off.

Oh, my dear wife and children, would to God you could know how I have been travailing in birth for you all, that no one of you may fail of the grace of God through Jesus Christ; that no one of you may be blind to the truth and glorious light of his Word, in which life and immortality are brought to light. I beseech you, every one, to make the Bible your daily and nightly study, with a child-like, honest, candid, teachable spirit of love and respect for your husband and father. And I beseech the God of my fathers to open all your eyes to the discovery of the truth. You cannot imagine how much you may soon need the consolations of the Christian religion.

* * *

I mention this as a reason for endeavoring to leave a valuable copy of the Bible, to be carefully preserved in remembrance of me, to so many of my posterity, instead of some other book at equal cost.

I beseech you all to live in habitual contentment with moderate circumstances and gains of worldly store, and earnestly to teach this to your children and children's children after you, by example as well as precept. Be determined to know by experience, as soon as may be, whether Bible instruction is of divine origin or not. Be sure to owe no man anything, but to love one another. John Rogers[3] wrote to his children: "Abhor that arrant whore of Rome." John Brown writes to his children to abhor, with undying hatred also, that sum of all villanies,—slavery. Remember, "he that is slow to anger is better than the mighty," and "he that ruleth his spirit than he that taketh a city." Remember also that "they being wise shall shine, and they that turn many to righteousness, as the stars for ever and ever."

And now, dearly beloved family, to God and the work of his grace I commend you all.

Your affectionate husband and father,
John Brown.

---

3. English clergyman (c. 1500–55), translator of the Bible into English and first English martyr for Protestantism during the reign of Mary I.

NOTE BEFORE THE GALLOWS

Charlestown, Va., Dec, 2, 1859.

I, John Brown, am now quite *certain* that the crimes of this *guilty land* will never be purged away but with *blood*. I had, as I now think vainly, flattered myself that without very much bloodshed it might be done.

Study Questions

1. In his words to the court, what does John Brown proclaim to have been his objective at Harpers Ferry? Why did he "feel no consciousness of guilt" for what he had done? What are his most important final instructions to his family?

2. Why in his courtroom speech does John Brown specifically reference the New Testament? How might his anti-slavery activities have been influenced by the Old Testament example of Moses as well? Where would John Brown most likely fit on the American religious landscape today?

3. Brown predicted that his "seeming disaster would ultimately result in the most glorious success." What did he mean by this? What, if anything, did he accomplish in the last weeks of his life?

4. What does Brown's final note prophesy about the coming civil war? Was he right? Did this make his violent resistance to slavery at Harpers Ferry and elsewhere more or less defensible? Explain fully.

CIVIL WAR AND RECONSTRUCTION

ALEXANDER STEPHENS

Comments on the Confederacy (1861)

Henry Cleveland, *Alexander H. Stephens in Public and Private With Letters and Speeches, Before, During, and Since The War* (Philadelphia, 1866), p. 721.

The new constitution has put at rest, *forever*, all the agitating questions relating to our peculiar institution—African slavery, as it exists amongst us—the proper *status* of the Negro in our form of civilization. This was the immediate cause of the late rupture and present revolution. Jefferson in his forecast has anticipated this as the "rock upon which the old Union would split." He was right. What was conjecture with him, is now a realized fact. But whether he fully comprehended the great truth upon which that rock *stood* and *stands* may be doubted. The prevailing ideas entertained by him and most of the leading statesmen at the time of the formation of the old constitution, were that the enslavement of the African was in violation of the laws of nature; that it was wrong in *principle*, socially, morally, and politically. It was an evil they knew not well how to deal with, but the general opinion of the men of that day was that, somehow or other in the order of Providence, the institution would be evanescent and pass away. This idea, though not incorporated in the constitution, was the prevailing idea at the time. . . . Those ideas, however, were fundamentally wrong. They rested upon the assumption of the equality of the races. . . .

Our new government is founded upon exactly the opposite idea; its foundations are laid, its corner-stone rests upon the great truth that the negro is not equal to the white man; that slavery—subordination to the superior race—is his natural and normal condition. (Applause.)

This our new government, is the first, in the history of the world, based upon this great physical, philosophical, and moral truth.

ABRAHAM LINCOLN

The Gettysburg Address (1863)

Abraham Lincoln traveled to Gettysburg, Pennsylvania, on November 18, 1863, to speak the next day at the dedication of the national cemetery for the soldiers who had died there more than four months earlier in the epic three-day battle. Edward Everett, a renowned orator, was featured speaker that day and preceded Lincoln at the podium with a two-hour address that dramatically recounted the battle and fervently condemned the rebellion. Lincoln delivered his own carefully crafted remarks in just over two minutes. While reportedly receiving only polite applause from the assembled crowd, Lincoln's words would soon become permanently embedded in the national consciousness. Today, his Gettysburg Address is regarded as one of the greatest and most important presidential speeches in U.S. history.

As you read the Gettysburg Address, keep in mind the time frame. While the Confederates had undoubtedly suffered a major military blow at Gettysburg, the war continued with no immediate end in sight. The Emancipation Proclamation, issued in preliminary form on September 22, 1862, had now gone into effect, transforming the nature of the conflict by making it a war of liberation for the nation's four million slaves. This was the context in which Lincoln offered his thoughts on the "great civil war" then still raging.

From Orton H. Carmichael, *Lincoln's Gettysburg Address*, (New York: The Abington Press, 1917) 92.

Four score and seven years ago our fathers brought forth on this continent, a new nation, conceived in liberty, and dedicated to the proposition that all men are created equal.

Now we are engaged in a great civil war, testing whether that nation, or any nation so conceived and so dedicated, can long endure. We are met on a great battlefield of that war. We have come to dedicate a portion of that field, as a final resting place for those who here gave their lives that that nation might live. It is altogether fitting and proper that we should do this.

But, in a larger sense, we can not dedicate—we can not consecrate—we can not hallow—this ground. The brave men, living and dead, who struggled here, have consecrated it, far above our poor power to add or detract. The world will little note, nor long remember what we say here, but it can never forget what they did here. It is for us the living, rather, to be dedicated here to the unfinished work which they who fought here have thus far so nobly advanced. It is rather for us to be here dedicated to the great task remaining before us—that from these honored dead we take increased devotion to that cause for which they gave the last full measure of devotion—that we here highly resolve that these dead shall not have died in vain—that this nation, under God, shall have a new birth of freedom— and that government of the people, by the people, for the people, shall not perish from the earth.

Study Questions

1. Why does Lincoln direct himself not just to Americans but to the world? What insight is provided into this by his opening words, "Four score and seven years ago"? What would have been proved if the South had managed to win the war?

2. Would the cemetery being dedicated at Gettysburg contain the graves of Confederate as well as Union soldiers? Why or why not? What evidence is provided by Lincoln's remarks?

3. What does the Gettysburg Address reveal about Lincoln's view of the Declaration of Independence? How might his reference to "a new birth of freedom" be seen as a criticism of that document or of the Constitution?

4. Critique the Gettysburg Address as a piece of writing. What are the most essential features of Lincoln's style? What phrases are most memorable and why? How does this speech differ from presidential addresses today? How might such differences be explained?

ABRAHAM LINCOLN

Second Inaugural Address (1865)

President Abraham Lincoln won reelection in November 1864, prevailing over Democratic nominee and former Union general George McClellan with 55 percent of the popular vote and an overwhelming majority in the Electoral College. Due to growing death tolls and war-weariness in the North, Lincoln's prospects for victory had seemed doubtful until General William Sherman's entry into Atlanta on September 2 finally convinced much of the public that Union triumph was in view. By the time of the inauguration on March 4, 1865, Confederate resistance was cracking on all fronts, and Lee's surrender to Grant at Appomattox Courthouse, Virginia, which would practically end the war, was exactly five weeks distant.

Lincoln's second inaugural address was among the briefest in American history, less than one-fifth the length of his first. Scholars agree that Abraham Lincoln was among the very best writers ever to occupy the White House. As you read this document, take note of Lincoln's literary style: pay heed to the elements which make his voice distinctive and imagine the effect of his words on Americans of his and subsequent generations. Unswayed by Lincoln's appeal was his future assassin, John Wilkes Booth, who, while the president delivered this speech, stood in the audience just a few feet away. By his actions on Good Friday (April 14) of the same year, Booth would ensure that this speech was the last of the president's great public statements.

From Abraham Lincoln to Hannibal Hamlin. Available at *Abraham Lincoln Papers at the Library of Congress*, Manuscript Division (Washington, D. C.: American Memory Project, 2000–01), http://memory.loc.gov/ammem/ alhtml/alhome.html (accessed 2012).

Fellow Countrymen:

At this second appearing to take the oath of the presidential office, there is less occasion for an extended address than there was at the first. Then a statement, somewhat in detail, of a course to be pursued, seemed fitting and proper. Now, at the expiration of four years, during which public declarations have been constantly called forth on every point and phase of the great contest which still absorbs the attention, and engrosses the enerergies of the nation, little that is new could be presented. The progress of our arms, upon which all else chiefly depends, is as well known to the public as to myself; and it is, I trust, reasonably satisfactory and encouraging to all. With high hope for the future, no prediction in regard to it is ventured.

On the occasion corresponding to this four years ago, all thoughts were anxiously directed to an impending civil war. All dreaded it—all sought to avert it. While the inaugeral address was being delivered from this place, devoted altogether to *saving* the Union without war, insurgent agents were in the city seeking to *destroy* it without war—seeking to dissolve the Union, and divide effects, by negotiation. Both parties deprecated war; but one of them would *make* war rather than let the nation survive; and the other would *accept* war rather than let it perish. And the war came.

One eighth of the whole population were colored slaves, not distributed generally over the Union, but localized in the Southern part of it. These slaves constituted a peculiar and powerful interest. All knew that this interest was, somehow, the cause of the war. To strengthen, perpetuate, and extend this interest was the object for which the insurgents would rend the Union, even by war, while the government claimed no right to do more than to restrict the territorial enlargement of it. Neither party expected for the war, the magnitude, or the duration, which it has already attained. Neither anticipated that the *cause* of the conflict might cease with, or even before, the conflict itself should cease. Each looked for an easier triumph, and a result less fundamental and astounding. Both read the same Bible, and pray to the same God; and each invokes His aid against the other. It may seem strange that any men should dare to ask a just God's assistance in wringing their bread from the sweat of other men's faces; but let us judge not that we be not judged.[1] The prayers of both could not be answered; that of neither has been answered fully. The Almighty has His own purposes. "Woe unto the world because of offences; I for it must needs be that offences come; but woe to that man by whom the offence cometh!"[2] If we shall suppose that American Slavery is one of those offences which, in the providence of God, must needs come, but which, having continued through His appointed time, He now wills to remove, and that He gives to both North and South, this terrible war, as the woe due to those by whom the offence came, shall we discern therein any departure from those divine attributes which the believers in a Living God always ascribe to Him? Fondly do we hope—fervently do we pray—that this mighty scourge of war may speedily pass away. Yet, if God wills that it continue, until all the wealth piled by the bond-man's two hundred and fifty years of unrequited toil shall be sunk, and until every drop of blood drawn with the lash, shall be paid by another drawn with the sword, as was said three thousand years ago, so still it must be said "the judgments of the Lord, are true and righteous altogether."[3]

---

1. "Judge not, that ye be not judged. For with what judgment ye judge, ye shall be judged: and with what measure ye mete, it shall be measured to you again." (Matthew 7:1–2).

2. Matthew 18:7.

3. Psalm 19:9.

With malice toward none; with charity for all; with firmness in the right as God gives us to see the right, let us strive on to finish the work we are in; to bind up the nation's wounds; to care for him who shall have borne the battle, and for his widow, and his orphan—to do all which may achieve and cherish a just, and a lasting peace, among ourselves, and with all nations.

Study Questions

1. How does Lincoln explain the brevity of his speech? What does he most want to communicate in this limited space?

2. Fully analyze the following sentence: "And the war came." To what degree does it fit with the overall tone or wording of the inaugural address?

3. On what basis could both the Union and Confederacy claim God's support? What are Lincoln's insights on the will of God? For the sake of argument, assume that Lincoln was actually not very religious and was even skeptical in regard to God's existence. What would then account for the religious content of this speech?

4. How might white southerners have viewed Lincoln's speech at the time it was delivered? How might their feelings have changed some years after the war's conclusion?

MARY BOYKIN CHESNUT

Civil War Diary (1865)

Mary Boykin Chesnut (1823–1886) was born into South Carolina's planter aristoc-
racy, the daughter of Mary Boykin and Stephen Decatur Miller. Her father served as
both governor and U.S. senator. As a result of her family's elite status, she received a
fine education at a French boarding school in Charleston. In 1840 she married James
Chesnut, a Princeton-educated planter who would be elected to the U.S. Senate in
1858. He became a leading secessionist after Abraham Lincoln's election in 1860, and
during the Civil War, rose to the rank of Confederate brigadier general and aide to
President Jefferson Davis.

Thanks to her husband's connections, Mary Chesnut moved in the highest
social circles in the Confederate capital of Richmond, Virginia. Her friendships
with leading politicians, generals, and their wives (such as Varina Davis, wife of the
Confederate president Jefferson Davis) provided rich material for the detailed dia-
ries she kept through the war years. In the postwar era, Chesnut returned to writ-
ing as a form of relief from numerous personal and family tribulations. After
completing three novels, she started revising her war journals in the early 1880s.
They were first published as A Diary from Dixie in 1905, nearly two decades after
her passing. Chesnut's insights and details make these writings a prized source for
historians of the war years. The following entries were written as the Confederacy's
forces were collapsing in the final months of the conflict. As you read, consider how
this looming defeat would affect members of the South's slave-owning elite, includ-
ing the Chesnuts.

From *Mary Chesnut's Civil War* edited by C. Vann Woodward, published by
Yale University Press. Copyright © 1981 by C. Vann Woodward, Sally Bland
Metts, Barbara G. Carpenter, Sally Bland Johnson, and Katherine W. Herbert.
Reprinted by permission of the publisher.

February 23, 1865. Isabella and I were taking a walk. General Joseph E. Johnston[1] joined us. He explained to us all of Lee and Stonewall Jackson's mistakes. He was radiant and joyful. We had nothing to say. How could we? He always impresses me with the feeling that all of his sympathies are on the other side. Still, he was neither gruff nor rude today—as he can be when he

---

1. Confederate general (1807–91) known for his defensive tactics; in late February 1865 he was appointed by
Confederate President Jefferson Davis to command the remnants of the Army of Tennessee.

chooses. He said he was very angry to be ordered to take command again. He might well be in a genuine rage. This on-and-offing is enough to bewilder the coolest head. . . .

Letter from my husband—he is at Charlotte. He came near being taken prisoner in Columbia,[2] for he was asleep the morning of the 17th, when the Yankees blew up the RR depot. That woke him, of course. He found everybody had left Columbia and the town surrendered by the mayor, Colonel Goodwyn. Hampton and his command had been gone several hours. Isaac Hayne came away with General Chesnut. There was no fire in the town when they came away. They overtook Hampton's command at Meeks Mill. That night, from the hills where they encamped they saw the fire and knew the Yankees were burning the town—as we had every right to expect they would. (Such a letter. Says our retreat was disgraceful and unnecessary and that he nearly was taken prisoner.) . . .

Charleston and Wilmington—surrendered. I have no further use for a newspaper. I never want to see another one as long as I live.

Wade Hampton lieutenant general—too late.[3] If he had been lieutenant general and given the command in South Carolina six months ago, I believe he would have saved us. Achilles was sulking in his tent[4]—at such a time!

Shame, disgrace, beggary—all at once. Hard to bear.

Grand smash—

Rain—rain outside—inside naught but drowning floods of tears.

I could not bear it, so I rushed down in that rainstorm to the Martins. He met me at the door.

"Madame, Columbia is burned to the ground."

I bowed my head and sobbed aloud.

"Stop that," he said, trying to speak cheerfully. "Come here, wife. This woman cries with her whole heart—just as she laughs." But in spite of His words, his voice broke down—he was hardly calmer than myself.

February 26, 1865. Mrs. Munro offered me religious books which I declined, being already provided with the Lamentations of Jeremiah, the Penitential Psalms of David, the denunciations of Isaiah, and above all the patient wail of Job. Job is my comforter now.

And yet I would be so thankful to know it never would be any worse with me. My husband is well and ordered to join the Great Retreater.[5] I am bodily comfort-

---

2. Capital city of South Carolina.

3. Wade Hampton III (1818–1902), South Carolina planter and politician promoted to this rank on February 14, 1865.

4. Reference to Homer's The Iliad, in which the Greek hero Achilles detaches himself from the fight with the Trojans due to his anger over being deprived by his king of his rightful spoils of war.

5. A reference to General Johnston.

able, if somewhat dingily lodged, and I daily part with my raiment for food. We find no one who will exchange eatables for Confederate money. So we are devouring our clothes. Ellen is a maid—comme il y en a peu[6]—and if I do a little work it is quite enough to show me how dreadful it would be without her *if I should have to do it all.*

Appliances for social enjoyment are not wanting. Miss Middleton and Isabella often drink a cup of tea with me. One might search the whole world and not find two cleverer or more agreeable women. Miss M is brilliant and accomplished. She must have been a hard student all of her life. She knows everybody worth knowing, and she has been everywhere. Then she is so highbred, high-hearted, pure and true. She is so clean-minded she could not harbor a wrong thought. She is utterly unselfish, a devoted daughter and sister. She is one among the many larger brained women a kind Providence has thrown in my way—such as Mrs. McCord, daughter of Judge Cheves, Mary Preston Darby, Mrs. Emory, granddaughter of old Franklin the American wise man, and Mrs. Jefferson Davis. How I love to praise my friends. . . .

Of course, if this rain continues we must have a deluge.

As a ray of artificial sunshine, Mrs. Munro sent me an *Examiner.* Daniel thinks we are at the last gasp, and now England and France are bound to step in. England must know if the U.S.A. are triumphant they will tackle her next, and France must know she will have to give up Mexico[7]—en case.[8]

My faith fails me. It is too late. No help for us now—in God or man.

Also—that Thomas was now to ravage Georgia. Never. Sherman from all accounts has done that work once for all.[9] There will be no aftermath.

They say no living thing is found in Sherman's track—only *chimneys*, like telegraph poles, to carry the news of Sherman's army backward.

* * *

March 5, 1865. Is the sea drying up? Is it going up into mist and coming down on us in this waterspout? The rain—it raineth every day, and the weather represents our tearful despair on a large scale.

It is also Lent—quite convenient, for we have nothing to eat. So we fast and pray. And go draggling to church like drowned rats, to be preached at.

To think, there are men who dare so defile a church, a sacred sanctuary dedicated to God the Father, and we have to hold up our skirts and walk tiptoe, so

---

6. As there is little (French).

7. France's initial intervention into Mexico had resulted in their defeat by the Mexicans at the Battle of Pueblo on May 5, 1862, providing inspiration for the recognition of Cinco de Mayo ("Fifth of May").

8. In that case (French).

9. Union generals George H. Thomas (1816–70) and William T. Sherman (1820–91) defeated Confederate forces in Georgia, capturing Atlanta and devastating Confederate infrastructure.

covered is the floor, aisle, and pews with the dark shower of tobacco juice. "How do Americans expectorate?" I know where Dante[1] would place these—animals.

My letter from my husband was so—well, what in a woman you would call "heartbroken." So I began to get ready for a run up to Charlotte. My hat was on my head. My traveling bag in my hand.

Ellen was saying, "Which umbrella, ma'am?"

"Stop, Ellen, someone is speaking out there." A tap at the door. Miss McLean threw the door wide open, and in a triumphant voice:

"Permit me to announce General Chesnut!"

She goes off singing, "ah, does not a meeting like this make amends!"

We went after luncheon to see Mrs. Munro. J. C.[2] wanted to thank her for all her kindness to me. We had been seeing the rough side of life so long, the seamy side. I was awfully proud of him. I had ceased to think everybody had the air and manners of a gentleman. I know now, it is a thing to thank God for.

Mr. Chesnut knew Mr. Munro in our legislature long ago. So it was all very nice. Father O'Connell was there, fresh from Columbia. News at last. Sherman's men had burned the convent. Mrs. Munro had pinned her faith to Sherman because he was a Catholic—and now! Father O'Connell was there—he saw it. The nuns and girls marched to old Hampton house (Mrs. Preston's now) and so saved it. They walked between files of soldiers. Men were rolling tar barrels and lighting torches to fling over the house when the nuns came. Columbia is but dust and ashes—burned to the ground. Men, women, and children left there, houseless, homeless, without one particle of food—picking up the corn left by Sherman's horses in their picket ground and parching it to stay their hunger.

General Chesnut said he had sent Isaac Hayne with a party of scouts. They would go to Columbia and come back by Camden. So we will hear something definite from home through Isaac Hayne. . . .

Colonel Childs walked down to the train with us. He is an ardent Joe Johnston man, and his mission seemed to instruct that general in some particular. He said, "I mean to put him straight. I'm for him, up to the hub."

J. C. gave me his last cent. It was a sad parting—though his words were cheerful enough.

That lowering black future hangs there—all the same. The end of the war brings no hope of peace or security to us.

---

1. Italian poet Dante Alighieri (c. 1265–1321), whose *Inferno* places various sinners in specific circles of Hell.
2. That is, James Chesnut.

Mrs. Green, in a meek aside: "And I have to bear that, too." This I told to Allen. You see I have gone back to my Greens. Yarn is our circulating medium. It is the current coin of the realm. At a factory here, Mrs. Glover traded off a negro woman for yarn. The woman wanted to go there as a factory hand, so it suited all round. I held up my hands! Mrs. Munro said:

"Mrs. Glover knows she will be free in a few days. Besides, that's nothing. Yesterday a negro man was sold for a keg of nails."

"God's will be done," escaped from Mr. Martin's lips, in utter amazement.

"This shows slavery is in its death throes."

"General C said we were lighthearted at the ruin of the great, slave-owners. An unholy joy."

They will have no negroes now to lord it over. They can swell and peacock about and tyrannize now over only a small parcel of women and children—those only who are their very own family.

L etter from Quentin Washington:
    "I have given up," he writes. "The bitterness is over." But then he adds, "I will write to you no more—I have not the heart."

General Manigault told Miss Middleton that Sherman burnt out all families whose heads had signed the secession ordinance.[3] Members of legislature's houses were burned.

"And if he had thrown in the members of the legislature themselves, nobody would mind."

"They are in bad odor, but that would have created a worse—burning members, you know."

Ellen said I had a little piece of bread and a little molasses today for my dinner—and then Mrs. M sent to ask me to dine with her today. Providential! Jack Middleton writes from Richmond: "The wolf is at the door here. We dread starvation far more than we do Grant or Sherman. Famine—that is the word now."

A pril 7, 1865. Richmond has fallen—and I have no heart to write about it. Grant broke through our lines. Sherman cut through them. Stoneman is this side of Danville.[4]

They are too many for us.

Everything lost, in Richmond, even our archives.

---

3. South Carolina had been the first state to secede, adopting its secession ordinance on December 20, 1860.
4. Respectively, Union generals Ulysses S. Grant (1822–51), William Tecumseh Sherman (1820–91), and George Stoneman Jr. (1822–94).

Blue-black is our horizon. . . .

Madame F, the milliner, wants to go west. "Westward the star of empire takes its course,"[5] she whimpered.

General Hood[6] said, "You will all be obliged to go west, Texas, I mean. Your own country will be overrun." . . .

A pril 19, 1865. Just now Mr. Clay dashed upstairs, pale as a sheet. "General Lee has capitulated."[7]

I saw it reflected in Mary Darby's face before I heard him. She staggered to the table, sat down, and wept, aloud. Clay's eyes were not dry.

Quite beside herself, Mary shrieked, "Now we belong to negroes and Yankees!" Buck said, "I do not believe it."

* * *

General Preston[8] is very bitter. He says General Lee fought first well enough to make the Yankees more conceited and self-sufficient than ever, that they were too much for him. They pay us a compliment we would never pay them. We fought to get rid of Yankees and Yankee rule. We had no use for Yankees down here and no pleasure in their company. We wanted to separate from them for aye.

How different is their estimate of us. To keep the despised and iniquitous South within their borders, as part of their country, they are willing to enlist, millions of men at home and abroad and to spend billions. And we know they do not love fighting per se—nor spending their money. They are perfectly willing to have three killed for our one. We hear they have all grown rich—shoddy—whatever that is. Genuine Yankees can make a fortune trading jackknives.

"Somehow it is borne in on me that we will have to pay the piper."

"No. Blood can not be squeezed from a turnip. You can not pour anything out of an empty cup. We have no money, even for taxes or for their confiscation."

"All gone up the spout," cry the flippant. The sentimental sigh.

"We hang out harps by the rivers of Babylon and make our lament."[9]

---

5. First line of the well-known poem "Verses on the Prospect of Planting Arts and Learning in America" by the Anglo-Irish philosopher George Berkeley (1685–1753).

6. Confederate general John Bell Hood (1831–79), whose forces were defeated by Union armies in Georgia and Tennessee.

7. Confederate general Robert E. Lee (1807–70) surrendered to Union general Ulysses S. Grant at Appomattox Court House, Virginia, on April 9, 1865, effectively ending the Civil War

8. Confederate general John S. Preston of South Carolina (1809–81).

9. A reference to Psalm 137.

Study Questions

1. What was Chesnut's concern about the news from Columbia, South Carolina? Why do you think Sherman's soldiers committed so much destruction in that state?

2. Elaborate fully on Mary Chesnut's references to the book of Job. What particular economic hardships and mental traumas did Confederate civilians face? For white Christians of the South, what must have been the religious implications of the Confederacy's coming defeat?

3. Explain the references to England, France, and Mexico in Chesnut's entry of February 26, 1865. How did Chesnut and her circle ultimately explain the South's defeat?

4. With news of Lee's surrender, one of Chesnut's friends lamented "now we belong to negroes and Yankees." Were such concerns well founded? What postwar challenges would elite Southern families most likely have faced, given what Mary Chesnut reveals of conditions at the end of the war?